MW01253687

Aristotle on Knowledge of Nature and Modern Skepticism

Aristotle on Knowledge of Nature and Modern Skepticism

Nathan R. Colaner

LEXINGTON BOOKS
Lanham • Boulder • New York • London

Published by Lexington Books
An imprint of The Rowman & Littlefield Publishing Group, Inc.
4501 Forbes Boulevard, Suite 200, Lanham, Maryland 20706
www.rowman.com

Unit A, Whitacre Mews, 26-34 Stannary Street, London SE11 4AB, United Kingdom

British Library Cataloguing in Publication Information Available

Library of Congress Cataloging-in-Publication Data

Colaner, Nathan R.
Aristotle on knowledge of nature and modern skepticism / Nathan R. Colaner.
p. cm.
Includes bibliographical references and index.
ISBN 978-0-7391-7712-9 (cloth : alk. paper) -- ISBN 978-0-7391-7713-6 (electronic) 1.
Aristotle. 2. Knowledge, Theory of. I. Title.

B491.K6C57 2014
121.092--dc23
2014032156

Printed in the United States of America

For Jennifer, 11 wonderful years in

Table of Contents

List of Abbreviations   ix
Preface   xi
Introduction   1

Part One: Aristotle on Knowledge of Nature   9

   1. What *Epistēmē* Is Not   11
   2. The Principles of *Epistēmē*   29
   3. Pursuing the Principles: *Epagōgē*   49
   4. Grasping the Principles: *Nous*   71
   5. Using the Principles: Demonstration and Contemplation   93

Part Two: Aristotle on Modern Skepticism   113

   6. Hume and Kant on the Problem of Objective Validity   115
   7. Kant and Aristotle on Spontaneity   125
   8. Gettier and the Problem of Justification   141
   9. Descartes and the Problem of External World Skepticism   153
  10. The Problem of Intellectual Intuition   163
  11. Dialectic and Metaphysical Skepticism   175

Bibliography   187
Index   193

List of Abbreviations of Aristotle's Works

The abbreviations of Aristotle's works follow their Latinized title.

Abbreviation   Title

Cat.	*Categories*
DI	*De Interpretatione*
GA	*Generation of Animals*
Meta.	*Metaphysics*
EN	*Nicomachean Ethics*
DA	*On the Soul*
PA	*Parts of Animals*
Ph.	*Physics*
Pol.	*Politics*
An. Post.	*Posterior Analytics*
An. Pr.	*Prior Analytics*
Top.	*Topics*

Preface

In the humanities, there are two general biases with respect to the timeliness of ideas; a researcher may be favorably disposed to new ideas, or continually intrigued by the old ones. My own suspicion that fresh ideas may be found in supposedly stale places partly explains the existence of this work. Specifically, I wrote this book in hopes of raising the question of whether Aristotle's theory of knowledge is still relevant. I mean this question to be put in the tradition that implicitly first asked the question of Aristotle's ethics, and then explicitly of his philosophy of mind. It was perhaps G.E.M. Anscombe's 1958 "Modern Moral Philosophy"[1] that began to restore Aristotle's ethical theory to its proper place of interest, and probably Alasdair MacIntyre's 1981 work *After Virtue*[2] that will guarantee its continuing relevance. Aristotle's virtue ethics quickly became a legitimate contender to utilitarianism and deontology as evidenced by the amount of scholarship generated by the *Nicomachean Ethics*, not to mention the fact that any introductory ethics course taught these days would be bafflingly incomplete without a thorough treatment of virtue ethics. So the question, 'Is Aristotle's theory of ethics still relevant?,' was answered with a resounding 'yes.'

Perhaps inspired by the success of this project in ethics, an analogous version of this question was raised: 'Is Aristotle's philosophy of mind still relevant?'[3] The hope was that Aristotle's position was something like a forerunner of functionalism, which some philosophers were optimistic was a third way between the limiting alternatives of dualism and physicalism. This debate began to take form in the 1970s until it was brought to full light by the indispensable *Essays on Aristotle's De Anima*[4] in 1992. This time, the results of the Aristotelian resurrection were not obviously positive, first of all, because it seems that functionalism's heyday has come and gone in the philosophy of mind. And second, there is considerable opposition to the idea that it is even coherent to wrest Aristotle's philosophy of mind from his antiquated picture of living bodies.[5]

Despite these mixed results, I am convinced that it is now worthwhile to examine the relevancy question with regard to Aristotle's theory of knowledge. I think it goes without saying that such a project is very large and will not be completed by any single book, and certainly not this one. This, however, should not discourage anyone in the least from trying to provide resources helpful for its eventual answer.

Aristotle, as is well-known, was the most influential Western philosopher from his original work in the fourth century BCE until the scientific revolution more than two millennia later. To confine a very long, complicated, and interesting story to a single sentence, Aristotle's picture of reality relied heavily on forms (as in the opposition 'form' and 'matter'), and the system of physics embraced by the scientific revolution had no use for such irreducible entities. Aristotelian physics was very quickly and quietly moved to the museum of intellectual history. In turn, because of the close association between knowledge and what it seeks to know, Aristotle's epistemology was unceremoniously dumped from intellectual life as well. Notably, Aristotle's epistemology was not argued against, nor was it appropriated or revised; rather, it received a far worse penalty—complete obscurity. What happened next was that modern Western epistemology fumbled along with doctrines that many thinkers found had little to do with everyday life, such as Descartes' evil genius, Hume's claim that we can't know anything that we are not presently observing, and Kant's rescue of knowledge in the context of idealism. From an Aristotelian perspective, this is particularly tragic because his doctrine, as he sees it, is able to preserve most of our common intuitions about knowledge. It is worth wondering if any of these doctrines would ever have seen the light of day if Aristotle's framework of epistemology were understood properly.

To be clear, I do not wish to restore the forms to their prominence in physics. However, it is certainly not obvious that Aristotle's theory of knowledge only works in the context of his historically situated physics and metaphysics. If his epistemology is inextricably linked to his entire theoretical work, it is probably not worth asking whether Aristotle's epistemology is still relevant. But if it does not, then his theory of knowledge demands a fair hearing, and as far as I can tell, no serious, sustained attempt has been made to articulate his epistemology in a way that does not depend on his (mostly) outdated understanding of the cosmos.

There is another way to approach this problem, and that is along the lines of the distinction between Aristotle's physics and his biology. The basic idea is that while large portions Aristotle's physics might belong exclusively to intellectual history, contemporary biology is still working out Aristotle's insights. This point was put most forcefully by Max Delbrück, who once remarked that Aristotle should be posthumously awarded the Noble prize for discovering DNA.[6] If forms could be interpreted merely as genetic sequences that are passed from parents to children, Aristotle comes out looking pretty good. To my mind this immediately raises important questions, such as whether Aristotle's theory of knowledge was more linked to his biology than to his physics, and if so, whether his theory of knowledge is similarly forward-thinking.

Nevertheless, I remain silent on whether Aristotle's epistemology is more favorably interpreted as working without the forms at all, or as working with the forms reconstructed according to contemporary biology. I am not withholding my opinion on the matter, I just do not (yet) have a reasoned opinion to give. But I think I do not need to decide on the matter in order to stand behind this book, simply because my project is more modest. My first task is to lay out Aristotle's theory of knowledge in such a way that its appeal does not depend on prior or simultaneous acceptance of his picture of the hylomorphic world. Then, I want to raise some issues that have occurred to the epistemologists of the modern world, and propose a direction that Aristotle's epistemology plausibly could have taken, leaving open the possibility that it would have been better to take that direction. My hope is that readers of this book will emerge with a 'Perhaps, let's investigate further' answer to the question 'Is Aristotle's epistemology still relevant?'

I should also say that I have been influenced by two of Aristotle's interpreters in particular whose work has generated much of the critical thinking behind this book, namely Richard Sorabji and Charles Kahn. To be clear, I have not consulted with them personally, nor have they commented on any part of the book, but it is not exaggerating to say that much of this work is a dialogue with these thinkers. I have not always agreed with their interpretations, although my attempts to articulate why exactly I find myself in disagreement with their views have generated long passages or even entire chapters. Finally, I would like to thank commenters at a 2011 Eastern American Philosophical Association colloquium session who commented on an essay of mine—"What Is Thought That Thinks Itself?"—that served as an important study for this book, as well as the participants in the 2012 and 2013 Northwest Ancient Philosophy Society and the 2013 Ancient Philosophy Society at Notre Dame University, who listened to and helpfully commented on large portions of chapters 3 and 4, which became the heart of this book.

Nathan Colaner
Seattle University

Notes

1. G.E.M. Anscome, "Modern Moral Philosophy," Philosophy 33, no. 124 (January 1958), 1-19.
2. Alasdair MacIntyre, *After Virtue: A Study in Moral Theory* (Notre Dame: University of Notre Dame Press, 1981).
3. See especially Burnyeat's and Cohen's contributions to *Essays on Aristotle's De Anima*, eds. Martha Nussbuam and Amélie Oksenberg Rorty (Oxford: Oxford University Press, 1992), 15-26, 57-74.
4. *Essays on Aristotle's De Anima*, ed. Martha Nussbuam and Amélie Oksenberg Rorty (Oxford: Oxford University Press, 1992).
5. Specifically, this is Burnyeat's objection in *Essays on Aristotle's De Anima*.
6. Max Delbrück, "How Aristotle discovered DNA" (American Institute of Physics, Cambridge, MA, 1974).

Introduction

It is not terribly controversial to recognize that there is a way to seek knowledge of mathematics on the one hand, and a way to seek knowledge of what is ostensibly the external world on the other. We may further divide the study of the external world into the study of nature (*phusis*), and the study of the ultimate principles of nature, which is sometimes called metaphysics (although not by Aristotle). I am here concerned mostly with Aristotle's claims about the knowledge of nature. He has much to say on this topic, which would seem to make it easier to give a general account of his view. This is not so in this case, however, partly because he does not express his views in one place, as there is no central Aristotelian treatise on knowledge. Rather, there are non-redundant epistemological doctrines to be found in nearly every major work, even those not obviously associated with theoretical philosophy. And while it is true that the *Posterior Analytics* is a fairly systematic attempt to explain demonstrations—the kind of deductions that yield *epistēmē*, this work does not address many issues necessary for understanding demonstration as a method, nor how demonstration has anything to do with knowledge of nature. Aristotle does address these topics, but only in bits and pieces over the corpus. For instance, he most clearly reveals *epistēmē*'s relationship to other kinds of knowledge in a middle chapter of the *Nicomachean Ethics*. The result of this fragmentation is that his remarks come across as miscellaneous, random, ad-hoc, and in some cases, contradictory. In fact, some may wonder whether there is anything like an Aristotelian account of knowledge at all.

This strikes me as unnecessarily pessimistic. While it may be true that Aristotle left many loose ends without a solution, it certainly does not follow that it is impossible to develop an account of knowledge of nature that is characteristically Aristotelian. In fact, the basic story is not overly complicated. Human knowers begin with nothing actual, but only the power of perception. The activity of perception, when it is accompanied by memory, produces a kind of concept in the mind that is best thought of as a perceptible universal. This concept is universal in the sense that it is not bound to a particular; it is perceptible because it is in images. Examples of this are concepts such as 'human' and 'circle,' and it is these concepts that are 'more familiar to us.' Thus, the first process Aristotle describes is the one that lays out how what is more familiar to us becomes more familiar to us in the first place. There is a second task here, namely, to get what is more familiar by nature from what is more familiar to us. Through proper use of these perceptible universals we come to have a different kind of universal— the kind of universal that *is* more familiar by nature. These are variously called definitions, essences, forms, and formal causes, examples of which are statements that express what it is to be a human, or what it is to be a circle. To emphasize their continuity with perceptible universals, I will call them 'definitional universals.' Aristotle sometimes calls this entire process of establishing definitional universals in the soul '*epagōgē*,' translated into English as 'induction.' He calls our familiarity with them '*nous*.'

Definitional universals are epistemologically primitive because they serve as the first principles of demonstration, and *epistēmē* comes about only from a demonstration (or explanation) based on these definitions. What are demonstrated are the other causes—material causes, and efficient causes, and in the case of non-organic things, final causes. It is of these three causes that we have *epistēmē*. Of the formal cause, we don't have *epistēmē*, since our awareness of it is a result of *epagōgē*, not demonstration. Demonstration is a process that delivers an explanation, while *epagōgē* delivers a simple awareness of what is by empirical means.

This, at least, is the story I tell in the third chapter, "Pursuing the Principles: *Epagōgē*.' This and chapter 4 form the heart of the first and most important part of the book—'Aristotle on Knowledge of Nature.' There is, of course, some necessary preliminary work. The first chapter, titled 'What *Epistēmē* is Not,' is an account of the kinds of statements that we in contemporary times call 'knowledge' that Aristotle would not call '*epistēmē*.' This is typically because Aristotle uses other words to express our familiarity with certain things, such as *doxa, nous, technē*, or *phronēsis*. *Epistēmē* is only possible as the result of a demonstration carried out correctly and in the context of a theoretical science. It turns out that this makes most of our everyday knowledge claims—even when true—something other than *epistēmē*. I begin the second chapter, 'The Principles of *Epistēmē*,' by considering Aristotle's claim that *epistēmē* must be based on principles. In order for the principles to be appropriate for generating *epistēmē*, they must be true, primitive, immediate, more familiar than the conclusion, prior to the conclusion, and explanatory of the conclusion. Five of these six requirements are quite complicated (the uncomplicated one being 'priority').

In the rest of the second chapter, I take up the requirements that the principles be true, primitive, and immediate. The truth requirement might seem obvious, but is not, for Aristotle actually requires that they be necessarily true. This presents an obvious relevance problem, because it is today difficult or impossible to believe that truths about nature are necessary truths. It is not difficult, however, to regain relevance here; we must simply see Aristotle's mistake about the nature of definitions of essences as an immediate implication of his mistake about the eternality of essences. Furthermore, there is no reason to believe that Aristotle's theory is suddenly unworkable if we note that essences are in fact not eternal. In the same spirit, Aristotle also says that the principles of demonstration must be immediate, by which he means that they cannot require their own demonstration, on pains of infinite regress. This doctrine, which strikes some as an *ad hoc* way to save the possibility of knowledge, is not *ad hoc* at all since Aristotle's theory of definition actually implies it. The solution is simply that demonstrations are explanations of middle terms, but definitions that are 'unmiddled;' this means that they are simply brute facts about the world that we discover through *epagōgē* that literally have no explanation. Hence, there could not in principle be demonstrations of definitions. And, for the one who points out that natural science no longer believes in unexplainable definitions of essences since all essences have at least an evolutionary explanation, I will once again point out that this complaint is neatly tucked away as about Aristotle's doctrine of the eternality of the world.

The fourth chapter is what I believe is my most original contribution to the interpretation of Aristotle's theory of knowledge. In it, I turn to the requirement that the principles be 'better known' than the conclusion. This doctrine implies that we must have a kind of knowledge of the definitions of essences that is somehow more precise than the *epistēmē* we come to have of what is demonstrated. This kind of knowledge is called *nous*, and it is gained through *epagōgē*. It is clear enough what it is to have *epistēmē* of something: one has *epistēmē* if and only if one is able to explain why a truth in a theoretical science is true. But what does it mean to have *nous* of a definition? I argue that the first step is to pull apart Aristotle's references to the images 'touching' and 'grasping,' both of which are sometimes lumped together as images of knowing *nous*. It is not an unreasonable *prima facie* assumption to believe that touching and grasping are the same kind of activity since they share a genus, but in fact they differ to the same degree as 'being acted upon' and 'acting,' respectively. A detailed analysis of Aristotle's texts reveals this as a consistent and important difference. By a process that Aristotle consistently calls *to noein*, we come to have what are called '*noēmata*,' which are concepts that cannot be true or false because they are non-assertive *logoi*, an example of which is a concept such as 'two-legged animal.' The most plausible reconstruction of the texts leads to the conclusion that this process is intuitive, even though it involves the mind instead of sensation; this means that this intuition in this case is intellectual rather than sensible. To emphasize, Aristotle thinks of *to noein* as a process of touching or making contact with *noēmata*, clearly indicating that *to noein* is modeled on the process of sense-perception.

The image of touch also indicates that this intuitive process is passive; 'grasping,' however, is not. It is only when we grasp a definitional universal that we have *nous*. The distinctiveness of the activity of 'grasping' may be found in Aristotle's complicated theory of definition. There is a formidably difficult collection of texts in which Aristotle appears to some interpreters to vacillate between believing that the first principles of demonstration are concepts, and that they are propositions. This is perhaps a natural way to categorize these texts, but there are certain passages that make this 'concept/proposition' interpretation impossible. Another attempt to make sense of this maze of passages is the interpretation that classifies definitions as identity statements. This would explain why Aristotle sometimes says that it is not possible to be in error about definitions, since if one defines 'human' as 'four-legged animal,' one has not erred but rather failed to identify 'two-legged' and 'human.' Identity statements on the other hand can be true, and this would explain Aristotle's doctrine that definitions can be true but not false.

This interpretation, however, does not work either. The crucial observation is that Aristotle (unhelpfully) sometimes thinks of definitions as statements such as 'humans are two-legged animals,' and sometimes as statements such as 'two-legged animal.' The latter definition has two terms and so is a *logos* and not a singular concept, yet is a non-assertive *logos* because it lacks a verb (*rēma*). Both kinds of definitions count as *logoi*, but only definitions in the first sense are assertions or predications. I believe that this interpretation is the only one that can make sense of Aristotle's various pronouncements that definitions could be premises of demonstration, yet definitions cannot be false. This analysis also completes the explanation of the difference between 'touching' and 'grasping;' I believe Aristotle's doctrine is that definitions as non-assertive *logoi* are touched, while definitions as assertions are grasped.

Chapters one and two explain the importance of the principles for Aristotle, and chapters 3 and 4 are accounts of how human knowers come to have them. Chapter 5, then, is about their use. I have had several occasions to mention one of their uses, namely as principles of demonstrations. But Aristotle also makes much of a different kind of use, which he calls contemplation. I argue that contemplation (*to theorein*), like *to noein*, is a process of intuiting the essences of things. The difference is that now these essences that are intuited are not part of the external world, but the mind. This is then, an active intuition. To be more precise, these essences *are* the mind, since the mind is nothing actual until it first intuits the forms. This, then, is a self-referential process. It is less obvious that contemplation has any significance for contemporary epistemology, nor that we can make sense of a *nous* that is the constitution of essences. Nevertheless, it is worth mentioning as a part of Aristotle's picture of knowledge, as he believes that contemplating is the most worthwhile activity available for human beings.

The second part of the book strikes a decidedly different tone. With respect to getting a general picture of Aristotle's actual doctrine, I have sought to be systematic in the sense that I have tried to interpret and comment on every passage that has major bearing on Aristotle's account of knowledge, and to smooth over those passages that seem to contain conflicting doctrines (at least where smoothing seems appropriate). The result is what I hope is a complete and coherent picture of Aristotelian epistemology. The second part of the book, however, is not coherent or systematic. I have chosen various epistemological problems that seem to me to be of central importance, and suggested the ways that Aristotle's doctrine might address those problems. These chapters are shorter, and should be read as exploratory essays that call for original research, rather than as essays that themselves work out that research. The title, "Aristotle on Modern Skepticism," already seems odd, given the reality of time's arrow. However, I do in fact mean to say that Aristotle's doctrines took into account and avoided certain problems that plagued the moderns, resulting in a surprising sort of dialogue.

Chapters 6 and 7 should be taken together, as they represent a problem and its proposed solution, respectively. I call this the problem of objective validity, which is a problem Kant identified in the traditions of both rationalism and empiricism, and which subsequently motivated much of his doctrine of transcendental idealism. The problem is that our concepts may be subjectively necessary in the sense that they are indispensable for us as knowers of the world, and so to that extent valid. However, their subjective validity does not imply their objective validity. That is, just because a concept is necessary for us, it very well may not represent how the world is in itself. Kant defers to Hume to explain how empiricism fails this test, but he goes on with equal force to criticize the rationalist tradition for assuming that what is subjectively valid is also objectively necessary. The concern is that, for all we know, an omniscient being simply 'implanted' the innate cognitive categories with which we find ourselves, which is of course no guarantee that they actually reflect reality. Kant's solution is to leave the underlying metaphysical picture of both theories—transcendental realism, for transcendental idealism, in hopes that knowledge may be found in the latter doctrine. If Kant is right about this, this is bad news for anyone who believes in both the possibility of knowledge and that the world is external to the mind.

Chapter 7 is concerned to articulate and compare Kant's and then Aristotle's solution to this problem. In a thought experiment, Kant asks us to imagine what he calls the *intellectus archetypus*, which is a being that knows intellectual objects by creating them. One implication of this kind of cognition is that discursivity is unnecessary for it, since the intuition does not to deliver sensible objects to it. Another feature of this cognition is that it is completely spontaneous—there is not receptivity in any part of it. It is the spontaneity of this cognition that guarantees knowledge. A human cognition, by contrast, is an *intellectus ectypus*, which uses intuition and concepts separately to generate knowledge. Furthermore, the intuition is sensible and receptive. There is spontaneity here, but the spontaneity exists all at the level of concepts. Because of this spontaneity, there is a kind of knowledge is available for human cognition. But because the concepts merely receive the manifold of intuition, we have no right to make judgments about the ultimate principles of reality. So in the case of both the *intellectus intuitus* and *intellectus ectypus*, spontaneity is the necessary and sufficient condition of knowledge. It turns out that Aristotle, like Kant after him, insists that we do not simply find our minds stocked with concepts; rather, those concepts arise from our own experience with the world. However, Kant and Aristotle would agree that they do not come about by abstracting the contents of experience, as the empiricist would argue. The result is that Aristotle also places spontaneity at the heart of his epistemology.

Chapter 8 addresses what is probably one of the most curious periods of Western epistemology, and that is the nearly universal acceptance of the idea that Gettier-style examples undermine 'traditional' justification analysis. Given Aristotle's status as the most important philosopher in Gettier's tradition, we should assume that Aristotle was supposed to be caught in this criticism. Aristotle, however, insists that *epistēmē* is not forthcoming when 1) no inference is involved, 2) false beliefs are used as premises, 3) justificatory premises are formed from testimony and/or perceptual beliefs, or 4) there are no immediate principles of demonstration. Since Gettier recognized no such limitations on justification as evidenced by his examples, we cannot be sure what he would say in response to Aristotle on these points. But in order to get a direct comparison, let's dismiss all of Aristotle's carefully thought-out epistemic rules, and imagine Aristotle considering whether one knows that 'The man with 10 coins in his pocket will get the job.' What would Aristotle have said about that example on Gettier's terms? As it turns out, we do not have to imagine, for Aristotle has sufficiently addressed these kinds of arguments. What he says that is relevant to them mostly occurs in *Posterior Analytics* I.13, where he works to distinguish demonstrations of the fact, deductions of the fact, and demonstrations of the reason why. Sometimes a demonstration yields a fact, and yet it fails to explain that fact. In such cases, we do not have *epistēmē*, since *epistēmē* can only result from a certain kind of explanation. Since we do not explain why 'the man with 10 coins in his pocket will get the job' in the justification of it, we cannot have *epistēmē*. At best, we have either deducted or demonstrated the fact. This shows that Aristotle critiqued Gettier's problem two and a half millennia before the problem was formulated.

Chapter 9 compares Aristotle's doctrine against perhaps the most well-known modern skeptical argument, namely Descartes' argument for external world skepticism. I believe that here, Aristotle's doctrines are once again remarkably prescient. Of course, no one has been able to solve Descartes' actual problem, including, notably, Descartes himself. After all, a solution would require a knower to be able to eliminate all logically possible alternatives to her proposition each time she made a judgment. Aristotle was aware of skepticism of this character, but he was not phased by it. Why? It is because he embraced a form of knowledge that relied heavily on method. First of all, this means that knowledge claims cannot be made by those not trained in the philosophical sciences (although they can make *doxa* claims). And second, what is important about these methods is that they are reliable ways to generate truth claims, not that they eliminate all logically possible alternative worlds. It is possible that Aristotle's casual dismissal of external world skepticism together with his focus on reliable ways to generate truth makes him something of a forerunner to externalism, which is a popular response to external world skepticism among contemporary epistemologists.

Chapter 10 returns to Kant, and to a problem discussed at some length in chapter 4, namely, intellectual intuition. As chapter 4 has it, intellectual intuition forms a central part of Aristotle's account of how we come to know first principles of demonstration. Kant does not speak often of intellectual intuition, although as it turns out, his rejection of it is at the very heart of his epistemology. Kant begins the first part of the *Critique of Pure Reason* by insisting that all intuition is sensible; intellectual intuition, therefore, does not exist. Why does Kant believe this? In a 1772 letter, he describes an epiphany he had: intuition is affection, and sensible objects affect us; furthermore, intellectual objects do not. The result is that the concept of intellectual intuition is incoherent. This presupposition, as will be appreciated by readers of the first *Critique*, is central to his epistemology. But of course, to argue against intellectual intuition would require explaining how we can know that intellectual objects do not affect us, although

Kant apparently never gives such an explanation, even though many philosophers are content with Kant's rejection. This observation may be coupled with the fact that Aristotle does make such an argument. If this is right, then the doctrine of intellectual intuition was dismissed without a fair hearing.

Chapter 11 strikes a far different tone, as this is the lone chapter where I chastise Aristotle without giving him hope of revising the particular doctrine; the issue, specifically, is dialectic, which is Aristotle's method for gaining metaphysical knowledge. Here, I contend that the skeptic (Kant in this case) successfully undermines Aristotle's method. Aristotle's method of dialectic is mercifully straightforward, considering the complicated passages in which Plato constructs his theory of dialectic. For Aristotle, one simply begins inquiry by setting down a reputable opinion (*endoxa*), then subjects it to critical analysis by examining its implications. If the implications of the *endoxa* are contradictory or absurd, then the *endoxa* itself must be discarded; this is simply a '*modus tollens*' style argument. After several rounds of this, the pretenders to truth are exposed. When there is only a single *endoxa* remaining, that *endoxa* has been established as true. Kant describes the relevant fallacy as 'subreption,' which is a failure to consider the difference between what it subjectively necessary and what is objectively valid in a metaphysical context. He makes his point by considering other kinds of truth claims. In mathematics, for example, subreption is not possible, and so it is not necessary to guard against it. This is so because human cognizers construct mathematical space, such that there is a perfect coincidence between what it subjectively valid and what it objectively necessary. In metaphysics, however, this is not so. The result is that just because we are able to undermine, say, the doctrine that the universe did not come to be in space and time, does not prove that it is eternal. Therefore, the use of dialectic in metaphysics is therefore an illegitimate way to generate truth claims.

There are three limitations to the second part of this work. First, I do not claim that Aristotle has actually solved the various skeptical problems (with the exception of chapter 8), merely that his epistemology is relevant to them, such that there is a potential for an Aristotelian solution that has so far been apparently unexplored. Second, while I claim that Aristotle has developed epistemological resources that may be relevant for modern epistemology, I do not consider any skeptical arguments of the ancient world, many of which Aristotle would have been aware. This is a rich tradition, but it is not what this book is about. Third, I do not consider any skeptical attacks on Aristotle's own work—either the extant attacks of ancient epistemology, or the possible attacks that could be developed from modern and contemporary epistemology. None of these limitations, however, affect my goal of showing that Aristotle's theory of knowledge should at least be part of the contemporary dialogue.

There is another possible criticism that is bound to come up in relation to the second part of the book, which is that it is not possible to compare Aristotle's epistemology to any modern or contemporary view of knowledge, because the contexts in which their respective philosophies were expressed are hopelessly different. I do not see how this view as I expressed it can be defended. It is certainly true that there are many contextual differences between Aristotle's world and ours that are both unspoken and important. But it does not follow for that reason that the two worlds cannot be compared; it merely follows that the differences must be addressed and evaluated, and not passed over in silence. It is, of course, worthwhile to worry about whether I have addressed all those differences sufficiently. If not, then I am happy to accept criticism on those grounds. But this is a very different kind of criticism from an *a priori* criticism that would unreflectively assert that Aristotle's views on knowledge just cannot be compared with contemporary ones.

Part One:

Aristotle on Knowledge of Nature

Chapter One
What *Epistēmē* Is Not

Five Restrictions on *Epistēmē*

In contemporary times, we use the word 'knowledge' in many contexts; we know (or at least someone knows) that the coffee is brewing, that trees lose their leaves in autumn, that the ball landed on the roof, the winner of last year's World Series, how spleens work, the best way to counsel troubled teenagers, the definition of a tiger, what parts a computer needs, who John is, and how to build houses. In the case of some ancient Greek authors, '*epistēmē*' can be translated as 'knowledge' without any important difficulty; this is not at all true with Aristotle. He certainly is no skeptic, although he would say that at most only two of those sample knowledge claims count as instances of *epistēmē*, namely, the ones involving trees and spleens. And even then, they may or may not be instances of *epistēmē*, depending on whether the knowledge claim was made in the right way. This is so simply because Aristotle places important restrictions on what *epistēmē* is. He restricts his use of the term in several ways: *epistēmē* only results from knowledge claims 1) that occur in the context of a science 2) that is a theoretical science 3) that results from demonstrations 4) that are demonstrations that give genuine explanations and 5) that are based on appropriate principles. The first four restrictions are the concern of the present chapter.[1]

The first restriction concerns knowledge claims that are not part of a larger body of knowledge called a 'science,' organized by principles. However, there is even some knowledge based on principles—namely, knowledge of how to make or how to do something, that does not count as *epistēmē*; as the second restriction specifies, *epistēmē* only occurs in the context of a science that is theoretical. The third restriction has the effect of excluding otherwise legitimate philosophical methods in theoretical science—namely, *epagōgē* and dialectic—that do not issue in explanations. The correct use of them leads to kinds of knowledge that are nevertheless not *epistēmē*. The fourth concerns pseudo-explanations, that is, arguments that seem to explain but do not; this is true whether these explanations occur in the context of a science or not.

An understandable initial reaction to these restrictions is to conclude that they are too onerous, and that any concept of knowledge surely must be more inclusive. I suggest two considerations before jumping to such a conclusion; first, although many things we say we 'know' are not true objects of *epistēmē* for Aristotle, he does not thereby classify them as matters of ignorance in the manner of a skeptic, for he carefully describes other kinds of 'knowledge' that are not *epistēmē*. There are, notably, craft-knowledge (*technē*), practical wisdom (*phronēsis*), incidental knowledge or opinion (*doxa*), and comprehension (*nous*). Second, it is prudent to reserve judgment about these restrictions until we see how a failure to restrict *epistēmē* properly lead to much modern and contemporary skepticism. Perhaps it was Aristotle's careful restrictions that kept mainstream philosophy away from the debilitating kind of skepticism for so long, and perhaps that is a tradition that we should reconsider.

The First Restriction: Knowledge Claims Not Made in the Context of a Science

We often make knowledge claims about things that are not part of a larger body of knowledge; these include certain events, features or characteristics of beings, and other states-of-affairs. A knowledge claim belongs to a larger body of knowledge only if it is concerned with a being that shares some kind of generic unity with others beings. Aristotle calls such a class of beings a science (*epistēmē*), and, confusingly enough, he also calls knowledge about beings in such a class *epistēmē*; hence, some even prefer to translate *epistēmē* as 'scientific knowledge.' There are no hard and fast rules to determine what the requisite connection of these beings must be, but this doesn't seem to bother Aristotle, nor should it. He just notes that different sciences are required for different groupings of beings:

> There is a science [*epistēmē*] that investigates being as being and the attributes that belong to this in virtue of its own nature. Now this is not the same as any of the so-called special sciences; for none of these others deals generally with being as being. They cut off a part of being and investigate the attributes of this part—this is what the mathematical sciences for instance do (*Meta.* IV.1 1003a22-26).[2]

In this passage, Aristotle refers to the science that investigates being as being, now classified as his 'metaphysics.' But there are also specific sciences that examine not being itself, but certain kinds of beings. Again, it is difficult to give a precise account here, but paradigm examples serve well enough. For example, it is not controversial that numbers and figures deserve their own science, and that plants do as well, and that mathematics and botany are very different sciences. As such, one may have *epistēmē* (knowledge) about certain truths in the *epistēmē* (science) of mathematics, and that same person may have very little *epistēmē* about the *epistēmē* of botany.

One sure sign that the considered domain of being is in fact a science is that the domain is organized by principles (*archai*, singular *archē*):

> Every science seeks certain principles [*archas*] and causes [*aitias*] for each of its objects—e.g., medicine and gymnastics and each of the other sciences, whether productive or mathematical. For each of these marks off a certain class of things for itself and busies itself about this as about something that exists and is...Of the sciences mentioned each somehow gets the what in some class of things and tries to prove the other truths, whether loosely or accurately (*Meta.* XI.7 1063b35-1064a6).

Any science has a certain set of principles that are foundational to it, and all the truths available within that science will be explained in reference to these principles.[3] In this passage, that is what Aristotle means when he says that the 'other truths' should be 'proved' on the basis of the principles of a science. It is fair to say then, that any science is organized by its principles.

Sumbebēkos and *Epistēmē*

But Aristotle's doctrine is even stronger, for principles are what make a group of things a science in the first place, such that any apparent class of things without principles is no science. It is worth noting that contemporary English retains this usage to a certain extent. Sometimes 'science' is short for 'science of nature,' but we also use the word the way Aristotle does when we refer to military science, or computer science, or the social sciences. When we classify these disciplines as sciences, what we mean is that they are organized by principles that may be taught and learned. Aristotle contrasts all of this with the accidental (*to sumbebēkos*, also translated as 'incidental' or 'coincidental') about which there can be "no scientific treatment" (*Meta.* 1026b4). No science of the accidental is possible simply because there are no principles of accidents. In an ontological sense, an accident is simply any predicate of a substance that is not a species or genus, but the concern here is not accidental predicates as opposed to substantial ones, but accidents in an epistemological sense[4;] this is simply a question about the presence or absence of principle that can explain the truth in question. An epistemological accident is a certain kind of truth that may be either of an event or of a feature of something—generically, they are accidental states of affairs.[5] In the following passage, Aristotle gives an example of both an accidental event and an accidental feature:

> We call an accident [*sumbebēkos*] that which attaches to something and can be truly asserted, but neither of necessity nor usually, e.g., if one in digging a hole for a plant found treasure. This—the finding of treasure—happens by accident to the man who digs the hole; for neither does the one come of necessity from the other or after the other, nor, if a man plants, does he usually find treasure. And a musical man might be white; but since this does not happen of necessity nor usually, we call it an accident (*Meta.* VI.30 1025a14-21).

Let's assume that the things we are considering are true; it is true, then, that a particular person who was digging a hole for a flower happened upon buried treasure. Therefore the true explanation of the event of his discovering buried treasure was that the person was digging holes for plants. But just because this is a true explanation, no sane person would stock up flowers that needed planting as part of a systematic way to discover treasure. In Aristotle's terms, what is implicitly recognized by anyone with common sense here is that finding buried treasure does not *usually* happen (and certainly it does not *always* happen) in the course of planting. Even someone who is quite unaware of Aristotle's analysis of accidental happenings would be able to agree with this analysis.

The same analysis works in the case of features or characteristics of a particular being. Let's consider his builder example (rather than the example of the musical man, which makes exactly the same point).[6] Suppose there is a particular person who builds houses, and who is also a medical doctor. Despite this, no one who discovers that this builder is also a doctor will call a builder the next time he is sick. Obviously, the builder does not possess knowledge of healing insofar as he is a builder, but insofar as he is a medical professional. Aristotle chooses to say that he while he is building, he is a healer accidentally. Again, the test that anyone would use is that possessing knowledge of healing does not coincide with (i.e., is incidental to) possessing knowledge of building either of necessity or for the most part.

The 'always or for the most part' test that Aristotle sometimes proposes is to a certain extent reliable, but it can also be distracting, because it does not yet provide the reason that these truths are accidental. For instance, we may observe that our builder also goes to sleep every night. Therefore it is true that 'builders are sleepers,' and here we can skip right past 'most part' and go for 'always.' But even though 'always' is now in our analysis, and things that are 'always' a certain way can usually be known, it seems that this should once again count as accidental knowledge. This is because the builder does not need to sleep insofar as he is a builder, but insofar as he is an animal. If a putative knower tries to explain the builder's tendency to sleep at night by talking about how exhausting the construction of houses is, the attempted explanation would not rely on any principles. The only kind of explanation that could result in *epistēmē* will have to talk about animals in general, and why animals need sleep.

The real reason that no *epistēmē* of accidents is possible, then, is that accidental truths lack principles, and truths must be explained on the basis of principles if they are to be the objects of *epistēmē*:

> That a science of the accidental is not even possible, will be evident when we try to see what the accidental really is. We say that everything either is always and of necessity...or is for the most part, or is neither for the most part, nor always and of necessity, but merely as it chances [*etuchen*]...there are not causes and principles of the accidental, of the same kind as there are of what is in its own right (*Meta.* 1064b30-1065a8).

It is only when we possess explanations of these truths based on principles that we possess *epistēmē*. If a state of affairs cannot be explained by principles, then it is a matter of chance (*tuchē*). If it is a matter of chance, it probably happens rarely, but as my builder/sleeper example shows, this is not necessarily the case. So we may ask: what are the principles of a builder who has knowledge of medicine, or of finding treasure by planting trees? There simply are not principles that explain these truths. They are mere facts, and there is no scientific explanation of them. In the case of the builder who needs sleep, there is a principle that explains that. However, that principle was not touched upon here, and that makes this a pseudo-explanation.[7] It turns out, then, that if a body of truths has principles, then it is a science, and it is only of these truths that *epistēmē* is possible.

Doxa of Accidents

This first restriction on *epistēmē* is particularly important because it concerns a very large percentage of state of affairs of which we claim to have knowledge. Surely it is possible to know that the book is on the table, or the view of the sun is blocked by clouds, or that the table is in the room at the end of the hall. How could we accept the ramblings of anyone who denied these as real knowledge claims? According to a theme that will emerge, Aristotle does not want to say that one cannot have *any* kind of knowledge of these states of affairs, as a skeptic might claim. Rather, he merely denies that one can have *epistēmē* of them, and this leaves the possibility that belief or opinion (*doxa*) of them is possible. *Doxa* and judgment (*hypolēpsis*) are held in high regard by Aristotle, although they do not reach the higher epistemological honorific: "Let it be assumed that the states by virtue of which the soul possesses truth by way of affirmation or denial are five in number, i.e., *technē, epistēmē, phronēsis, sophia, nous*; for *doxa* and *hypolēpsis* may be mistaken" (*EN* VI.3 1139b15-18). This is a difficult doctrine to understand if one simply assumes that Aristotle means by 'belief' what contemporary epistemologists do. In modern times, knowledge is belief about something that is true and has a justification. Hence, I may have a belief that there is a book on the table, but lacking justification, I do not know that there is a book on the table. But you, having justified belief that there is a book on the table, know that the book is on the table.

This is not at all what Aristotle means by belief, for knowledge is not belief plus something. Rather, belief and knowledge are distinguished by their respective objects:

> What is knowable [*epistēton*], and knowledge [*epistēmē*], differ from what is opinable [*tou doxastou*], and opinion [*doxēs*], because understanding is universal and through necessities, and what is necessary cannot be otherwise. But there are some things that are true and are the case, but which can also be otherwise. So it is clear that understanding is not about these things, for then what can be otherwise could not be otherwise...hence it remains that opinion [*doxa*] is about what is true or false but can also be otherwise. This is belief [*hypolēpsis*] in a proposition that is immediate and not necessary (*Post. An.* II.33 88b30-89a3).

We have here a formula: belief or opinion (*doxa*) is judgment (*hypolēpsis*) about things that 'can be otherwise' or are contingent.[8] One of the doctrines that Aristotle announces here—that *epistēmē* has as its object truths that are necessary—is a difficult doctrine, and it will receive full treatment elsewhere.[9] For now, let us accept for the sake of argument Aristotle's claim that if a truth is a universal

definition of an essence, it is necessarily true. I want to focus on the less conten-
tious claim that *doxa* is *hypolēpsis* of non-necessary or contingent truths.

What makes these truths contingent? Aristotle sometimes makes the answer
seem very easy: a truth is contingent if it is about a particular. So instead of the
universal claim that giraffes are long-necked animals, we are considering a particular claim, such as that *this* giraffe is long-necked. Particular beings by definition involve matter, and change is present wherever matter is present. If
epistēmē is about what cannot be otherwise, but *doxa* is about what can be otherwise, the application of the criterion will be quite simple:

> There is neither definition nor demonstration of sensible individual substances,
> because they have matter whose nature is such that they are capable both of be-
> ing and of not being...just as knowledge [*epistēmē*] cannot be sometimes
> knowledge and sometimes ignorance, but the state that varies thus is opinion
> [*doxa*]...it is opinion that deals with that which can be otherwise than as it is
> (*Meta*. VII.15 1039b27-1040a1).

> Now what knowledge [*epistēmē*] is, if we are to speak exactly and not follow
> mere similarities, is plain from what follows. We all suppose that what we
> know is not capable of being otherwise; of things capable of being otherwise
> we do not know, when they have passed outside our observation, whether they
> exist or not (*EN* VI.3 1139b19-23).

It is inevitable that particular beings change, and *epistēmē* cannot have a changing object. It follows that *epistēmē* cannot be of particular beings. The
Nicomachean Ethics passage is worded somewhat awkwardly, but the sentiment
is clear enough: particular beings change, and they are therefore not suitable
objects of knowledge.

There is a better answer, however, and it is not so easy, as Aristotle himself
indicates elsewhere. The clue that there is more to the story here is that this doctrine puts the science of nature in an impossible position. Clearly, Aristotle
wants to say that one can achieve *epistēmē* in natural science. On the other hand,
natural science obviously treats beings that have matter essentially, and nothing
with matter behaves with perfect regularity and necessity.[10] Aristotle clearly
recognizes this fact and at least attempts to account for it, repeating often that
"all *epistēmē* is either of that which is always or of that which is for the most
part" (*Meta*. VI.2 1027a21). This concession is an easy way to make sure
knowledge of nature is possible. But this, of course, is also an admission that
any being in nature can be otherwise than as it is. And this, according to those
other passages, seems to make nature a realm of *doxa*. Something has to give.

Aristotle offers a clue to resolution in his discussion of the accidental:

> That there is no science of the accidental is obvious; for all science is either of
> that which is always or for the most part. For how else is one to learn or to
> teach another? The thing must be determined as occurring either always or for
> the most part, e.g., that honey-water is useful for a patient in a fever is true for
> the most part (*Meta*. VII.2 1027a20-24).

Some states of affairs have principles that explain them. In these cases, one who knows that these principles are true can share that knowledge, and one who seeks this knowledge can do so perfectly well. The student of nature would ask, for example, "Why is there sap running down that tree?" The teacher's answer would involve explaining the 'what it is to be' of a deciduous tree.[11] And so there is teaching and learning here, even though deciduous trees do not coagulate sap with perfect regularity. Nevertheless, the teacher already has knowledge of these matters, and the student comes to have it. Aristotle therefore does not appear to care whether there is perfect necessity or not, only whether there is a forthcoming explanation. Mathematicians have *epistēmē* since they can explain why the angles of triangles must equal 180 degrees, and so do botanists, since there are principles that explain the coagulation of sap.

As further evidence that this is the better explanation of *epistēmē*, consider that there are other closely related states-of-affairs where teaching and learning are absent: "Why is there sap on that rock?" The answer is that the rock happened to be resting under a tree that for the most part coagulates sap. The teaching and learning that occur here are of a weak sort—so weak, that Aristotle would not bother to call them teaching and learning at all. This is not the kind of explanation that rests on a principle, but a set of true facts strung together that have no deeper connection; this is easy to see because rocks in fact do not gather sap always or for the most part. About the former state of affairs, one may arrive at *epistēmē* via an explanation based on the principles of deciduousness. About the latter state of affairs, one may have *doxa* about the sap on the rocks, but not *epistēmē*. There does not seem to be any difference here whether we are considering Aristotle's analysis of events or characteristics of a being, for there may be *epistēmē* of events or characteristics depending on the kind of events of characteristics that they are. The event 'finding treasure' has an accidental efficient cause—planting flowers. One therefore has *doxa* that this particular man found treasure by planting flowers, but it is not possible to have *epistēmē* of this event.

But at best, this is a summary of what Aristotle wants. What is his justification for his claim that knowledge of nature is possible even though things is nature come to be only for the most part? The key is that the phrase 'possible for something to be otherwise' is ambiguous:

> In one it means to happen for the most part and falls short of necessity, e.g., a man's turning grey or growing or decaying, or generally what naturally belongs to a thing...In another way it means the indefinite, which can be both thus and not thus...generally what happens by chance [*tuchē*]...Science and demonstrative deductions are not concerned with things that are indefinite, because the middle term is uncertain; but they are concerned with things that are natural, and as a rule arguments and inquiries are made about things that are possible in this sense. Deductions indeed can be made about the former, but it is unusual at any rate to inquire about them (*An. Pr.* I.13 32b5-22).

This passage is indispensable for understanding the real difference between *epistēmē* and *doxa*. If something exists with something less than perfect necessity, we cannot say for that reason that it is contingent. And this is because some-thing may be truly contingent in the sense that it is 'indefinite' and 'happens by chance,' or something may be contingent in the sense that it only happens for the most part. We can have *epistēmē* about the mathematics, which exists with perfect necessity, and we may have *epistēmē* about nature, which comes to be only for the most part. Two plus two comes to be four, and humans grey with age, but it is not true that every human in history has lost hair pigment upon ag-ing. Hence, one truth is necessary and one is not. However, both truths are ob-jects of *epistēmē*, because it is not by chance that human grey with age even though it is not necessary. Whether a claim about a state of affairs can be knowledge, then, depends entirely on whether the knowledge claim can be ex-plained by principles. If not, one has *doxa* about it.[12] And so *epistēmē* and *doxa* are in fact distinguished because they have different objects; it is therefore not the case that *epistēmē* is of universals and *doxa* is of particulars.[13]

The Second Restriction: Knowledge Claims Not in the Context of a Theoretical Science

Another kind of knowledge claim that does not count as *epistēmē* are knowledge claims that are scientific in the sense that they are made in the con-text of a science, but not a theoretical science. Aristotle's most fundamental epistemological distinction concerns the rational part of the soul:

> We said before that there are two parts of the soul—that which possesses rea-son and that which is irrational; let us now draw a similar distinction within the part that possesses reason. And let it be assumed that there are two parts that possess reason—one by which we contemplate the kind of things whose princi-ples cannot be otherwise [*mē endechontai allōs echeiv*], and one by which we contemplate variable things [*ta endechomena*]; for where objects differ in kind the part of the soul answering to each of the two is different in kind...Let one of these parts be called the scientific [*to epistēmonikon*] and the other the calcu-lative [*to logistikon*] (*EN* VI.1 1139a3-12).

As noted, *epistēmē* is usually appropriately translated as 'science' or 'knowledge,' when the knowledge is in the context of a science. So in normal circumstances, it would be appropriate to render '*to epistēmonikon*' as 'the sci-entific intellect,' as is done in the current translation. But this does not take into account that Aristotle clearly intends to use the word 'science' more broadly. For reasons that will become clear, it is more accurate to think of *to epistēmonikon* as the theoretical intellect, where a theoretical intellect is one kind of scientific intellect. This intellect tries to know not sciences of any kind, but a particular kind of science—a kind whose 'principles cannot be otherwise.' Correspondingly, it will be helpful to call this kind of science 'theoretical science.' And if this terminology is accepted, the principles of such a science may be called theoretical principles.

Aristotle adds quickly in the passage that the 'calculative intellect' may also be called the deliberative intellect and is distinct from the other kind of intellect since "to deliberate [*bouleuesthai*] and to calculate are the same thing, but no one deliberates about what cannot be otherwise" (*EN* VI.1 1139a13-15). Again, it is clear from other parts of Aristotle's corpus that he does not mean to exclude the deliberative disciplines from the category of 'science,' for he speaks explicitly of practical and productive science, which are domains of the deliberative intellect.[14] Thus, it is more helpful to say that the distinction between *to epistēmonikon* and *to logistikon* is the difference between the theoretical intellect and the deliberative intellect, and implies the differences between theoretical and deliberative sciences and principles.

The deliberative intellect is concerned with principles that can be otherwise. This sense of 'otherwise' means that they are the subject of deliberation, which has nothing to do with the sense in which natural principles may be otherwise.[15] In turn, there are two kinds of deliberative intellect, because there two (non-theoretical) ways for principles to be otherwise: "Among things that can be otherwise are included both things made and things done; making and acting are different...so that the reasoned state of capacity to act is different from the reasoned state of capacity to make" (*EN* VI.4 1140a1-5).

The reasoned state of capacity to make is called '*technē*,' and the reasoned state of capacity to act is called '*phronēsis*.' So a person who knows how to build houses or fix computers has *technē*, which is a kind of intellectual virtue that corresponds to the English 'knowledge,' but not to Aristotle's *epistēmē*; *epistēmē* is rather "the state of capacity to demonstrate [*apodeiktikē*]" (*EN* VI.3 1139b32), and there are no demonstrations in sciences that rely on deliberation.[16] The same is true for someone who knows what to say to criminals with hostages or what kind of assistance to give the homeless or how to vote on the health care law. This person has *phronēsis* but not *epistēmē*.

In an important word choice that must foreshadow Aristotle's famously difficult discussion of the best and second best lives at the end of the *Nicomachean Ethics*,[17] he does not say that the theoretical intellect is merely the other kind of intellect, but rather implies that it has a better claim to be called what the intellect is:

> Of the part that is practical and intellectual the good state is truth in agreement with right desire...for good action and its opposite cannot exist without a combination of intellect and character. Intellect itself, however, moves nothing, but only the intellect which aims at an end and is practical; for this rules the productive intellect as well, since everyone who makes, makes for an end (*EN* VI.2 1139a29-b2).

Since making and acting are different functions, they have different excellences. As noted, since these functions both essentially involve deliberation, they both belong to the deliberative intellect. This is to be contrasted the intellect that Aristotle has called the 'intellect-itself,' which has as its objects principles that cannot be otherwise. For Aristotle, this is more properly knowledge because "we all suppose that what we know cannot be otherwise" (*EN* VI.3 1139b20-21). The generic unity of *phronēsis*, *technē*, and *epistēmē* is that they reason from principles. In this sense, they are all kinds of knowledge, and Aristotle in fact calls them all intellectual states "by virtue of which the soul possesses truth" (*EN* VI.3 1139b15). But the important point is that *phronēsis* and *technē* are not specific kinds of *epistēmē*, and this is an indispensable feature of Aristotle's analysis of knowledge.

The Third Restriction: Non-Demonstrative Knowledge in Theoretical Science

Epagōgē

Aristotle reflected deeply on his own philosophical method (*methodos*). Without it, a philosopher would be distracted by every piece of information that came to her attention, making it more difficult or even impossible to seek the truth in any kind of systematic way. A philosophical method will have a starting point, a goal, and a characteristic way of proceeding. What is most important in a discussion of restrictions on episteme is to find out what the goal of the method in question is. For Aristotle, the only philosophical method that aims to arrive at *epistēmē* is demonstration, for "*epistēmē*...is a state of capacity to demonstrate" (*EN* VI.3 1139b31-32). Even though demonstration is the only method that yields *epistēmē*, it is not the only method necessary for philosophical investigation. The first division in philosophical method is between deduction and induction:

> All teaching an intellectual learning come about from already existing knowledge [*gnōseos*]...both deductive [*sullogismos*] and inductive [*epagōgē*] arguments proceed in this way; for both produce their teaching through what we are already aware of [*proginōskomenōn*], the former getting their premises as from men who grasp them, the latter proving the universal through the particular's being clear (*An. Post.* I.1 71a1-9).

There is a further division in deductive methods, for there is both dialectic and demonstration. These are both deductive because "something other than what is stated follows of necessity from their being so" (*An. Pr.* I.1 24b19-20). *Epagōgē* is different because it does not make inferences from already known premises, but from some kind of observation of particulars.[18]

Aristotle is not particularly clear about the exact relationship between demonstration and dialectic. The relationship between demonstration and *epagōgē*, fortunately, is much clearer. As noted, a demonstration is a kind of deductive argument, and deductive arguments must start with premises. Demonstrations begin with a very particular kind of premise called 'principles': "now we have said earlier that it is not possible to understand demonstration if we are not aware of the primitive, immediate, principles [*archai*]" (*An. Post.* II.19 99b20-21). And these kinds of principles can only be gained by *epagōgē*: "Now induction [*epagōgē*] is of first principles and of the universal and deduction proceeds from universals. There are therefore principles from which deduction proceeds, which are not reached by deduction; it is therefore by *epagōgē* that they are acquired" (*EN* VI.3 113928-31).[19] *Epistēmē* is gained by demonstration. Demonstration, however, could never take place without using certain principles as premises, and these principles are gained by *epagōgē*. In this way, *epagōgē* is necessary but not sufficient for gaining *epistēmē* in the theoretical sciences.

Dialectic

Induction is a philosophical method distinct from demonstration; induction starts with appearances (*phainomena*) and ends with *nous* of definitions (*horismoi*), which are called principles (*archai*). Demonstration then starts with these immediate principles and ends with *epistēmē*. Demonstration is a kind of deduction, but there is another kind of deduction featured in Aristotle's epistemology, and this is so because there is another starting point for deductive arguments besides principles. It follows that this kind of deduction is not dependent on induction:

> Our treatise proposes to find a line of inquiry [*methodou*] whereby we shall be able to reason from reputable opinions [*endoxa*] about any subject presented to us...Now a deduction is an argument which, certain things being laid down, something other than these necessarily comes about through them. It is a demonstration when the premises from which the deduction starts are true and primitive...and it is a dialectical deduction, if it reasons from reputable opinions (*Top.* I.1 100a20-30).

Aristotle clearly means to develop a philosophical method that is deductive but not demonstrative. The difference is that in the case of demonstration, the premises (or at least one of the premises) are principles gained through induction, and are true in the special sense announced in the *Posterior Analytics*.[20] But the premises of a deductive argument will not always be like this, for some premises are principles resulting from conceptual analysis.

Which concepts are we supposed to analyze in this conceptual analysis? Aristotle calls these concepts '*endoxa*,' traditionally translated as 'reputable opinions.' The idea is that it is unnecessary to take any and all opinions (*doxa*) into account, because opinions are sometimes born from a good deal of careful reflection and sometimes from none at all. About *endoxa*, Aristotle notes that "those opinions are reputable that are accepted by everyone or by the majority, or by the most notable and reputable of them" (*Top.* I.1 100b20-22).[21]

In any event, what makes a deductive argument dialectical is that it starts with these *endoxa* rather the primitive, immediate, principles with which demonstration begins. Also unlike demonstration, which is a specific method with specific rules terminating in a specific kind of knowledge, dialectic is somewhat of a 'catch-all' method, relevant for many different things. In fact, it is not even exclusively a philosophical method, for it is the appropriate method whenever there are concepts that need to be analyzed, whether those concepts are philosophical or not:

> [Dialectic is useful for] intellectual training, casual encounters, and the philo-sophical sciences. That it is useful as a training is obvious on the face of it. The possession of a plan of inquiry will enable us more easily to argue about the subject proposed. For the purpose of casual encounters, it is useful because when we have counted up the opinions held by most people, we shall meet them on the ground not of other people's convictions but of their own, shifting the ground of any argument that they appear to us to state unsoundly (*Top.* I.2 101a26-34).

The specifics of this passage may be debated, but Aristotle clearly believes that dialectical arguments are the kind of arguments that regular people make in eve-ryday conversation, whether the concepts being tested and examined are philo-sophical or not. Even a person completely uninterested in real philosophy will benefit from being a skilled dialectician in either 'intellectual training' or 'casual encounters' (whatever those may be exactly), since it is not really possible to live a human life that never needs to evaluate concepts.

But important for our purposes is that dialectic is also useful for the 'philo-sophical sciences':

> For the study of the philosophical sciences [*tas philosophian epistemas*] it is useful, because the ability to puzzle on both sides of a subject will make us more easily detect the truth and error about the several points that arise. It has a further use in relation to the principles used in the several sciences...it is through reputable opinions about them that these have to be discussed, and this task belongs properly, or most appropriately, to dialectic; for dialectic is a pro-cess of criticism wherein lies the path to the principles of all inquiries (*Top.* I.2 101a34-101b4).

Aristotle does not often use the phrase 'philosophical science,' but we may be confident that he does not mean it as synonymous with 'theoretical science,' given his own use of dialectic for both theoretical and ethical matters.[22] A 'phil-osophical science' therefore is probably a theoretical or a practical science, but not a productive one, for production is not philosophical in nature. If so, dialec-tic is a method that is relevant for obtaining both *epistēmē* and *phronēsis*, but not *technē*.

But how, exactly, is dialectic useful for the philosophical sciences? There is a mainstream tradition based on the work of Owen and Irwin[23] that holds that dialectic is *the* method for Aristotelian philosophical sciences, pointing to Aristotle's remark at the end of this paragraph that "dialectic is a process of criticism wherein lies the path to the principles of *all* inquiries" (*Top.* I.2 101b3-4, my emphasis). I will elsewhere, at length, give reasons to show that this is mistaken.[24] But for now, we may observe that Aristotle simply does *not* say in that sentence that *all* scientific principles *whatsoever* come from dialectic; he says explicitly that he is referring to the principles that are used for several sciences, and these are a special kind of principles elsewhere called axioms.[25] Axioms— such as the law of non-contradiction—can only be arrived at by going through the *exdoxa*. Or as Aristotle's puts it, 'it is only through reputable opinions about [these kinds of principles] that they have to be discussed.' Once we are knowledgeable about the law of non-contradiction, for example, we may use it in any number of sciences, for this principle is as true in mathematics as it is in botany. But not all principles are like this; some principles are used for a particular science—these principles are definitions (*horismoi*), such as the definition that expresses the essence of a horse. It would be quite surprising if anyone could produce a single example of how a *horismos* could be gained by using dialectic rather than induction. It is false, then, that 'dialectic is a process of criticism wherein lies the path to the principles of *all* inquiries.' It appears to be quite true, however, that dialectic is required for gaining axioms, which is all we should suppose Aristotle meant there.

So much for that proof text supporting the claim the dialectic is Aristotle's method in general. The usual suspects for other proof texts come from Aristotle's discussions of 'incontinence' and 'place,' respectively:

> We must, as in all other cases, set the phenomena before us and, after first discussing the difficulties, go on to prove [*deiknunai*], if possible, the truth of all the reputable opinions about these affections, or failing this, of the greater number and the most authoritative; for if we both resolve the difficulties and leave the reputable opinions undisturbed, we shall have proved the case sufficiently (*EN* 1145b1-7).

> We ought to try to conduct our inquiry into what place is in such a way as not only to solve the difficulties connected with it, but also to show that the attributes supposed to belong to it really belong to it, and further make it clear the cause of the trouble and the difficulties about it. In that way, each point will be proved in the most satisfactory manner (*Ph.* IV. 4 211a6-11).

Both of these passages indicate that we must start with *endoxa*, and then if possible 'prove' that those *endoxa* are true after examining their difficulties. According to Aristotle's classification, these arguments would be deductive, and dialectical.

Owen takes this as further evidence that dialectic is Aristotle's general philosophical method, for these two passages clearly show that dialectic is useful in ethics and natural science. But Owen is taking too much here. Consider this passage from later in the *Topics* where Aristotle reflects on the propositions that may be gained with dialectic:

Of propositions...there are...three divisions; for some are ethical propositions, some are in natural science, while some are logical. Propositions such as the following are ethical, e.g., "Ought one rather to obey one's parents or the laws, if they disagree?'; such as this are logical, e.g., 'Is the knowledge of opposites the same or not?'; e.g., while such as this are in natural science, e.g., 'Is the universe eternal or not?' (*Top.* I.14 105b19-25).

In each of these cases, the path to knowledge here necessarily begins with *endoxa*. What the reasoning does next is to test the opinions by considering counterexamples, implications, etc. This is the very definition of dialectic.

Does this not show that Aristotle's main philosophical method is dialectic? Dialectic gets practical wisdom, which is not *epistēmē* but *phronēsis*. We also gain knowledge of logical and/or metaphysical principles through dialectic. And clearly, we get knowledge of a *kind* of principle in natural science via dialectic. But note that the natural scientist must have more than the knowledge of principles such as the definition of place, the universe, motion, etc., where 'definition' here translates *ti estin*—literally, 'what it is.' This is so because for demonstrations to occur, the natural scientist *also* must have knowledge of a different kind of definition—a *horismoi*—such as the definition of a human being or a deciduous tree. This is only gained through *epagōgē*, and this kind of knowledge is called *nous*. So the dialectical method is necessary for getting *some* principles of demonstration in natural science, but it is not sufficient, for *epagōgē* is also needed for a different kind of necessary principle. When in possession of both of those kinds of principles, demonstration may occur, yielding *epistēmē*. In this way, dialectic does not gain *epistēmē* directly, although it is relevant for the process. But dialectic is just one of Aristotle's philosophical methods, along with *epagōgē* and demonstration. And only demonstration yields *epistēmē*.

The Fourth Restriction:
Pseudo-Explanations

The first three restrictions show the sense in which *epistēmē* results only from demonstrations that occur in the context of theoretical science. An explanation comes through a demonstration (*apodeixis*), and demonstrations are very particular kinds of deduction (*syllogismos*). Aristotle sets out his theory of deduction in the *Prior Analytics*, a work is arguably the most seminal in the history of Western philosophy, as anyone wishing to do serious philosophy must be familiar to some extent with Aristotle's theory of deduction. His subsequent work, the *Posterior Analytics*, is concerned to set out his theory of demonstration. A demonstration is a deduction that follows certain rules and meets certain conditions, and in doing so yields *epistēmē*. But importantly, a deduction can appear to be a demonstration and yet fail to really be one, as Aristotle announces after giving certain criteria for demonstration: "there will be deduction [*syllogismos*] even without these conditions, but there will not be demonstration [*apodeixis*]; for it will not produce *epistēmē*" (*An. Post.* I.2 71b23-24). When an argument seems to be an explanative demonstration, but is not, I will call it a 'pseudo-explanation.' When an argument lacks the certain conditions referred to in *Post. An.* 71b, it is a pseudo-explanation. By 'these conditions,' Aristotle is referring to the requirement that the deduction must be based on appropriate principles. What a principle is, and what makes one appropriate is a complex topic and the fifth restriction on *epistēmē*, and will be more fully treated in chapters 2-4.

So one case of pseudo-explanation occurs when there is something that resembles an explanation but is not based on appropriate principles. But even if the principles are appropriate, Aristotle believes that it is still possible to give demonstrations on the basis of the principles and yet fail to give real explanations, and so fail to gain *epistēmē*. I count this as the fourth restriction on *epistēmē*; these are more subtle kinds of 'pseudo-explanations.' There are two kinds of this kind of pseudo-explanation—merely apparent demonstrations, and non-explanatory demonstrations. There is a famous passage in the *Posterior Analytics* that announces these distinctions:

> Knowing [*epistathai*] the fact [*to oti*] and the reason why [*to dioti*] differ, first in the same science—and in that in two ways: in one way, if the deduction [*sullogismos*] does not come about through immediates [*di' ameson*] (for the primitive explanation is not assumed, but knowledge of the reason why occurs in virtue of the primitive explanation [*proton aition*]); in another, if it is through immediates but not through the explanation but through the more familiar of the converting terms. For nothing prevents the nonexplanatory one of the counterpredicated terms from being more familiar, so that demonstration will occur through this (*An. Post.* 78a23-29).

One kind of knowledge claim that does not count as *epistēmē* is a fact, such as "the cat is in the tree." First of all, this claim is not in the context of a science, and so could not be *epistēmē*. But even if we could imagine that there is a non-accidental science about 'cats in trees,' the knowledge claim did not result from an argument, but from a simple observation. In the current passage, however, Aristotle is considering two cases where the knowledge claim results from a sound, deductive argument that very well may be in a scientific context, that nevertheless does not yield *epistēmē*.

Three kinds of sound deduction are in play in the 71b passage: 1) a deduction that is not a demonstration at all, 2) a demonstration that issues in an explanation, and 3) a demonstration that does not issue in an explanation. The first possibility results in a deduction of the fact, the second a demonstration of the reason why, and the third, a demonstration of the fact. Of course, 2) results in *epistēmē* , but it is tempting to believe that 1) and 3) do also, since Aristotle says that it is possible to know (*epistathai*) the fact (*to oti*) in these cases. However, I think we should not make too much of this wording, for Aristotle elsewhere draws a sharp distinction between 'to know' (*epistathai*) and actually 'to have knowledge' (*to epistēmēn echein*)[26]—that is, genuinely to possess *epistēmē*—such that Aristotle can speak of a person 'knowing' without committing to say that the person has real *epistēmē*. Given this, it makes more sense to believe that after processes 1) or 3), we do not possess *epistēmē*, but neither do we lack knowledge completely. I suggest that, once again, *doxa* is the best word here. But whatever we decide to call this kind of familiarity, the important point is that they are not instances of *epistēmē*, since they are not real explanations.[27]

On Translating '*Epistēmē*' as 'Knowledge'

This chapter began with a list of things that ordinary people (whether philosophically inclined or not) claim to know, and then observed throughout the course of the chapter that hardly any of them count as instances of Aristotelian *epistēmē*. Specifically, most of that list concerns knowledge claims that are made outside of a science, or outside of a theoretical science, or a knowledge claim that is not the result of an explanation. That leaves only knowledge of leaves changing colors in autumn and knowledge of how spleens work are genuine instances of *epistēmē* from the initial list, and then, only if that knowledge was not gained by any kind of pseudo-demonstration. If Aristotelian *epistēmē* and the contemporary meaning of knowledge are so different, this raises a question: should we just find a different word than 'knowledge' to translate '*epistēmē*'?

Given these restrictions, it is not unreasonable to consider 'scientific knowledge,' 'explanatory knowledge,' or 'demonstrative knowledge' as possible translations. All of these have the advantage that they highlight an important feature of *epistēmē*, although at the same time they also leave out specific Aristotelian restrictions. For example, 'scientific knowledge' is not an overly useful translation, because while it makes clear that *epistēmē* can only occur in the context of a science, it seems to allow the misunderstandings that it may be in the context of a practical science, or as a result of induction. And 'demonstrative' or 'explanatory' knowledge of course leaves out the important qualification that *epistēmē* must be scientific.

Perhaps for these reasons, Jonathan Barnes rejects these translations and opts for 'understanding.'[28] Besides the advantage of maintaining word for word correspondence, 'understanding' also has the advantage of being vague enough that is seems to call for further clarification, as we have seen is necessary for Aristotelian *epistēmē*. For this reason, I do not think that Barnes' translation is a bad one, but it seems unnecessary, for if we already have to flag the word 'understanding' and explain the several exceptions that I have explained in this chapter, why not just use 'knowledge'? This has the advantage, at least, of staying closer to the traditional definition of epistemology—'theory of knowledge.' Aristotle's definition of 'knowledge' is certainly complicated, but so what?

Whose definition of knowledge in the entire history of philosophy is not filled with caveats? This is analogous to the inability of English translators to render Aristotle's concept of *'eudaimonia'* with any word or simple phrase. Most translators use 'happiness' before listing a series of warnings about how *eudaimonia* does not mean happiness, at least not in any contemporary sense. In the same way, *'epistēmē'* does not have a word in English that describes what Aristotle has in mind, but I don't see this as a real barrier, provided we keep the points made in this chapter in mind. I therefore will translate *epistēmē* as 'knowledge,' or when useful, I will leave it untranslated.[29]

Notes

1. The last restriction is by far the most complicated, and is reviewed in chapters 2-4.

2. All quotations of Aristotle are from: Aristotle, *The Complete Works of Aristotle: The Revised Oxford Translation*, ed. Jonathan Barnes (Princeton: Princeton University Press, 1984). This edition never contains the original Greek, so all insertions of the Greek over the English translation are my revisions. Other revisions will be noted. For instance, I consistently use 'knowledge' instead of 'understanding' (see n. 35).

3. See also *Ph.* 194b16-20, and *EN* 1139b24-31.

4. Aristotle makes it clear that he intends such a distinction at *Meta* VI.30 1025a30-34. For the full doctrine, see *Cat.* 5. For this reason (apparently), 'accident' in the ontological sense is sometimes translated 'property.'

5. It is useful, however, to hold on to this distinction, for sometimes Aristotle speaks as through only definitions of substances can count as principles of demonstration (*An. Post.* II.3 90b29-32). But then, just as clearly, he refers to the principles of events (*An. Post.* II.12).

6. *Meta* 1026b35-1027a2.

7. See pp. 24-26.

8. This passage also notes that *nous* is also a type of *hypolēpsis*, although I will leave this claim aside, since this is not the way Aristotle normally describes *hypolēpsis*. It is more usual to associate it with *doxa* and discursive reasoning in general.

9. See pp. 36-37.

10. Or at least nothing with matter under the heavenly bodies, as Aristotle mistakenly believes that the heavenly bodies move with perfect circularity.

11. See Aristotle's example in *An. Post.* II.16-17.

12. Also see *An. Post.* II.12 96a8-18.

13. This is also well-supported by *An. Post.* I.33 89b1-3.

14. *Meta.* XI.7.

15. It would be more accurate to say that they cannot be manipulated are still be theoretical principles. For example, it is indeed possible to modify the genes of plants. However, Aristotle might say (with good reason) that the scientists doing such genetic modifications are engaging in practical disciplines, even if the principles of genetic plant life are theoretical principles in other contexts.

16. *EN.* VI.5 1140a33-1140b4.

17. *EN.* X.7-8.

18. See pp. 47-50.

19. Also see *An. Post.* II.19 100a3-4.

20. *An. Post.* I.2 71b20-24.

21. Aristotle might be accused of resting this doctrine on a vicious circle, because we will not truly know the difference between opinions worth considering and those not worth considering until we actually consider them. But for the sake of argument, let us agree with Aristotle on the general principle that some opinions obviously demand our immediate attention, but not all do.

22. *EN* VI.2 1145b1-7.

23. T.I Irwin, "Ways to First Principles: Aristotle's Methods of Discovery, " *Philosophical Topics* 15, no. 2 (Fall 1987): 109-134.

G.E.L. Owen, "*Tithenai ta Phainomena,*" in *Articles on Aristotle: Vol. 1 Science,* ed. J. Barnes, M. Schofield, and R. Sorabji (Great Britain: Gerald Duckworth & Company Limited, 1975).

24. See pp. 57-61.

25. *An. Post.* I.2 72a15-24.

26. *An. Post.* 74b21-24.

27. Chapter 8: "Gettier and the Problem of Justification" gives a more detailed treatment of this topic, since these mistakes are committed by Gettier in his famous problem.

28. He is the editor of the *Revised Oxford Translation*, revising it according to this standard.

29. Correspondingly, I will change 'understanding' to 'knowledge' in quotations from the Revised Oxford Translation, as I have already done throughout this present chapter.

Chapter Two
The Principles of *Epistēmē*

The Criteria for Principles

The first chapter describes four restrictions that Aristotle puts on *epistēmē*. The present chapter begins an examination of a fifth, which is surely the most complicated of the restrictions. It is that *epistēmē* must be supported by a very particular kind of premise. Aristotle is fairly consistent is calling these premises 'principles' (*archai*); probably Aristotle's most well-known general description of the principles of *epistēmē* is at the beginning of the second book of the *Posterior Analytics*:

> If then, *epistēmē* is as we posited, it is necessary for demonstrative understanding in particular to depend on things that are true and primitive [*prōton*] and immediate [*amesos*] and more familiar than and prior to and explanatory of the conclusion (for in this way the principles [*ai archai*] will also be appropriate [*oikeiai*] to what is being proved) (*An. Post.* II.1 71b20-23).

The claim is that if principles can be used in demonstration, they must be appropriate or fitting for the task. Aristotle here seems to give six separate criteria for appropriate principles of episteme: they must be 1) true, 2) primitive, 3) immediate, 4) more familiar than the conclusion, 5) prior to the conclusion, and 6) explanatory of the conclusion. This chapter is concerned with the first three criteria.

Although this list promises to provide straightforward organization to Aristotle's otherwise disparate discussions of and references to the principles, there are complications. It is possible to believe that 2) and 3) are basically synonymous; I think that they are importantly different, and in what follows I give what I take to be Aristotle's distinct defenses of them. It has also been suggested that 1) is as straightforward as it is uncontroversial—of course a sound argument must have true premises—although I have already shown in the first chapter that it is not, for by 'true' Aristotle means 'necessarily true.' The present chapter is directly concerned with these first three. Criteria 4) and 6) are sufficiently complicated to merit their own chapters (4 and 5, respectively), while 5) appears to be nothing more than an obvious corollary of any of the other criteria, save the first. Indeed, 'priority' is surely implied in the literal meaning of the very term *ai archai*, which more precisely means 'first principles.'

According to *Endoxa*, the Principles are *Prōtōn*

Unlike many influential philosophers throughout the Western tradition, Aristotle is not suspicious of appearances. Thus, he does not have a tendency to begin an inquiry by searching for the reality behind the appearances; rather, the favor is in the direction of the appearances, and Aristotle will wait for a compelling reason to abandon them. Appearances or phenomena can certainly refer to literal perceptions, although *endoxa*, or reputable opinions, may also be considered as kinds of appearances.[1] And although *endoxa* are different kinds of phenomena, the goal is the same as in the case of perceptions: "if we both resolve the difficulties and leave the reputable opinions undisturbed, we shall have proved the case sufficiently" (*EN* VII.1 1145b6-7).[2]

It is not controversial that Aristotle sometimes relies on *endoxa* to begin an inquiry into practical disciplines, such as the field of ethics.[3] But he never suggests that *endoxa* cannot be used outside of the practical disciplines. In fact, Aristotle uses *endoxa* all the time. For instance, he says that "we must, *as in all other cases*, set the phenomena before us, and, after first discussing the difficulties, go on to prove, if possible, the truth of all the reputable opinions...or failing this, of the greater number and the most authoritative" (*EN* VII.1 1145b2-6, italics mine). And so it should not be surprising if Aristotle begins with *endoxa* in various discussions of knowledge. So it appears that Aristotle plans to answer the question, "What is the object of knowledge?" in the same way as he answers many philosophical questions, namely by starting with the *endoxa*; I will refer to these as the 'epistemic *endoxa*.'

There are at least three places[4] in Aristotle's corpus when he seems to approach the topic of knowledge indirectly, via *endoxa*; in these passage we find important epistemological doctrines introduced only with the phrase 'we think we know...when....' The first two of these are similar in that they express one important feature of knowledge, namely that it must begin with something primary, or prior: "... obviously that which is primarily [*prōton*] is the 'what' [*ti estin*]...And we think we know [*oiometha eidenai*] each thing most fully, when we know [*gnōmen*] what it is...rather than when we know [*ismen*] its quality, its quantity, or where it is..." (*Meta.* VII.1 1028a14-1028b3). In *Physics* II.3, he uses the same general language, although there he speaks not of a primary as a 'what,' but as a cause and a 'why': "Knowledge is the object of our inquiry, and men do not think they know [*oiometha eidenai*] a thing till they have grasped [*labōmen*] the 'why' [*to dia ti*] of it (which is to grasp [*labein*] its primary cause [*tēn prōtēn aitian*])" (*Ph.* II.3 194b18-29).

One way to investigate Aristotle's meaning here is to examine his word choices. To be sure, there are nuances—some noteworthy—between the meanings of *gignōskō* (conjuageted here as *gnōmen*), *oida* (*eidenai*, *ismen*), and *lambano* (*labōmen*, *labein*); the most important is that Aristotle consistently uses *lambano* to mean a grasp of something, evoking the metaphor of touch.[5] But *gignōskō* and *oida* simply refer to 'knowledge' in general; we could do worse than to think of knowledge as *oida* or *gignōskō* as a general sort of familiarity with some object.

There are also specific ways to be familiar with something, of course, one of which is *epistēmē*. *Epistēmē* is a familiarity that comes from demonstrating, which is Aristotle's way to describe a certain kind of explanation. One reason *epistēmē* stands out from other kinds of familiarity—such as *doxa* (belief)—is that *epistēmē* must be based on a certain kind of principle. As Aristotle says, a truth can only be demonstrated "on the basis of the first principles of its science" (*An. Pr.* I.1 24a30). And if the first principle is to be appropriate (*oikeion*) to the truth demonstrated, it must be *prōton*. In the *Physics* passage, Aristotle calls this 'the primary cause' [*tēn prōtēn aitian*]. In the *Metaphysics* passage it was just '*prōton*,' which Ross translates as 'primary.' Throughout the *Posterior Analytics*, Ross translates *prōton* as 'primitive'[6], so when Aristotle uses the noun form—'*ta prōta*'—it is reasonably translated as 'the primitives' (100b4). But what makes a principle *prōton*?

Essences as *Prōtōn*

It is tempting to understand 'primary' in terms of the fifth criterion, 'priority,' such that a *prōtōn* principle is simply one that is 'prior to the conclusion.' On this reading, the principles would be primary not because their object is primary, but only in the sense that they are prior relative to the demonstrated conclusions. This is not what Aristotle meant. The complicated story begins earlier, in the *Categories*. Here, Aristotle uses the word 'primary' quite differently, to refer to individuals:

> A substance [*ousia*]—that which is called a substance most strictly, primarily [*prōtōs*], and most of all—is that which is neither said of a subject [*kath hypokeimenou*] nor in a subject [*en hypokeimenoi*], e.g., the individual man or the individual horse. The species in which the things primarily called substances are, are called secondary substances [*deuterai ousiai*], as also are the genera of these species (*Cat.* 5 2a12-17).

Aristotle thus identifies a primary substance in a negative way, as that which is not predicated in a subject or of a subject; the only candidate left is the subject itself, and so substance is subject. For example, a color such as 'brown' is said in a subject, while a species like 'horse' is said of a subject; only individual horses can be 'brown horses,' and those individuals are not themselves predicated of anything. As such, they are *hypokeimenon*. 'Horse' and 'brown' are alike in being predicates, but they are different kind of predicates since the species and genus (horse, animal) of an individual horse are predicates that reveal what it is. Predicating 'brown' of the horse gives us information about the horse, but it does not tell us what it is since a horse may be any number of colors while being what it is. These two kinds of predicates are therefore essential (*kath' auto*) and accidental (*kata sumbebēkos*) predicates, respectively.[7]

Because species and genus tell us what kind of substance an individual is, Aristotle in turn thinks of them as kinds of substances. They are not, however, primary substance, but secondary; they merely "reveal the primary substance" (2b30). Only an individual substance (*tode ti*) is a primary substance. Aristotle's chief reason appears to be that species and genera would not exist if they were no existing individual. The predicate 'horse' exists, but only because there are existing individual horses. The accidental predicates also give us information about the primary substance, but they tell us about the features it may or may not have, not about the kind of substance it is. So they are also dependent on an individual for their existence, but in Aristotle's technical vocabulary, they are 'said in' a subject. Because of the special relation the species and genus have to the subject, they are 'said of' a subject. The important point, however, is that both terms express dependence on the fundamental subject (*hypokeimenon*).

Aristotle's summary of the previous view of substance in *Metaphysics Zeta* is certainly reminiscent of the main points made in the *Categories*:

> The word 'substance' [*ousia*] is applied, if not in more senses, still at least to four main objects; for both the essence [*to ti ēn einai*] and the universal [*katholou*] and the genus [*genos*] are thought to be the substance of each thing, and fourthly the substratum [*hypokeimenon*]. Now the substratum is that of which other things are predicated, while it is itself not predicated of anything else. And so we must first determine the nature of this; for that which underlies a thing primarily is thought to be in the truest sense its substance (*Meta.* VII.3 1028b35-1029a1).

The connection of this passage to the *Categories* is reasonably straightforward. There, a subject or substratum was identified as primary substance, and species and genus—which are both universal and essential predicates—had a claim to be a kind of substance as well.

But the subsequent discussion in *Zeta* takes a different turn. From an epistemological perspective, what is most important is that primary substance now seems to be what signifies the substance; importantly, this means that primary substance itself is an object of knowledge. In the *Categories*, "only [species and genera], of things predicated, reveal the primary substance [*dēloi tēn prōtēn ousian*]" (2b30); primary substances were ontologically basic, but secondary substances were epistemologically basic, because we only know about primary substance through the secondary substance. Now, in *Zeta*, "the what, which indicates the substance" is said to be *prōton*. This is worth a fuller quote:

> Obviously that which is primarily [*prōton*] is the 'what' [*ti estin*] which indicates the substance [*sēmainei tēn ousian*] of the thing...Therefore that which is primarily and is simply (not is something) must be substance. Now there are several senses in which a thing is said to be primary; but substance is primary in every sense—in formula, *in order of knowledge* [*gnōsei*], in time...And we

think we know [*eidenai*] each thing most fully, when we know [*gnōmen*] what it is...rather than when we know its quality, its quantity, or where it is (*Meta.* VII.1 1028a14-1028b3, emphasis mine).

This subtle but significant change in the doctrine of substance is due to complicating factors introduced in the meantime by the *Physics*. In *Physics* I.7, Aristotle is concerned with the principles that would explain the phenomenon of change:

We have now stated the number of the principles of natural objects that are subject to generation, and how the number is reached; and it is clear that there must be something underlying the contraries, and that the contraries must be two...The underlying nature [*ē hypokeimenē phusis*] can be known by analogy. For as the bronze is to the statue, or the matter and the formless before receiving form to any thing that has form, so is the underlying nature to substance, i.e., the 'this' [*tode ti*] or existent (*Ph.* I.7 191a2-12).

In this highly consequential passage, Aristotle indicates two distinctions that will dominate subsequent Western intellectual history, namely between form and matter, and potentiality and actuality. Aristotle calls these principles 'necessary' because absolute, coming to be from nothing is impossible. Rather, there is privation (a kind of potential form), the form that something actually has, and the matter that survives the change from potential to actual form.

This challenges the doctrine of the *Categories* because there, what underlies as the ultimate bearer of predication just was a *tode ti*; there was nothing more to the story because the individual was identical to the subject or underlying thing. Now, however, matter underlies the *tode ti*, which makes the individual a composite of form and matter. The individual, therefore, is not fundamental. Aristotle immediately realizes that the matter/form distinction raises a question that he must return to later: "whether the form or what underlies the form is the substance [*ousia*] is not yet clear" (*Ph.* I.7 191a19-20).

This is the complicated background against which Aristotle asks the question in *Zeta*, 'What is substance?' He refers to the negative criterion concerning predication developed in the *Categories* again—that substance is the bearer of predicates, but is not predicated of anything—but rejects it this time:

We have now outlined the nature of substance, showing that it is that which is not predicated of a subject, but of which all else is predicated. But we must not merely state the matter thus; for this is not enough. The statement itself is obscure, and further, on this view, matter becomes substance (*Meta.* VII.3 1029a7-10).

When this criterion was applied in the *Categories*, what turned out to be a subject was an individual. But in the wake of the form/matter distinction, this criterion names the matter as the subject. Aristotle complains that this method of naming the substance is 'obscure,' but Aristotle's real argument against it is this:

this criterion identifies matter as the subject, but matter is not subject, and so the criterion must have been wrong.

And indeed, a few lines later he names three new criteria that are clearly meant to replace the first: separability (*chōriston*), individuality (*tode ti*), and priority:

> For those who adopt this point of view [of the *Categories*], then, it follows that matter is substance. But this is impossible; for both separability and individuality are thought to belong chiefly to substance. And so form and the compound of form and matter would be thought to be substance, rather than matter. The substance compounded of both [*tēn ex amphoin ousian*], i.e., of matter and shape, may be dismissed; for it is posterior and its nature is obvious (*Meta.* VII.3 1029a29-32).

Formless matter fails to be separable and/or individual,[8] while the compound is not prior by definition, since it is composed of matter and form.

The candidate that survives is form (*eidos*).[9] Aristotle quickly adds that the investigation into form is both necessary and difficult, although he turns abruptly not to an investigation into *eidos*, but into *to ti ēn einai* (1029b13)—literally, 'what it is to be something'; translated into Latin as '*essentia*,' 'essence' in English. What he means is that "the essence of each thing is what it is said to be in virtue of itself [*kath' auto*]" (1029b14). Aristotle's failure to immediately investigate *eidos* is understandable given his identification of form and essence: "by form [*eidos*] I mean the essence [*to ti ēn einai*] of each thing and its primary substance" (1032b1-2) and "I call the essence substance without matter" (1032b14).

It is obvious that something is different about Aristotle's doctrine of substance, but it is not so obvious what that is. Thus, a consequential question: what has changed about Aristotle's doctrine of substance from the early *Categories* to the mature *Metaphysics*, and what has not? What has not changed is Aristotle's belief that he is saying something fundamentally different about substance than Plato, and that Plato was wrong. If it can be said that for Plato, a universal as a knowable Form [*Eidos*] is a primary substance and that individual substances were secondary, then the *Categories* completely reverses this. There, the particular is primary, and the species and genus are predicable, universal, secondary substances that reveal the nature of the primary substance.

It is tempting to believe that Aristotle has now come around to Plato's side in the *Metaphysics*, for now form is primary substance, and forms are universal. Aristotle is, however, doing something much more subtle: he is attempting to find a middle ground between the early doctrine of the *Categories* on the one hand, and Platonism on the other. I think that two follow-up arguments make this clear (although the logic of the arguments themselves is far from clear)—one in VII.6, and another VII.13. In VII.6, Aristotle asks "whether each thing and its essence are the same or different" (1031a15) and concludes via a particularly obscure argument that they are the same, and that separating the two—as believers in the Forms do—would be "absurd" (1031b28). In VII.13, he rails against the possibility that universals as Forms could be substance, for no universal "indicates a this, but rather a such" (1039a2).

For all the extreme consternation that these two passages have caused,[10] I do not believe that Aristotle's general intentions in *Metaphysics Zeta* are particularly mysterious: he wants to name essence as primary substance, but he does not want to give the impression that he is becoming a Platonist by simply reversing the *Categories*, such that universals are now primary, and particulars secondary. One way to understand this subtle maneuver is to note that the *Categories* asks the question, "What is substance?," and the answer is 'subject.' But given the complications of the form/matter distinction, Aristotle must now ask a different question: "What *makes* a subject a substance?," or at least "What is the substance of x?," where x is some *tode ti*. Thus, it is at least possible that *Zeta* did not mean to question whether an individual is a primary substance, but what makes an individual a primary substance. It turns out that an individual is a substance because of its essence.

Indeed, Aristotle adds, tellingly, that "substance is of two kinds, the concrete thing [*sunolon*] and the formula [*logos*]" (*Meta.* VII.15 1039b20). A *sunolon* is literally a 'thing all together'; what is all together is the matter and the form,[11] and so a *sunolon* is a compound substance—a particular. Substance as *logos* is meant to pick out the essence that makes a particular what it is. This re-affirms that Aristotle is not simply jettisoning the individual when it comes to a discussion of substance. In respect of these passages and word-choices, my own judgment is that it is best to think of Aristotelian substance as either essence, or 'enmattered essence' (the horseness of individual horses); strictly speaking, a compound is not a substance (some particular horse), but neither is an abstract, universal essence ('Horse'). Whether Aristotle has effectively articulated a middle ground between his own *Categories* and Platonism is, of course, another matter, but I believe that it was his intention to do so. If I am right about this, Aristotle never gives up his belief that substance is whatever a subject is, although his idea about what that is has changed. In the *Categories*, it was an individual (which now must be regarded as a compound of form and matter), and in the *Physics*, it was (at least for a few lines) matter. The three new criteria lead him to reject both of these possibilities in favor of a third candidate, form.

This emphasizes the connection that the mature doctrine of essence has with his doctrine of the principles of knowledge. In the *Categories*, secondary substances as essences were the objects of knowledge, rather than primary substance. After the complicated arguments of *Zeta* VI and elsewhere, substance as essence is decidedly *prōton* (1032b2). And, while essences are knowable, what is really important about them is that knowledge of essences is what makes explanation possible; as such, knowable essences *are* the principles of knowledge: "there is knowledge [*epistēmē*] of each thing only when we know [*gnōmen*] its essence" (*Meta.* VII.6 1031b6). This is what Aristotle means in the *An. Post.* I.2 passage when he says that appropriate *archai* are *prōton*.

The Principles as Necessarily True

In the list at *Posterior Analytics* 71b20-23 where Aristotle requires that appropriate principles of demonstration be primary, he also says that they must be true. It may be thought that truth is the most unremarkable of these requirements, for there is no controversy that in order to have a sound argument—let alone a demonstrative one—the premises must be true. However, there is another *endoxa* that implies that the 'truth' requirement is more complicated:

> We all suppose that what we know [*epistametha*] is not capable of being otherwise [*mē endexesthai allōs echein*]; of things capable of being otherwise we do not know, when they have passed outside our observation, whether they exist or not. Therefore the object of knowledge is of necessity [*anagkēs*] (*EN* VI.3 1139b20-23).

The reference to 'what we know' is to demonstrated knowledge, and so the claim here is that demonstrated knowledge must be of necessary truths. By itself, this claim is not particularly striking or controversial, because demonstrated knowledge is based on principles: "Knowledge [*epistēmē*] is belief [*hypolēpsis*] about things that are eternal and necessary, and there are principles of everything that is demonstrated [*tōn apodeiktōn*] and of all knowledge, for knowledge involves reasoning [*meta logou*]" (*EN* VI.6 1140b31-3). Since the reasoning in question preserves the necessity, it is the fact that the principles are of necessary truths in the first place that means that demonstrated knowledge will be of necessary truths. Thus, the real question here is why Aristotle would say that the principles of knowledge must be necessary.

The origin of the difficulty is found in his distinction between kinds of principles:

> We said before that there are two parts of the soul—that which possesses reason and that which is irrational; let us now draw a similar distinction within the part that possesses reason. And let it be assumed that there are two parts that possess reason—one by which we contemplate the kind of things whose principles cannot be otherwise, and one by which we contemplate variable things [*ta endexomena*]; for where objects differ in kind the part of the soul answering to each of the two is different in kind...Let one of these parts be called the scientific [*to epistēmonikon*] and the other the calculative [*to logistikon*] (*EN* VI.1 1139a3-12).

As noted in the first chapter, this division may be described as between theoretical intellect/sciences/principles on the one hand, and deliberative intellect/sciences/principles on the other. In which of the two categories does Aristotle put the science of nature? It might be assumed that because things in nature come to be always or for the most part, that Aristotle would count natural science as one of the sciences with variable principles, alongside the practical and productive sciences.

This point is only emphasized by noting that the principles of natural science are strikingly unlike other theoretical principles, such as those of mathematics:

> Natural bodies contain surfaces and volumes, lines and points, and these are the subject-matter of mathematics...Now the mathematician, though he too treats of these things, nevertheless does not treat of them as the limits of a natural body; nor does he consider the attributes indicated as the attributes of such bodies. That is why he separates them (*Ph.* II.2 193b23-33).

When 'surfaces and volumes' in natural bodies change, it is of no consequence to the mathematician, since she is not interested in them insofar as they are in natural bodies. Rather, she 'separates' them from matter in her treatment of them. This is significant, because it is matter that introduces change, and it is change that introduces irregularity, imperfection, generation, and corruption. Absent change, it is easy to understand why Aristotle classifies mathematical principles as necessary.

A principle of nature, however, cannot separate the matter in the same way as a mathematician separates the concept 'concavity' from concave material things, as Aristotle explains with his favorite example:

> And since each of the sciences must somehow know the 'what' [*to ti estin*] and use this as a principle [*archē*], we must not fail to observe how the natural philosopher should define things and how he must state the formula of the substance [*ho tēs ousias logos*]—whether as akin to snub or rather to concave. For of these the formula of the snub includes the matter of the thing, but that of the concave is independent of the matter; for snubness is found in a nose, so that its formula includes the nose—for the snub is a concaved nose. Evidently then the formula of flesh and the eye and the other parts must always be stated without eliminating the matter (*Meta.* XI.7 1064a19-28).

As noted, mathematical objects are separable in thought, and so matter is not of interest to the mathematician *qua* mathematician. But the formula or account of any natural substance is like the account of 'snub'; since only noses are snub, any explanation of snubness that did not reference matter will be an insufficient account.[12]

Despite that fact that natural science seems to have 'variable' principles and should thus be counted with practical and productive sciences, Aristotle consistently maintains a distinction between these disciplines and natural science: "There is a science of nature [*hē peri phuseōs epistēmē*], and evidently it must be different both from practical [*praktikēs*] and from productive [*poiētikēs*] science" (*Meta.* XI.7 1064a10-11). This makes it impossible to believe that Aristotle meant to include natural science as one of the sciences with principles that can be otherwise.

Natural and Necessary? Some Failed Interpretive Possibilities

The inclusion of natural science as a theoretical science presents an obvious interpretive difficulty; how could Aristotle say that a science is made up of truths that are necessary, yet also that natural principles must refer to matter, and that things with matter often come to be only for the most part? The most obvious possible explanations are four. First, Aristotle could have simply been wrong, or worse—contradicted himself. Second, maybe there is a way to re-describe natural science to show that it meets the standard of a necessary theoretical science after all. Third, perhaps Aristotle meant to leave a third category for a science in between "incapable of being otherwise" and those concerned with "making and doing," The fourth possibility—the one that I will argue for—is that when Aristotle's doctrine of necessity is described correctly, natural science is an easy fit after all.

Different versions of the first possibility are endorsed by even the most sympathetic scholars. Richard Sorabji's seminal article from several decades ago as well as C.D.C. Reeve's more recent work deserve special mention here.[13] In Sorabji's article on Aristotle's definitions, he shows conclusively that Aristotle does not mean that principles of nature are analytically true simply because they are necessary. This is because necessity may also be *de re* necessity, and the case is strong for believing that this is what Aristotle intended. Sorabji, however, ultimately finds fault with Aristotle because he believes that Aristotle does not successfully show how principles of nature are necessary at all, and that it is better to believe that they are rather contingent. Reeve's criticism is a bit more serious: he claims that Aristotle simply contradicted himself on this point, saying that Aristotle has a "consistency problem" on this issue.[14]

I think that they are both right to recommend that Aristotle drop his claim about necessity in natural science, but both criticisms are based on a misunderstanding about why Aristotle makes this assertion in the first place. I will show that his mistake is not an epistemological one, but rather a metaphysical one, and that the metaphysical claim may be expunged without doing any serious damage to this theory of knowledge of nature. I will confront these arguments in due course.

On to the second possibility: perhaps is it possible to re-describe natural science to show that it does concern necessity after all. In fact, Aristotle does ascribe a sort of necessity to natural science:

> As regards what is of necessity [*anagkēs*], we must ask whether the necessity is hypothetical [*hypotheseōs*], or simple [*haplōs*] as well. The current view [i.e., the view that it is hypothetical] places what is of necessity in the process of production, just as if one were to suppose that the wall of a house necessarily comes to be because what is heavy is naturally carried downwards and what is

light to the top...Whereas, though the wall does not come to be without these, it is not due to these, except as its material cause: it comes to be for the sake of sheltering and guarding certain things. Similarly in all other things which involve that for the sake of which...What is necessary, then, is necessary on a hypothesis, not as an end. Necessity is in the matter, while that for the sake of which is in the definition (*Ph.* II.9 199b33-200a14).

And so there is *haplōs* (simple, unqualified, absolute) necessity—the sort that attaches to mathematics—and there is hypothetical necessity. The latter kind of necessity merely requires that *if* there is to be a horse, there must be such and such matter for the skin, etc.; there is no requirement that there must be a horse in the first place. This kind of necessity could rightly be called 'material necessity.' If then, a science is theoretical because it deals with necessity, then perhaps natural science is theoretical for that reason.

This, however, is not a serious possibility for two reasons. First, about this object of knowledge that cannot be otherwise, Aristotle says that "it is eternal; for things that are necessary *in the unqualified sense* are all eternal; and things that are eternal are ungenerated and imperishable" (*EN* VI.3 1139b23-25, my italics). This doesn't describe the objects of natural science, for those have only hypothetical necessity, rather than 'unqualified' necessity; equally as obviously, they are temporal, generated, and perishable. Second, Aristotle notes that productive sciences also deal with hypothetical necessity, and they are properly excluded from theoretical sciences. It therefore does not seem promising to believe that natural science is theoretical on the basis of material necessity.

But Aristotle's introduction of hypothetical necessity suggests a third possibility, which is that natural science is neither theoretical nor deliberative:

> For there is absolute necessity, manifested in eternal phenomena, and there is hypothetical necessity, manifested in everything that is generated as in everything that is produced by art, be it a house or what may be...So also is it with the productions of nature. This mode of necessity, however, and the mode of demonstration are *different in natural science from what they are in the theoretical sciences* (we have spoken of these elsewhere). For in the latter the starting point is that which is, in the former that which may be (*PA* I.1 639b24-29)

This suggests a division of theoretical sciences into natural and theoretical proper, which is based on the kind of necessity that obtains of the principles—unqualified or hypothetical. This division seems quite sensible, and further is a remarkably tidy way to define the term 'metaphysics,' since metaphysics could describe any properly theoretical science, while physics could be a different discipline entirely. Mathematical first principles would be included in theoretical science proper. Things are even better in theology since matter is not involved at all, for theology deals with things are "separable and unmovable" (*Meta.* XI.8 1064b11).[15]

A first note is that this possibility contradicts other place where Aristotle believes that there is no such distinction to be made: The above quote aside,

Aristotle expresses several times that there are only three divisions of sciences: "...natural science [*tēn phusikēn epistēmē*] must be neither practical [*praktikēn*] nor productive [*poiētikēn*], but theoretical [*theōrētikēn*] (for it must fall into one of these classes) (*Meta.* XI.7 1064a16-19).[16] Furthermore, there is good evidence that Aristotle actually intends this tri-fold classification. This is because he gives a justification for why he allows these three and no others. Consider a passage in the *Topics*, where he says, regarding the sciences, that they are "classified as speculative, practical, and productive; and each of these denotes a relation; for it speculates upon something, and produces something, and does something" (*Top.* VI.6 145a15-18).

The tri-fold division is therefore not based on the nature of the principles themselves, but the way the human intellect is related to principles. In the case of theology, mathematics, and natural science, the role of human intellect is to *speculate* or form *theories*. And when we have the kind of first principles that are objects of speculation, it is possible to demonstrate, and thus, to possess knowledge: This, then, is one way that our intellect might relate to first principles. Thus, whether principles involve absolute or hypothetical necessity is irrelevant to classifying them as theoretical principles. For the most part, carrots are orange and have a certain amount of vitamin A, but it is not necessary that this particular carrot come to be orange or to come to have a certain vitamin content. Obviously, an indefinite number of things could have happened that might prevent this typical production. The kind of knowledge we have about carrots, however, is theoretical.

The domain of the first kind of intellect, then, is not things that exist by necessity, but rather are sciences about which we *speculate*, and it is possible to speculate about necessary principles and about principles of particulars that come to be for the most part. This is meant to contrast with the relation our intellect has to first principles in the other main branch of sciences, about which we *deliberate*:

> In the case of productive science the principle of production is *in the producer* and not in the product, and is either an art [*technē*] or some other capacity. And similarly in practical science the movement is not in the thing done, but rather *in the doers*. But the science of the natural philosopher deals with things that have *in themselves* a principle of movement (*Meta.* XI.7 1064a10-17, my emphasis).

It must be pointed out that the principle of motion being external or internal cannot alone be divide theoretical and deliberative science any more than necessity, for the other theoretical sciences sometimes deal with immovable substances.[17] However, Aristotle's distinction that the principles of movement may exist *'in themselves'* or *in agents* is significant. That is to say, one science requires speculation because agency is not involved, and this is true of all the theoretical sciences, whether they involve immovable substances or not.

Why Natural Principles are Necessarily True

The fourth possibility begins by re-examining what makes something necessary in the first place. Aristotle's comments about substance in *Zeta*.15 reveal much about his position:

> Since substance is of two kinds, the concrete thing and the formula (I mean that one kind of substance is the formula taken with the matter, while another kind is the formula in its generality), substances in the former sense are capable of destruction (for they are also capable of generation), but there is no destruction of the formula... (*Meta.* VII.15 1039b20-24).

Aristotle refers to substance in two senses—in one sense as a formula with matter, and in another as a formula without matter. Concrete things or compounds are generated and destroyed, and are thus clearly not eternal; this particular horse was born and will die. This is because "they have matter whose nature is such that they are capable both of being and of not being" (*Meta.* VII.15 1039b29-30).[18] This is why Aristotle says "if all thought is either practical or productive or theoretical, natural science must be theoretical, but it will theorize about such being as admit of being moved, and only about that kind of substance which in respect of its formula is for the most part inseparable from matter" (*Meta.* VI.1 1025b25-27).

This is precisely the same reason that individual substances come to be always or for the most part—it is because they are enmattered. Whether we are referring to the temporality of a compound (this horse will perish) or the 'for-the-most-part' of a compound (horses have four legs, but this one was born with three), matter is essentially involved. This means that any individual substance can be otherwise, which means that it cannot be an object of knowledge:

> Knowledge cannot be sometimes knowledge and sometimes ignorance, but the state that varies thus is opinion...it is opinion that deals with that which can be otherwise than as it is...Therefore when one of those who aim at definition defines any individual, he must recognize that his definition may always be overthrown; for it is not possible to define such things (*Meta.* VII.14 1039a32-1040a7).

In this passage, Aristotle focuses on the fact that any individual will pass away. For this reason, there can be no knowledge of it, because true knowledge, according to Aristotle, cannot become untrue.

But does Aristotle mean to say that the individual cannot be known only because that individual can pass away? The individual can become different from itself, but more important, the individual can fail to become like its principle. That is to say, what Aristotle is concerned with is that individuals can change, and perishing is only one way of being otherwise. There are obviously others, as the case of the horse that was generated with three legs makes clear. There is a small difference: in the case of a horse perishing, it cannot be an object of knowledge because it has the potential to become different from how it actually is: alive. But individual horses also have the potential to become different than the essence of horseness by losing a leg. If there were a horse born with three legs, a contemporary scientist would likely seek it out specifically because it is anomalous. Aristotle, however, seems to be uninterested in such deformities—individuals, and *a fortiori* deformed individuals, can at best be objects of opinion. There is no knowledge to be had of a three-legged horse.

The case is quite different with the 'formula in its generality,' i.e., the essence, for "there is no destruction of the formula in the sense that it is ever in the course of being destroyed; for there is no generation of it" (*Meta.* VII.15 1039b23-24). This means, simply, that an essence is not capable of being otherwise. Therefore, a particular horse, whether well-formed or deformed, is not an object of knowledge, but a definition of an essence of horseness is; it is a principle that is not capable of being otherwise. The principle is necessary for that reason.

This idea has been considered and rejected by Sorabji, but unjustifiably so. He considers the point that Aristotle "believes the kinds studied by scientists are everlasting, and that what is everlastingly the case about an everlasting subject is necessarily the case about it."[19] Against this consideration, he observes that "the definitional connection is (part of) the reason for the necessity," and therefore that "everlastingness is not *on its own* the source of necessity."[20] Indeed, the relation of the subject and predicate must be a very particular sort of connection is order for the proposition to count as a definition of an essence; if a proposition is not a definition of an essence, it cannot serve as a principle. In particular, Sorabji refers to the requirement developed in *An. Post* 1.4-6 that a "subject must be definable in terms of the predicate or *vice versa.*"[21]

The possibility overlooked by Sorabji is that the requisite definitional connection between the subject and predicate is created *by* its eternality. This is why Aristotle consistently associates absolute (i.e., non-hypothetical) necessity with what is eternal.[22] For example, it is part of human essence to be rational, but not to be musical. Why? In one case—and in this sense Sorabji is correct—it is because man cannot be defined in terms of musical or vice-versa. This is why Aristotle says that "a white man is not always or for the most part musical, but since this sometimes happens, it must be accidental" (*Meta.* VI.2 1027a9-10). 'Musical' is predicated accidentally, not essentially of man, and the reason given here is that this happens only sometimes, as opposed to always or for the most part. But consider a counter-factual: suppose all or almost all humans were musical, the species 'human' did not become musical at any time, and the species would never become un-musical. In that case, 'man is musical' would have the requisite definitional connection. And it would have it because it is an eternal truth, and because that principle is eternally true, it is not capable of being otherwise. Aristotle leaves us to suppose that we learn that musical is an accidental predicate simply by mundane empirical processes.

Aristotle, of course, is wrong about all this, since species evolve and devolve. Importantly, though, Aristotle has not made an epistemological mistake here, but a metaphysical one. Given his mistaken belief that true definitions of essences are ungenerated an indestructible, he mistakenly calls them 'necessary.' And this means that it is a mistake to worry that Aristotle contradicted himself when he classified natural principles as necessary, theoretical principles that cannot be otherwise. Nor should we be disappointed that Aristotle does not give justification for this doctrine, as Sorabji suggests, for Aristotle, as I interpret him, does give a justification for his doctrine that definitions of essences are eternal, namely, that their essences are also.

The Principles as Immediate

The third characteristic that Aristotle mentions in his list is that the principles must be immediate. This characteristic is necessary because it is possible to wonder whether any kind of knowledge of primitive principles is even possible. Aristotle addresses unnamed skeptics who raise that very question: "Now some think that because one must understand [*epistathai*] the primitives there is no understanding at all" (*An. Post.* I.3 72b5-6). The skeptic here emphasizes that if all demonstration is based on premises that themselves need to be demonstrated, there are two equally bad possible outcomes. One is that demonstration might continue *ad infinitum*. But if there are no primitive propositions, then demonstration would not be grounded in anything at all because "it is impossible to go through infinitely many things" (*An. Post.* I.3 72b10).

The first possibility, then, is that there are no principles at all. The other possibility is that the chain does come to stop and is based on principles: "if it comes to a stop and there are principles, they say that these are unknowable since there is no demonstration of them, which alone they say is understanding" (*An. Post.* I.3 72b10-12). Here there are principles prior to the conclusion, and so it is possible to engage in something resembling demonstration. But on this model knowledge is *only* gained by demonstration, and since it is not possible to demonstrate the principles, it is not possible to know them. Since knowledge cannot be based on ignorance, there is no knowledge in this case either, even if there is a kind of deduction.

There is another possibility that seems to allow the possibility of knowledge on the same assumption: "The other party agrees about understanding; for it, they say, occurs only through demonstration. But they argue that nothing prevents there being demonstration of everything; for it is possible for the demonstration to come about in a circle and reciprocally" (*An. Post.* I.3 72b15-17). Aristotle identifies two problems with this possibility. There is, first of all, a *reductio* argument that if we were to apply this method, we could prove anything whatsoever (73a5). But Aristotle's real concern is that this method violates the principle of priority: "it is impossible for the same things at the same time to be prior and posterior to the same things" in the same sense (72b26-29).

Despite the fact that Aristotle does not believe that demonstration can be reciprocal, he does not give in to the skeptic. His solution is quite simple:

> but we say that neither is all understanding demonstrative [*epistēmēn apodeiktikēn*], but in the case of the immediates [*tōn amesōn*] it is nondemonstrable [*anapodeikton*]…and we also say that there is not only understanding but also some principle of understanding [*archēn epistēmēs*] by which we become familiar with the definitions (*An. Post.* I.3 72b19-25).

This passage is potentially confusing because of Aristotle's unfortunate choice to use *epistēmē* to mean both any kind of knowledge is the context of a theoretical science, as well as demonstrative knowledge. When *epistēmē* means demonstration (*apodeiktikos*), the phrase '*apodeiktikēn epistēmēn*' is redundant. Aristotle is clearly using *epistēmē* in the other way here, and thus it refers to any kind of general knowledge (*gnōsis*) that occurs in the context of a theoretical science. The solution offered here, then, is that *gnōsis* in the context of a theoretical science may be either demonstrative or non-demonstrative. Other contexts make clear that the principle of understanding that is non-demonstrative is *nous*, such that we have *nous* of the principles, and *epistēmē* of the results of demonstration. *Nous* and *epistēmē* are therefore the two kinds of knowledge that are possible in the context of a theoretical science.

But Aristotle's solution raises an important question: why, exactly, does he say that the first principles of a science may be known without demonstration? If he declares that the principles are not demonstrated simply in order to avoid an infinite regress problem, we should be unimpressed. If this were the case, of course, it would not in any way indicate that there actually is non-demonstrative knowledge; it would simply point out that if there is to be demonstration, then there must be non-demonstrative knowledge on which the demonstration depends. Aristotle even suggests this interpretation later in that paragraph: "if it is necessary to understand the things that are prior and on which demonstration depends, and it comes to a stop at some time, it is necessary for these immediates to be non-demonstrable. So as to that we argue thus" (*An. Post.* I.3 72b20-23).

There is, however, more to the argument; Aristotle suggests this by referring to the principles as 'immediate' (*amesos*). The meaning of 'immediate' is somewhat obscured by the surrounding texts, where Aristotle attempts what looks like a definition of 'immediate,' but is not:

> Depending on things that are primitive is depending on appropriate principles; for I call the same thing primitive and a principle. A principle of a demonstration is an immediate proposition [*protasis amesos*], and an immediate proposition is one to which there is no other prior (*An. Post.* I.2 72a6-9).

If an immediate proposition is immediate *because* there is no prior proposition, then it will not be significantly different from a primary proposition, for a primary must be prior. This is what a straightforward reading of this passage indicates. But as it turns out, this is exactly backwards—it is not immediate *because* there is no prior proposition; rather, there is no prior proposition *because* it is immediate. That is, its immediacy makes is impossible for there to be a prior proposition. That is why Aristotle says that an immediate proposition is not simply not demonstrated, but that it is 'non-demonstrable'; he means exactly that—one is unable to give a demonstration of it.

Whatever makes it immediate, then, is some feature of it other than its priority. The question is what makes it impossible to give a demonstration in this case. A clue is found by looking at the Greek term—*amesos*—which literally means 'unmiddled.' Aristotle is referring to terminology introduced in the *Prior Analytics*, which is a work devoted to deduction in general, rather than demonstration, a specific kind of deduction (hence its priority):

> Whenever three terms are so related to one another that the last is in the middle as in a whole, and the middle is either in, or not in, the first as in a whole, the extremes must be related by perfect deduction. I call that term middle [*meson*] that both is itself in another and contains another in itself: in position also this comes in the middle (*An. Pr.* I.4 25b31-36).

A middle term is the one that connects the 'extremes' in a valid deduction. So in the argument 'Socrates is a man, all men are mortal, therefore Socrates is mortal,' Socrates and mortal are the extreme terms, and 'man' links them together as the middle term.

In the *Posterior Analytics*, which is concerned with demonstration specifically, the middle term doesn't simply make a deduction possible, but allows the possibility of understanding. That is to say, a demonstration gives an explanation, and the explanation comes through the middle term. Aristotle addresses this issue explicitly in *An. Post.* II.16:

> Let shedding leaves be *A*, broad-leaved *B*, vine *C*. Well, if *A* belongs to *B* (for everything broad-leaved sheds its leaves) and *B* belongs to *C* (for every vine is broad-leaved), then *A* belongs to *C* and every vine sheds its leaves. *B*, the middle-term, is explanatory (98b5-11).

This is the way in which the explanation comes through the middle term.

This example of a demonstration, it turns out, has the effect of emphasizing what Aristotle meant by an unmiddled proposition. In this example, this demonstration is of the proposition that all vines are leaf-shedders. This demonstration is based on the observation that all vines are broad-leaved, and ultimately on the principle that all broad-leaved plants are leaf-shedders. Is this principle unmiddled?

Aristotle explains in the next chapter that it is not:

> If you were to take the primitive middle term, it is an account of shedding leaves. For there will be a middle term in the other direction (that all are such and such); and then a middle for this (that the sap solidifies or something else of that sort). What is shedding leaves? The solidifying of sap at the connection of the seed (*An. Post.* II.17 99a25-29).

Aristotle announces that the principle of the first syllogism is in fact not unmiddled, and this is because there is a further middle term that is able to explain the fact that all broad—leaved plants are lead-shedders. The explanation is that sap collects on broad-leaved plants, and when it reaches a sufficient weight, it causes the leaf to fall.

What explains that principle? Surely something does, but it is also clear that for Aristotle, we will eventually reach a principle that is not in need of an explanation. And this will be because it is not possible to give an explanation of it; we will discover some brute fact about the world—an essence, the 'what it is to be' of a deciduous tree—and knowledge of it can only be gained through inductive processes. Of course, since this knowledge does not issue from an explanation, it cannot be called *epistēmē*. But since this is a kind of knowledge, it is able to serve as a principle of demonstration. This same analysis can be given in the case of animal substances: 'Horses are four-legged animals.' What explains horses being four-legged? For Aristotle, nothing does, because the species horse has always had four legs, and always will.[23]

A proposition has a middle, therefore, if there is a third term through which it can be explained. A proposition lacks a middle (i.e., is *amesos*) if no such third term could be introduced. Aristotle introduces the term '*amesos*' to describe first principles and their manner of know-ability. Another way to understand this claim is to note that this principle also works for non-essential (i.e., accidental) predications, albeit in a different way. For example 'this cloak is wool' does indeed have a middle term. In fact, it has many middle terms, since there are many kinds of explanations that can be given here. But whatever path one follows, it will not lead to some eternal, brute fact about the world. In fact, if my analysis of *amesos* is correct, then *by definition* it will not terminate in some eternal, brute fact about the world, for in that case it would be essential and not accidental.

Conclusion

The requirement that the principles be unmiddled is in addition to the requirements that they be *prōton* and true. The analyses of the terms '*amesos*' and '*prōton*' also serve to make clear the priority requirement, since an *amesos* proposition is one to which there is not prior because nothing explains it, and a *prōton* principle also requires priority. This leaves only two criteria from the list at 71b20-23 unaccounted for, namely that the principles must be 'more familiar than' and 'explanatory of' the conclusion. These are the two most complicated of the criteria, and will require chapters of their own. In chapter 4, I develop Aristotle's account of *nous*, which is the only intellectual state that is "more precise" (*An. Post.* II.19 100b9) than *epistēmē*. *Nous* is of principles, which is why principles are more familiar than what is demonstrated based on them. In chapter 5, I give an overview of Aristotle's method of demonstration, which is a syllogism that is 'explanatory of' its conclusion; this method itself receives greater treatment in chapter 6. First, however, in chapter 3, I make some general claims about *epagōgē*, which is the process by which *nous* is established.

Notes

1. G.E.L. Owen, *"Tithenai ta Phainomena,"* in *Articles on Aristotle: Vol. 1 Science*, ed. J. Barnes, M. Schofield, and R. Sorabji (Great Britain: Gerald Duckworth & Company Limited, 1975).

2. Or in Kraut's formulation, "Aristotle says that our first priority should be to preserve all of the *endoxa*; that is, to find a way to show that apparently conflicting views are really in agreement, when their ambiguities are recognized." Richard Kraut, "How to Justify Ethical Propositions: Aristotle's Method," in *The Blackwell Guide to Aristotle's Nicomachean Ethics*, ed. Richard Kraut (Oxford, UK: Blackwell Publishing Ltd., 2008), 82.

3. For example, in the case of *akrasia.*

4. The first two are given immediately below. The third is in *EN* VI.3 1139b19-23, addressed already on page 16 and again on page 36.

5. See pages 75-76.

6. For instance, in *An Post* 71b21 and 100a16.

7. Cf. *Meta* IV. 7 1017a7.

8. Aristotle does not follow his argument through here, and so it is not clear why matter is off the table as a candidate for primary substance. But it is clear that is it is.

9. In the logical works, *eidos* meant the species, as opposed to genus. Now, Aristotle clearly uses it to be form as opposed to matter.

10. There may be as many different particular analyses of *Metaphysics Zeta* as there are ancient philosophers. My comments here are not meant as a specific challenge to any one interpretation, but rather a general set of statements about the contours of the chapter.

11. Cf. *Meta.* 1037a32.

12. Also, see *Meta.* 1064a10-27.

13. Richard Sorabji, "Definitions: why necessary and in what way?," in *Aristotle on Science: the Posterior Analytics*, ed. Enrico Berti (Padua, 1981).

C.D.C Reeve, *Substantial Knowledge: Aristotle's Metaphysics* (Indianapolis: Hackett Publishing Company, Inc., 2000).

14. Reeve, *Aristotle*, 27-38.

15. Reeve makes this point. A science is made more or less exact based on the degree to which matter is involved (38-42).

16. Cf. *Meta* 1025a25-28.

17. *Meta.* 1026a7-23.

18. Aristotle may be referring to the intelligible matter of mathematics as the other kind of matter.

19. Sorabji, "Definitions," 235.

20. Sorabji, "Definitions," 236.

21. Sorabji, "Definitions," 236.

22. Cf. *PA* 639b24.

23. This makes obvious a very large chasm between Aristotelian science of nature and a modern one, as an evolutionary explanation would go on to explain the survival benefits of horses being four-legged. For a modern biologist, then, that horses are four-legged in certainly not a brute fact of the way the world is, for something must explain how it got that way.

Chapter Three
Pursuing the Principles: *Epagōgē*

The First Stage of *Epagōgē*

There is reasoning from principles—that is, reasoning that uses principles as its ultimate basis. Aristotle classifies this sort of thinking as 'deduction' (*syllogismos*). But all reasoning could not be from principles unless we were aware of all the principles from birth—a possibility that Aristotle clearly rejects.[1]

Therefore, there must be a kind of reasoning useful for getting the principles in the first place. Aristotle calls this *epagōgē*, typically translated as 'induction':

> And all teaching...proceeds sometimes through induction [*epagōgē*] and sometimes through deduction [*syllogismos*]. Now induction is of first principles and of the universal and deduction proceeds *from* universals. There are therefore principles from which deduction proceeds that are not reached by deduction; it is therefore by induction that they are acquired (*EN* VI.3 1139b26-31).

The word '*epagōgē*' shows up in various and sometimes unexpected places in his corpus, such that it is quite difficult to give a simple definition—or even a complicated one—of *epagōgē*.[2] But clearly, one meaning of *epagōgē* picks out the method that is appropriate for establishing the kinds of universals that are the definitions of essences and the principles of demonstration, and this is how I will use the word.

There are several difficulties associated with appreciating this general method, the first of which is Aristotle's disorienting uses of 'particular' and 'universal' in his various discussions of this method. For instance, in the opening passages of the *Posterior Analytics*, Aristotle says both that inductive arguments prove "the universal [*katholou*] through the particular's [*to kath hekaston*] being clear" (I.1 71a9) and that what is "prior and more familiar in relation to us [is] what is nearer in perception...and the particulars are nearest" (I.2 72a3-5). Universals are not initially familiar to us, but are more familiar by nature. This seems to be consistent with much else Aristotle has to say about *epagōgē*, although from this perspective, the meaning of *Physics* I.1 is confusing: "we must advance from universals [*katholou*] to particulars [*ta kath hekasta*]; for it is a whole that is more knowable to sense-perception, and a universal is a kind of whole..." (*Ph.* I.1 184a22-25). In an effort to save Aristotle from an apparent contradiction, some translators render *katholou* as 'comprehensive' in the latter part of the phrase.[3] Others, such as LeBlond, are content to believe that these sorts of inconsistencies (and he is here thinking specifically of *Physics* I.1) provide evidence of a "perceptible vacillation" in Aristotle's scientific method.[4]

However, these passages only appear contradictory when it is assumed that *epagōgē* only needs to account for the transition from particular to universal. It is better to think of *epagōgē* in distinct stages. There is the more well-known description of *epagōgē* as the movement from what is more familiar to us to what is more familiar by nature. However, there is evidence that Aristotle also intended *epagōgē* to describe how what is more familiar to us becomes more familiar to us in the first place. And Aristotle maintains that both objects of familiarity are universal: what is initially familiar to beings with perception and memory is a sort of perceptible universal, while what is more familiar by nature is what may be called a definitional universal, useful as a principle of demonstration. In *Physics* I.1, Aristotle says that he means by '*ta kath hekasta*' not a perceptible particular, but the distinguished elements in a definition (which contrasts sharply with his other various uses of *ta kath hekasta*). *Epagōgē* therefore must be interpreted as a two-stage process, where the first stage—referred to in *An. Post.* I.2—describes how what is more familiar to us becomes more familiar to us in the first place, i.e., how we become familiar with perceptible universals from perceptible particulars. In the second stage—referred to in *Physics* 1.1—Aristotle prescribes rules for getting the definitional universal from the perceptible universal.

Perceptible Universals in *An. Post.* II.19 and *Physics* I.1

Aristotle's references to *epagōgē* at the beginning of the *Posterior Analytics* are given more detail in its last chapter. He begins II.19 by noting that all animals have perception, but only some are able to retain perceptions:

> So from perception there comes memory, as we call it, and from memory...experience [*empeiria*]... And from experience, or from the whole universal [*pantos tou katholou*] that has come to rest in the soul (the one apart from the many, whatever is one and the same in all those things), there comes a principle [*archē*] of skill and of knowledge—of skill if it deals with how things come about, of knowledge if it deals with what is the case (*An. Post.* II.19 100a4-9).

In this passage, Aristotle says that first principles come from experience (*ek empeirias*)—or, what amounts to the same, from the whole universal (*pan katholou*). It is possible to believe that the phrase 'whole universal' as simply another name for a first principle, so there really is not any gap between whole universals and first principles. The observation that principles come *from* whole universals is already one reason to be hesitant in our endorsement the position that a whole universal just is a principle of demonstration.[5] If we reject the idea that there is no gap between *pan katholou* and first principles, we should expect to find Aristotle elsewhere describing a kind of universal that both is more closely tied to experience and that is not the kind of universal that is useful in demonstration. As it turns out, Aristotle does this not only in the remaining passage but elsewhere.

Aristotle admits that this description of *epagōgē* at 100a4-9 is not terribly clear, so he re-describes the same process in the very next paragraph. There are two parts of the paragraph, separated in the text by the word '*palin*' at 100b1. The first is this:

> When one of the undifferentiated things [*tōn adiaphorōn enos*] makes a stand, there is a primitive universal [*proton katholou*] in the mind (for though one perceives the particular [*to kath hekaston*], perception is of the universal [*tou katholou*]—e.g., of man but not of Callias the man) (*An. Post.* II.19 100a15-18).

Whole universals are thus equated with primitive universals, an example of which is the concept 'man.' It is worth noting from the outset of our analysis that there is no reason to presume that a *proton katholou* is primitive relative to the other elements of demonstration (as are first principles) rather than to some further refined concepts that are themselves first principles. Indeed, the latter position receives some support by noting that the primitive universal is incomplete, for "a stand is made in these until what has no parts [*amerē*] and is universal stands" (100a2-3).

If we take seriously the alternative that a stand is made in primitive, 'part-full' universals until some sort of 'part-less' universal stands, then it is possible to affirm the agreement between *An. Post.* I.2 and *Physics* I.1 (hereafter I.2 and I.1). There, Aristotle says that

> What is to us plain and clear at first is rather confused masses [*ta sugkekhumena*], the elements and principles of which become known to us later by analysis [*diairousi*]. Thus we must advance from universals [*ek tōn katholou*] to particulars [*ta kath hekasta*]; for it is a whole [*holos*] that is more knowable to sense-perception and a universal is a kind of whole, comprehending many things within it, like parts [*merē*]. Much the same thing happens in the relation of the name to the formula. A name, e.g., 'circle,' means vaguely [*adioristōs*] a sort of whole; its definition [*horismos*] analyses [*diaipei*] this into particulars [*ta kath hekasta*] (*Ph.* I.1 184a22-b11).

If the process of *epagōgē* is simply the process of getting universals from particulars, then it must be assumed that *katholou* is being used in a non-technical way here, and thus for the sake of clarity may be translated as something other than 'universal.' But if *epagōgē* describes both the journey from particulars to perceptible universals, and then from perceptible to definitional universals, we may instead believe that passage is referring simply to the latter part of the process.

The agreement of this passage with I.2 is made more compelling by attending to Aristotle's specific wording there: "I call prior and more familiar in relation to us what is nearer [*ta enguteron*] to perception, prior and more familiar *simpliciter* what is furthest away. What is most universal [*ta katholou malista*] is furthest away, and the particulars are nearest..." (*An. Post.* I.2 72a3-5). Particulars are near, but for that must we presume that they are what are more familiar to us? Aristotle simply says that what is more familiar to us is 'nearer' to perception, which does nothing to show that they are *ta kath hekasta* and not perceptible universals. To be sure, *ta kath hekasta* are near to perception, but perceptible universals are also. This is perhaps emphasized by Aristotle's curious choice of the phrase *ta katholou malista* (what is universal especially, above all) rather than simply 'universal.' This indicates that another universal is there—one that is less universal, but still universal in a sense.

One puzzle remains: if the passages agree, then why does Aristotle describe the final object of familiarity as 'particular' in I.1, rather than as what is 'most universal'? The answer has the advantage of being remarkably simple. Aristotle is explicit that in I.1 he means by '*ta kath hekasta*' the distinguished elements of the definition, while in I.2 '*ta kath hekasta*' are the particular things that are objects of perception. Aristotle is thus giving *ta kath hekasta* not a fixed meaning, but what is relatively more specific; hence it can mean a perceptible particular (more specific relative to a universal) or the differentiae of a definition (more specific relative to other general adjectives). This is perhaps unfortunate, since it makes it even more difficult to interpret his dense technical vocabulary. But in Aristotle's defense, he was perfectly clear about when *ta kath hekasta* was meant as a particular thing and when as an element of a definition. There is therefore no real inconsistency here.

Perceptible Universals as Less Universal

What could Aristotle mean by implying that universals may be part-full or part-less? And in what sense is a part-less universal more universal? In II.19, just as in I.1, Aristotle describes a universal that becomes familiar to us in perception. This sort of universal has parts in II.19, and is 'confused masses' in I.1, which are clarified by some further process. In II.19, what eventually stands is part-less, while in I.1 Aristotle describes it as a definition. In both passages, the universal that is available in perception is a concept like 'man' or 'circle.' In I.1 it is confused and vague and unanalyzed; thus "a child begins by calling all men father, and all women mother, but later on distinguishes [*diorizei*] them" (*Ph.* I.1 184b13-14).[6] And although in II.19 Aristotle does not specifically say that perceptible universals are confused or vague, he does state that they are undifferentiated and must be further refined until one comes to possess a universal that is part-less (*amerē*).

Derivatives of the word *meros* show up in some interesting places in Aristotle's logical works. One such instance is in *An. Pr.* I.1, where he contrasts a universal proposition with an *en merei* one, typically translated into English as 'particular': "By universal I mean a statement that something belongs to all or none of something; by particular that it belongs to some or not to some or not to all" (*An. Pr.* I.1 24a16-19). This obviously becomes the basis of Aristotle's doctrine of validity, where all propositions are universal affirmative or negative, particular affirmative or negative, and deductive arguments are valid or invalid on the basis of the combination of propositions.

But let's imagine a necessary time early in our investigation of the world when we did not know which propositions were particular and which universal. Suppose I did not know whether, for example, "All adult males have mustaches" or rather that merely "Some adult males have mustaches." If my own father were mustached, and if he only spent time with other mustached men, and if the postman were mustached, no one would think me dull child if I entertained the possibility that 'mustached' were a universal property of adult males.

In II.19, when we have enough perceptions retained in memory to have experience, Aristotle says that "experience, or...the whole universal...has come to rest in the soul (the one apart from the many, whatever is one and the same in all those things)" (*An. Post.* II.19 100a6-7). 'Those things' refers to the objects of my *actual* experience that currently reside in my soul, not to all cases of that kind of thing that there are *potential* objects of my experience. One thing that is one and the same in my experience of adult males is mustaches. My concept 'adult male' certainly needs to be refined through further induction, but as long as I say "Some adult males (and perhaps all, if further induction shows) have mustaches," there is nothing wrong with this statement.[7] That is to say—in the language of *An. Pr.* I.1—that as long as my statement takes the form of an *en merei* judgment, it is appropriate to my initial experiences.

This judgment about 'some males' is obviously not universal in one sense—'*katholou*' can mean a proposition in which a predicate belongs to all or none of a subject. In my early stages of induction, I am not certain whether 'mustached' is a universal predicate of 'adult male.' Thus, I do not have a *katholou* in this sense, but my *en merei* statement is *katholou* in another—it is a particular judgment about the whole group of adult males with whom I am acquainted.[8] The stricter sense of *katholou* refers to predicates that attach to subjects universally. The more general sense of *katholou* simply means that I have a concept of a group or whole (*holos*). The word '*katholou*,' therefore, is by itself ambiguous, for a judgment can be '*katholou katholou*' or '*en merei katholou*.'

This language is retained in I.1. Aristotle concludes that passage by noting that

A universal is a kind of whole, comprehending many things within it, like parts...A name, e.g.. 'circle,' means vaguely a sort of whole: its definition analyses this into particulars. Similarly a child begins calling all men father, and all women mother, but later on distinguishes each of them (*Ph.* I.1 184a25-184b14).

To be sure, a definition is a universal. But there is obviously another kind of universal here—a universal only in the sense that it is a notion about a whole. One who has only made it to this stage may believe falsely—as indeed is the case here—that "All adult males are fathers"; he can only make particular judgments legitimately. But there are also universals that are universal because they are about a whole species *and also* because they include or exclude a predicate from the whole species—definitional universals are this type of universal.

Aristotle's language in *An. Post.* I.31 echoes this observation:

> Nor can one understand by perception. For even if perception is of what is such and such [*tou toioude*], and not of individuals [*toude tinos*], still one necessarily perceives an individual and at a place and at a time, and it is impossible to perceive what is universal and holds in every case; for that is not an individual not at a time; for then it would not be universal—for it is what is always and everywhere that we call universal (*An. Post.* I.31 87b29-34).

Aristotle here calls what is truly universal what is true 'always and everywhere.' This is consistent with his other statements about what is universal in both senses. And he mentions the individual, which as enmattered, shows up necessarily in time and space. Any judgment about individuals will therefore be non-universal in both senses; it will not be about a *holos*, and *a fortiori* cannot be about all or none of a *holos*. But he indicates another sort of judgment, this one based in perception; it is not universal in the predicative sense, but it is about a *holos*—a such and such; in the words of II.19, a judgment about 'man' and not Callias the man.

I want to conclude by considering a passage in *De Anima* III.3—another context, to be sure, but an important one, as Aristotle returns to the sense in which confusion, vagueness, and/or lack of distinction are introduced via perception:

> Perception of the special objects of sense is never in error or admits the least possible amount of falsehood. Next comes perception that what is incidental [*sumbebēkenai*] to the objects of perception *is* incidental to them: in this case certainly we may be deceived; for while the perception that there is white before us cannot be false, the perception that what is white is this or that may be false (*DA* III.3 428b18-22).

The perception of special objects of sense involves the perceiver taking on the sensible form without the matter.[9] Here, truth and falsity are impossible, as there is only taking on the form or not taking it on. But Aristotle clearly believes that this is not all there is to perception, for it also involves attributing properties to objects. He here describes an error that results from attaching a predicate to an object of perception that doesn't belong to it. His example implies that he has in mind individual objects of perception, rather than perceptible universals. However, this account points to an analogous error in the case of universals.[10] As an example of the latter case, a cloistered Greek child may believe that 'white' or 'mustached' or 'father' is a universal property of adult males based on perception and experience. Further inductive processes reveal to him his naiveté about this species-concept. Aristotle is optimistic that this refinement process will eventually lead to first principles that are necessarily true and hence, appropriate for *epistēmē*.

The Second Stage of *Epagōgē* as Empirical

After getting the perceptible universal—'horse,' for example—one knows *that* horse *is*, in the sense that she knows that the species 'horse' exists and is the kind of thing that has an essence and a definition. But knowing *that it is* is a rather primitive form of knowledge, for I am not yet familiar with *what a horse is*. Thus far I have described only the first stage of *epagōgē*, which consists in the journey from perception of particulars to what it more familiar to us, namely perceptible universals; thus, the first stage of *epagōgē* describes how what is more familiar to us becomes more familiar in the first place. Now Aristotle must explain how what is more familiar to us becomes identical with what is more familiar by nature, and what is more familiar by nature are essences. The question, then, is about how we come to know essences, and whether such a process is essentially empirical.

In *An. Post.* II.19 and elsewhere Aristotle is quite brief when describing the journey from particulars to perceptible universals. I excused this brevity because it is not any great task to come to a possession of a perceptible universal; all creatures endowed with perception and memory can and will do it. The journey from perceptible universals to definitional universals, however, will have to be philosophically rigorous. After all, it ends in knowledge of necessary truths about the world. Those truths should be harder to come by, the journey filled with traps. Already some might be justifiably suspicious that such a process could not be empirical.

Because of its philosophical complexity, we should expect Aristotle to be somewhat detailed about this second stage of the journey that terminates in certain knowledge of necessary truths. Yet, some commentators believe that Aristotle takes no great pains to elaborate on this process either. For instance, Kahn says that

> Even if Aristotle's inductive account may pass muster as an explanation for our common sense grasp of universal concepts, that is, for the kind of tacit knowledge of universals that is implicit in our mastery of a language, how can it explain the deeper grasp of essences required as an adequate basis for science…Is Aristotle aware of this gap between vulgar and scientific conceptualization?[11]

What I have called 'perceptible universals'—those universals accessible with perception and memory—are roughly what Kahn calls the vulgar universals, assessable to 'common sense.' Kahn concludes that Aristotle was aware that there needed to be a journey from these first universals to essences, but he believes that Aristotle does not himself elaborate on it.

Kahn's work mainly concerns the *Posterior Analytics* and the *De Anima*, and it is true that in those books, Aristotle refers to but does not develop the path from perceptible to definitional universals. But this is to miss the fact Aristotle gives us some highly-detailed examples of how to do this process elsewhere. Furthermore, before he does so, he announces what his method will be. It begins with an empirical examination of the parts of a subject:

> In the first place we must look to the constituent parts of animals. For it is relative to these parts, first and foremost, that animals in their entirety differ from one another: either in the fact that some have this or that, while they have not that or this...Now the parts are obvious enough to perception. However, with a view of observing due order and sequence and of combining reason with perception, we shall proceed to enumerate the parts.... (*HA* I.6 491a14-25)

Once we know that something is—i.e., once we have the perceptible universal—we begin the second stage of *epagōgē* by investigating the parts of our subject in the only way we can—empirically. Naturally, this investigation will not be successful if we do not also use reason, but this still counts as an empirical investigation since it depends on data derived from sense experience.

Going through the parts, however, is not the same as investigating the material cause. When we empirically investigate the parts of a human, say, it is not necessary or even important that we understand why the parts we are observing must be *just these parts* and not any others. We simply observe the parts as they are. But to discover the material cause is to discover why these parts are necessary for the generation of the particular substance in question. This is, indeed, Aristotle's doctrine of hypothetical necessity. This is why Aristotle says that

> the fittest mode, then, of treatment is to say, a man has such and such parts, because the essence of man is such and such, and because they are the necessary conditions of his existence, or, if we cannot quite say this then the next thing to it, namely, that it is either quite impossible for a man to exist without them, or, at any rate, that it is good that they should be there (*PA* I.1 640a33-640b1).

Here in the introductory book of the *Parts of Animals*, Aristotle is saying that knowledge of why there must be these parts and not other parts comes after knowledge of the essence. This is clearly different from observing what parts there in fact are. Therefore, the phrase 'investigating the parts of a species' is ambiguous, for it could refer to an investigation that there are in fact such and such parts of a species, or it could refer to an investigation of why it is necessary that there are these parts and no others. The former investigation precedes the knowledge of the essence, while the latter investigation of hypothetical necessity follows knowledge of the essence.

The point I am making is emphasized by the other passages where Aristotle intends to reveal his method:

> We must take animals species by species, and discuss their particularities severally... *After this* we shall pass on to the discussion of causes. For to do this when the investigation of the details is complete is the natural method; for from them the subjects and the premises of our proof become clear (*HA* I.6 491a5-14, my emphasis).

> Ought the student of nature follow the plan adopted by the mathematicians in their astronomical demonstrations, and *after considering* the phenomena presented by animals, and their several parts, *proceed subsequently to treat of the causes and the reason why*: or ought he follow some other method?...The best course appears to be that we should follow the method already mentioned with the phenomena presented by each group of animals, and, when this is done, *proceed afterwards* to state the causes of those phenomena—in the case of generation too (*PA* I.1 639b7-640a17, my italics).

These passages, taken from the opening sections of the *History of Animals* and *Parts of Animals* respectively, describe the same method. This method starts by taking the particularities of animals 'species by species' (*HA*), or what it the same, the 'phenomena presented by each group of animals' (*PA*). That is to say, the path from perceptible universals to definitional universals begins by examining the parts of the being in question. In the *HA* passage, the 'premises of our proof become clear' from such an investigation. Since at this stage, we are still establishing first principles, rather than demonstrating from them, this is the second stage of *epagōgē*. The *PA* passage makes this same point in slightly different language. The investigation into the phenomena (in this case, the parts of animals) allows the investigator to go on to treat 'the cause and the reason why.' This is the 'natural method' of investigation. The process of gaining knowledge the essences, then, is thoroughly empirical.

From Nominal to Essential Definitions

When we are confronted with a being, we naturally try to become familiar with it by defining it. This will take the form of a phrase (or account or formula): "a definition is always a phrase [*logos*] of a certain kind" (*Top.* I.5 102a5-6). The kind of definition that Aristotle is interested in expresses an essence, but it is clear that a definition does not always state an essence: "Since a definition is said to be an account of what a thing is, it is evident that one type will be an account of what the name, or a different name-like account [*logos onomatōdēs*], signifies" (*An. Post.* II.10 93b29-31). The tradition has reasonably called this a

'nominal definition,' since it is a *logos* that merely signifies the name, as contrasted with an essential definition, which is an account of why it is, or at least
what is it to be that thing.[12]

There are three cases in which a definition is nominal, one having to do
with the kind of thing that is being defined, the other two having to do with the
kind of definition. First the former possibility: simply asking what a thing is is
not a technical question, for we can ask in a mundane sense what a cloak is, or
what a pale man is, or what the *Illiad* is. Those things are substances in a loose
sense, since they are bearers of predicates and not predicated of anything else.
Because of this, the answer to the question, 'What is this?' counts as a *logos*.
While there is nothing wrong with such everyday inquiries, Aristotle sometimes
speaks as though he wants to reserve the term 'definition' (*horismos*) for real
substances—that is, beings that are enmattered essences. Not all beings are like
this, however:

> But is being a cloak an essence at all? Probably not. For the essence is what
> something is; but when one thing is said of another, that is not what a 'this'
> [*tode ti*] is, e.g., white man is not what a 'this' is since being a 'this' belongs
> only to substances. Therefore there is an essence only of those things whose
> formula [*logos*] is a definition [*horismos*] (*Meta*. VII.4 1030a2-6).

Anything that *is* something, i.e., that exists, will have a formula (*logos*) corresponding to what it is, where a formula is simply a statement "that this attribute
belongs to this subject" (*Meta*. VII.4 1030a16). So a sensible and potentially
informative answer to the question, 'What is the *Illiad*?' is 'A book authored by
Homer.' Likewise, a cloak is something, and so it will have a formula. However,
neither a book nor a cloak is a real *tode ti*. We might say then that the book and
the cloak are 'accidental substances'; they are substances since they are at least
bearers of predicates, but the *logos* that expresses their 'what it is' does not also
express their essence, and so they cannot be called essential substances. We
should thereby believe that the *logos* of them is merely a 'name-like account,'
i.e., a nominal definition.

This is the sense in which a definition may be nominal owing to the kind of
thing it is defining. But a definition may also be nominal because it is lacking
something—namely, an account of 'why it is.' In *An. Post*. II.1-10 and elsewhere, Aristotle describes the process of going from the initial, nominal definition, to the definition that gives the 'why it is.' This process is what I have referred to as the process of going from the perceptible universal to the
definitional universal. The evidence for this begins in II.1, where Aristotle says,
regarding substances, that there are two things we seek: if it is (*ei esti*), and what
it is (*ti estin*).[13] Aristotle insists that these two questions may be asked of a single substance, but never simultaneously. Rather, the question of whether it is
must proceed the question of what it is: "it is clear that...we cannot grasp what it
is to be something without grasping the fact that it is; for it is impossible to

know what a thing is if we are ignorant of whether it is" (*An. Post.* II.8 93a19-21).

If it is conceded that Aristotle's nominal definitions map onto my perceptible universals, then this doctrine makes perfect sense. When we first become familiar with a universal, like 'human,' we first must recognize that this is the kind of thing that deserves a definition. So we recognize that there is a sort of animal that is its own species—'human.' This is equivalent to believing that a human is a certain kind of animal. We then proceed to get the essential definition based on our familiarity with the nominal definition, or as I have it, we seek the definitional universal from the perceptible universal. This is equivalent to seeking to know that kind of animal that human is.[14] This interpretation fits well with Aristotle's examples:

> as to whether it is, sometimes we grasp...something of the object itself—e.g., of thunder, that it is a sort of noise of the clouds; and of eclipse, that it is a sort of privation of light; and of man, that he is a sort of animal; and of soul, that it is something moving itself (*An. Post.* II.8 93a21-24).

Our next move is to go beyond the nominal definition; for instance, we are familiar with 'human,' and recognize that it is a kind of animal, but we do not know what kind of animal. In other words, we now are interested in the differentia, and once we come to know it, we will have the essential definition.

This also implies the possibility of a third kind of nominal definition, because one may attempt to get beyond the nominal definition to the essential definition, but fails to do so:

> It is better to try to come to know what is posterior through what it prior, inasmuch as such a way of procedure is more scientific. Of course, in dealing with persons who cannot recognize things through terms of that kind, it may be necessary to frame the account through terms that are familiar to them...definitions of this kind...explain the prior by the posterior...One must, however, not fail to observe that those who define in this way cannot show the essence of what they define, unless it so happens that the same thing is more familiar both to us and also without qualification, since a correct definition must define a thing through its genus and differentia, and these belong to the order of things that are without qualification more familiar than, and prior to, the species (*Top.* VI.4 141b15-27).

What is 'prior' (more familiar by nature) is in this case presumably the differentia, while what is 'posterior' (more familiar to an individual) is either a property or accident.[15] It is possible to define what is prior through what is posterior, but that kind of definition 'cannot show the essence,' even though it is about a real substance. There are, then, at least three types of nominal definitions: 1) definitions that are about accidental substances, 2) definitions of the perceptible universal that at best only the species in the genus, and then 3) definitions that try to locate a species within a genus by means of a differentia, but fail, and give another kind of characteristic. In a discussion of *epagōgē*, the second sense is of course the most important of the three, since it is a precursor to having the kind of definition that will be useful for demonstration.

Does Natural Science Need Dialectic?

It is uncontroversial that the first stage of *epagōgē* is empirical, and I have indicated that the second stage is essentially empirical as well. But what about dialectic? Is it not to be found in 'the discussion of causes' in the *History of Animals* or when we 'treat of the causes,' as it is described in the *Parts of Animals*? Dialectic is indeed part of natural science as a precursor to demonstration, but it is not a part of getting the definitions of essences. My defense of this position will be somewhat tedious, but I think necessary. It is helpful to begin by addressing this commonly misinterpreted passage:

> [Dialectic] has a further use in relation to the principles used in the several sciences. For it is impossible to discuss them [i.e., these general principles] at all from the principles proper to the particular science in hand, seeing that the principles [of particular sciences] are primitive in relation to everything else: it is through reputable opinions about them [the general principles] that these have to be discussed, and this task belongs properly, or most appropriately, to dialectic; for dialectic is a process of criticism wherein lies the path to the principles of all inquiries (*Top.* I.2 101a37-b4).

Some commentators take the phrase 'the principles of all inquiries' to mean 'first principles of all kinds.'[16] This interpretation is not supported by the text, which simply says that dialectic is useful for discovering principles *common* to several sciences. Aristotle simply meant that one cannot get to such general principles from the principles of particular sciences; rather, it is necessary to get to those general principles by dialectic. I will argue that this is an exact description of what happens in the *Physics*, as Aristotle uses dialectic to get the general principles of *phusis*—principles that are useful for several particular sciences of nature. And at the beginning of the *Physics*, Aristotle uses dialectic to refute Parmenides, and thus to get principles that are useful for sciences of both mathematics and nature. But how could dialectic ever be used to get principles of plant or animal life, for example?

Rather, when the process of getting essential definitions (*horismoi*) is discussed in any detail, dialectic is nowhere to be found. Why, then, has the belief that dialectic has a part in *epagōgē* persisted so? The reasons, it seems, are two; first, there is the general (and vague) sense that dialectic has a place in establishing first principles in natural philosophy. I think that this is true in a way, although I do not think that this is true because dialectic assists in obtaining *horismos*; this will be the main argument of the subsequent sections. The second reason is the concern that real definitions of natural essences could surely never be gained by simple empirical processes. The premises required for demonstration must be necessary and eternal, among other criteria. Such standards seem to demand something more substantial than mere empirical methods. Kahn expresses the worry this way:

> Does Aristotle suppose that such complex scientific concepts of the structure and function of living things are reached by a continuation and refinement of the process he calls *epagōgē*? The answer to this question must be "yes," since *epagōgē* is the only process Aristotle recognizes as leading from sense experience to universal or essential knowledge...there are many loose ends in Aristotle's theory of knowledge, and this seems to be one of the problems he never considers in any detail.[17]

The commentators I will consider next would respond to Kahn by first agreeing that *epagōgē* by itself could not yield necessary and eternal essences, but in fact Aristotle uses dialectic to get such essences. My own response is to highlight the passages from *Parts and Animals* and *History of Animals* that indicate Aristotle's belief that empirical methods can in fact get essences without the assistance of dialectic, and Aristotle's description of the process of getting essential definition in *Posterior Analytics* II, where all that is needed is a search for the differentia. In what sense does dialectic needed in that process? An examination of Aristotle's analysis of the epistemological journey to knowledge of essences will show the sense in which dialectic is necessary.

Dialectic in Natural Science

I offer a theory about Aristotle's method of obtaining principles of demonstration in natural science that would resolve two related and long-standing interpretive difficulties. The first is why this method is sometimes dialectical, and sometimes empirical. It is now rather common to believe that Aristotle arrives at first principles sometimes by empirical methods, sometimes by dialectical methods.[18] Philosophers who do this, however, typically do not give a clear, principled reason that explains why Aristotle uses different methods at different times. A failure to insist on clarity here leads to the belief that Aristotle was fairly haphazard in the application of his method.[19] The second problem is the relation of a definition (*horismos*) to a *hypothesis*, since both are kinds of first principles.[20] In general, these problems are resolved by observing that, first of all, the phrase 'Aristotle's method in natural science' is already misleading, for it obscures the fact that any successful interpretation must rather speak of Aristotle's *methods*. But this is not going far enough, for it does not yet eliminate the possibilities that dialectic and empiricism work together to establish a single kind of first principle, nor that they are different ways to get at the same kind of principle. I argue that dialectic and empiricism are separate methods not only in the sense that they have different starting points, but also because they also produce different kinds of principles.

And in particular, these problems are resolved if it is first of all true that dialectic in natural science starts with *endoxa* and ends with definitions of the basic principles of *phusis*, such as motion, change, infinity, place, magnitude, etc. But Aristotle never refers to these kinds of definitions as '*horismoi*,' and this is apparently because they do not state any kind of formal or hylomorphic essence, as the *horismoi* of the investigating natural scientist must[21]; instead, Aristotle consistently uses the more general '*ti estin*' when describing the definitions of the principles of *phusis*.[22] Furthermore, when a philosopher's attention is turned toward nature and more or less away from dialectic, a dialectical principle in that case is called a '*hypothesis*,' since the basic principles of *phusis* are assumptions to the one actively investigating, much in the same way that the very existence of *phusis* is a hypothesis to the dialectician of the basic principles of *phusis*.[23] Demonstration in all sciences must use *horismoi* as principles, but the investigating natural scientist must also suppose the principles of *phusis*; otherwise real explanations would not be forthcoming in many cases.

In this way, dialectic is required for establishing principles in natural science that are hypotheses, but there is a distinct method by which *horismoi* are established; Aristotle typically calls this *epagōgē*.[24] This method, in turn, has two stages, the first of which is explicitly and exclusively empirical; the second stage necessarily relies variously on both empirical and logical processes, but there is no evidence—textual or otherwise—to suppose that dialectic is part of this process. In what follows, I introduce and interpret the passages in which Aristotle most explicitly insists on these points.

It is odd that Aristotle's commentators are able to produce arguments for and against the nature of his scientific method; of all the things that are ambiguous in Aristotle's writings, one would not anticipate this being one. Yet, some commentators point to passages that feature dialectic in natural science, while others drum up passages that point to Aristotle's affinity for empiricism.[25] What must be noted about this disagreement is that these commentators share the assumption that there is no equivocation on the phrase 'the principles of natural science;' thus, they take themselves to be disagreeing about how Aristotle characteristically establishes a single kind of principle. But this is to fail to appreciate that demonstration in natural science is more complicated than demonstration in other sciences,[26] and this is simply because nature is a principle of motion and change.[27] As a result, real explanations will require principles of *phusis* in general in addition to specific *horismoi*.

There are, in general, three kinds of analyses of the role of dialectic in natural science, all of which, it will turn out, face severe difficulties. The first, argued by Robert Bolton, is that dialectic has no role in natural science. His project is to reconcile the method of the *Physics* with that of the *Posterior Analytics*, or rather to reduce the former's method to empiricism:

> The correspondence between the *Physics* and the *Analytics* enables us now to draw a general conclusion about the method which Aristotle recommends in the *Physics* for natural science, namely that this method is exactly the one he describes in the *Posterior Analytics*. It is an immediate consequence of this that Aristotle's method is not dialectic.[28]

The second view, established by Owen and Irwin, is that Aristotle's method is basically dialectical, although he leaves room for empiricism; empiricism, however, is redundant because it cannot establish anything that dialectic cannot establish.[29] The third is that dialectic works together with empirical methods to establish a single kind of principle. Reeve, for instance, believes that empiricism gives us 'unanalyzed universals,' which makes one a person of experience. Dialectic (and specifically, aporematic) subjects those universals to analysis, yielding 'analyzed universals,' useful as first principles in demonstration: "Aporematic philosophy, then, is what the second stage of induction—the stage that culminates in understanding's grasp of analyzed universals—consists in."[30]

Against Bolton's view, we may note Aristotle insistence that dialectic is indeed relevant for a science of nature because it is necessary for reaching the principles of *phusis*:

> The science of nature is concerned with magnitudes and motion and time, and each of these is necessarily infinite or finite…it is incumbent on the person who treats of nature to discuss the infinite and to inquire whether there is such a thing or not, and if there is, what it is [*ti estin*]. The appropriateness to the science of this problem is clearly indicated; for all who have touched on this kind of science in a way worth considering have formulated views about the infinite, and…make it a principle of things (*Ph.* III.4 202b30-203a4).

In this passage, Aristotle require any physics 'worth considering' to establish principles that express the *ti estin* of such things as the infinite.[31] Aristotle apparently does not think much of any science that attempts to proceed without principles of this sort.

Importantly, Aristotle is not ambiguous about how to arrive at the *ti estin* of the infinite—he begins his own journey by considering the *endoxa* of Pythagorus, Plato, Democritus, and Anaxagoras, which amounts to an endorsement of the dialectical method in natural science.[32] But we are right to wonder exactly how extensive is the use of dialectic in natural science.

Dialectic is useful for establishing the *ti estin* of the principles of *phusis*. By these, I mean the principles of *phusis* in general, as opposed to the principles appropriate to a particular inquiry within natural science, such as geology or botany. These, however, require distinct inquiries, and are related as common and specific principles; this is so because the principles of motion and magnitude are not different for stars and horses and plants and rocks, but the principles of *phusis* will not be of use in any particular demonstration without a *horismos*. Importantly, definitions yielded by dialectic are not much like formal definitions, such as 'man is a terrestrial animal.' It would be impossible for them to be alike, as 'the infinite,' for example, does not have a form. The infinite must have a different kind of definition.

One clue that Aristotle intends a distinction is that he consistently uses the word *'horismos'* when referring to an essential definition, i.e., an expression of the form or essence (*to ti ēn einai*). But when he refers to principles established by dialectic, he consistently avoids *horismos*, instead using the more general *ti estin*. Throughout the *Physics*, Aristotle explicitly seeks—through dialectic—the *ti estin* of many things such as motion (200b12-14, 224b11), the infinite (202b30-35), place, (208a27-35), void (213a13), continuity, contact, and succession (226b19-21). But whenever the process of establishing *horismos* is clearly under discussion, he never speaks of dialectic, rather speaking of perception, memory, and other empirically-based processes.[33]

Hypotheses in Natural Science

Aristotle believes that grasping first principles is necessary before demonstrating a truth in any particular science. This will require definitions (*horismoi*), which state the essence of a thing by giving the genus and differentiae. But Aristotle believes that definitions are only one kind of first principle:

> I call an immediate principle of deduction a thesis [*thesin*] if it is not demonstrated, but it is not necessary to be grasped for all kinds of learning. If it is necessary for any learning, it is an axiom...A thesis that takes one of the parts of a contradiction—I mean that something is or is not—is a *hypothesis*; a definition [*horismos*] is without this feature, [even though] a definition is a thesis (*An. Post.* I.2 72a15-22).[34]

An axiom—such as the principle of non-contradiction—must be grasped in order to learn anything at all. Definitions and hypotheses are different in that they are first principles relevant only to a particular science or branch of sciences. Aristotle describes definitions at length in many different contexts, but mentions hypotheses by name a precious few times. This has led to much controversy about what they even are.

The sentence immediately following the quoted portion says this, according to Barnes: "For a definition is a *thesis* (for the arithmetician posits that a unit is what is quantitatively indivisible) but not a *hypothesis* (for what a unit is and that a unit is are not the same)" (*An. Post.* I.2 72a15-24).[35] Aristotle thus seems to indicate that a hypothesis has to do with the 'that-it-is' of a thing, while the definition has to do with the what. Thus, many commentators conclude that hy-

potheses are existence claims. On this view, definitions are predictive propositions, "a unit is such-and-such," while hypotheses are not—"this unit exists."

But the example given in this passage is highly ambiguous; Aristotle simply
says that a hypothesis of unit gives *to einai monada*, which need not be taken to
signify an existence claim about a particular unit. It is just as likely that it expresses the supposition that *there is* such a thing as a quantitatively divisible
thing because reality *is not* one and motionless. Indeed, Aristotle explicitly worries in the *Physics* that Melissus' position calls into question the very notion of
magnitude.[36] If so, this particular example simply shows that our mathematician
must not be caught up in the theory of monism in order to give the definition of
unit. This observation is to be combined with the fact that in other passages,
hypotheses are propositions used in deductions, which seems to indicate that
they are predications, rather than existential affirmations.[37] Furthermore, the
only obvious example Aristotle gives of a hypothesis—the hypothesis that nature is a principle of motion[38]—is a straightforward predication.

Hypotheses, therefore, are predicative principles useful in deduction. They
are also themselves provable, although they are, by definition, unproved:

> Whenever a man assumes without proving it himself although it is provable—if
> he assumes something that seems to be the case to the learner, he hypothesizes
> about it (and it is a hypothesis[39] not simpliciter but only in relation to the learn-
> er) (*An. Post.* I.10 76b27-30).

Aristotle has already stated one difference between hypotheses and definitions,
namely that hypotheses are assumptions of one part of a contradiction, while
definitions are necessarily true. They are also un-provable, and must be grasped.
But hypotheses are suppositions about some principles that are provable, yet
unproved from the perspective of a particular person.

Hypotheses are principles, and as such are useful for learning in physics.[40]
Furthermore, both are provable, although the physicist *qua* dialectician has actually proved the principles, while the one actively investigating has not, even
though she could. This is a bit of common sense—while investigating the principles of rock formation (e.g.), it is quite appropriate for the investigator to be
unconcerned with the *ti estin* of magnitude, place, succession. But it is not clear
what sort of geological truths she would be able to demonstrate if she had no
views whatsoever about the nature of motion and change. We must at least admit, then, that hypotheses simpliciter and dialectical principles of *phusis* have
much in common, if they are not identical.

It also seems that Aristotle believes that hypotheses are useful not only for
the physicist *qua* empirical investigator but also for the physicist *qua* dialectician. While there may be some dialectical controversy over the principle that
nature is a source of change, this does not affect the dialectical inquiry of the
physicist: "...objections involving the point that we have just raised do not affect the physicist; for it is a hypothesis that nature is a principle of motion."[41]

From the perspective of the physicist *qua* dialectician, it is entirely appropriate to call the principle that nature is a source of change a hypothesis. In fact, the dialectician of the principles of *phusis* must suppose that nature is not one and motionless as a condition of the inquiry.

This in no way implies, however, that the existence of *phusis* is a hypothesis in-itself, i.e., simpliciter; it is rather a hypothesis for the dialectician of the principles of *phusis*. Obviously, Aristotle himself certainly does not assume that Parmenides is wrong; rather, he explicitly proves that the theory is false at some length in *Physics* I.3 with his considerable dialectic skills. The physicist, however, need not deliver such a proof. What has been proved by Aristotle may be taken as hypothesis for the one investigating the principles of *phusis*. This means that a hypothesis is relative to the kind of inquiry one is undertaking. To the mathematician and the dialectician of *phusis*, it is a hypothesis that motionless monism is false. To the one empirically investigating some particular domain of *phusis*, the principles of *phusis* in general are hypotheses. This is why Aristotle insists that a hypothesis is never a hypothesis simpliciter.

It is possible to deny all this, and instead believe that Aristotle's method is strictly empirical by highlighting passages such as this:

> Now to investigate whether what exists is one and motionless *is not a contribution to the science of nature*...at the same time the holders of the theory of which we are speaking do incidentally raise physical questions, though nature is not their subject; so it will perhaps be as well to spend a few words on them, especially as their inquiry is not without scientific interest (*Ph.* I.2 184b26-185a20, italics mine).

The fact that Aristotle proceeds to give a dialectical proof of the falsity of motionless monism, combined with the fact that this particular investigation is not relevant to physics, might seem to indicate that the dialectical method is not part of the scientific method.[42] But this is to miss an important stage-direction of the *Physics*; Aristotle believes the whether nature is a principle of motion or not is indeed irrelevant for the physicist; a physicist, by definition, has already made a commitment on this issue. As such, we could do worse than to call this a metaphysical debate.

In the first sentence of I.4, Aristotle clearly announces his return to physics from his brief metaphysical detour. Aristotle then proceeds to establish, through dialectic, the *ti estin* of the infinite, motion, change, cause, etc. Unlike the dialectical refutation of Parmenides, these dialectical investigations are indeed relevant for physics, as these definitions are used as principles. In fact, we have seen Aristotle insist that a natural science that did not take a position on these principles is not worth considering.[43] For the physicist *qua* dialectician, the falsity of Parmenides' thesis is a hypothesis. But Aristotle goes on to establish the principles of *phusis* dialectically, and empiricism does not seem to be involved anywhere in those passages. This implies that a philosopher may be a dialectician of *phusis* or a dialectician of meta-*phusis*; and of course, sometimes a well-rounded philosopher will investigate some particular part of nature empirically. All these are philosophical activities in the broad sense, and a single person may engage in all of these kinds of philosophy at various times, as Aristotle himself does.

Notes

1. *An. Post.* 99b20-26.

2. There are some valiant attempts, however. See Richard McKirahan, "Aristotelian *Epagōgē* in *Prior Analytics* 2.21 and *Posterior Analytics* 1.1," *Journal of the History of Philosophy* 21, no. 1 (January 1993): 1-13.

3. Robert Bolton, "Aristotle's Method in Natural Science: Physics I," in *Aristotle's Physics: A Collection of Essays*, ed. Lindsay Judson (Oxford: Oxford University Press, 1991), 4.

4. Le Blond says that in Aristotle there is a "perceptible vacillation between a rationalist and an empiricist approach to science" (J.M. LeBlond, "Aristotle on Definition," *Articles on Aristotle*, ed. J. Barnes, M. Schofield, and R. Sorabji. Gerald Duckworth & Company Limited, 1976) n. 67.

5. It is no argument to say that Aristotle does nothing to describe in any detail the process of going from whole universals to principles in this passage, since he is discussing how perception's role in *epagōgē* steers through Meno's paradox in *An. Post.* 99b20-26.

6. It is not clear from this passage if the child is lacking information about the concept 'man' (believing that all men have children), the concept 'father' (believing that father is the word for 'adult male'), or both, but it does not matter in this context as the child is certainly in possession of a confused concept.

7. This is another reason to doubt that *pan katholou* refers to the principles of demonstration, for simple experience has led to a false predication of 'all males.'

8. Or at least I believe so. I may have excluded an adult male based on his lack of a mustache because of my mistaken belief about the universality of 'mustached.'

9. *DA* 424a16-27.

10. Aristotle's discussion of *sumbebēkos* in *Top.* I.5 102b4-26 makes this sufficiently clear.

11. Charles Kahn, "The Role of *Nous* in the Cognition of First Principles," in *Posterior Analytics* II 19. In *Aristotle on Science: The Posterior Analytics*, Enrico Berti, ed. (Padua, 1981), 386.

12. Aristotle uses the 'why it is' language throughout the second book of the *Posterior Analytics* to pick out an essential rather than a nominal definition, even though definitions of the essence are usually called the 'what it is.'

13. See *An. Post.* 89b23-35. We also seek the fact and the reason why, although these are of state-of-affairs, and not substances.

14. I am here aware that my analysis of the difference between nominal and essential definitions in this sense is in line with Bolton, and against many other interpretations,

such as David Demoss and Daniel Devereux, "Essence, Existence, and Nominal Definition in Aristotle's *Posterior Analytics* II 8-10," Phronesis 33, no. 2 (1988): 23-38.

   15. *Top.* I.5.

   16. See pages 22-23.

   17. Kahn 396.

   18. See Owen, G.E.L. *"Tithenai ta Phainomena," Articles on Aristotle*, ed. J. Barnes,
M. Schofield, and R. Sorabji (Gerald Duckworth & Company Limited, 1976); also Irwin,
T.H. "Ways to First Principles: Aristotle's Methods of Discoveries." *Philosophical Top-
ics* 15, no. 2 (1987).

   19. See n. 4.

   20. Contemporary commentaries on this problem are plentiful and seem to be inspired
by a seminal interpretation by W.D. Ross, *Aristotle's Prior and Posterior Analytics* (Oxford: Oxford University Press, 1949), 57.

   21. *Meta.* 1064a18-29. Cf. *Ph.* 193a30-193b6.

   22. *Ph.* 201b 33, 202b30-35, 208a27-35, 213a13, 224b11, 226b19-2.

   23. *Ph.* 185a1-4, 253b2-6.

   24. Given Aristotle's various uses of *epagōgē*, there are difficulties with supposing
that there is one definition of it. For one thing, Aristotle sometimes seems to use it as a
general description of the process of getting first principles. This at least distinguishes
this method from demonstration (Cf. *EN* 1139b27-31, *An. Post* 71a1-9). As a consequence, dialectic (at least some form of it) and aporematic would be types of *epagōgē*.
But it is also possible to confine the term to describe the process of seeking first principles when sense-perception is relevant (*An. Post.* 100b3-5). This is the way I use the
term, in any event.

   25. *Top.* I.2 101a34-101b4 is a typical proof text for the former position, *An. Pr.*
46a17-26 for the latter.

   26. See *Ph.* 198a14-26, where Aristotle describes the complexity of getting 'the what'
when motion must be accounted for.

   27. This is not to say that demonstration in other sciences never requires principles
other than *horismoi*. In mathematics, for example, a mathematician must suppose that
there are such things as magnitudes, which is to assume that monism is false (*An. Post.*
72a15-21). However, a physicist seeking definitions must assume this as a hypothesis in
addition to the principles of *phusis*.

   28. Bolton, 11.

   29. Owen admits that occasionally Aristotle allows for a 'physical' method separate
from a 'dialectical' method. These two methods, when both are available, typically reach
the same principle, as in the cases concerning infinite physical body or natural place. This
shows that dialectical method is distinguished from a physical method not because it
arrives at a different sort of principle, but because it proves more than the physical method. Other times, he claims that Aristotle uses empiricism to test, rather than to establish,
principles (Owen, 118). Bolton claims the reverse, that empirical methods establish principles, while dialectic may aid the process of establishing these same principles in limited
ways (Bolton, 21).

   30. Thus, empiricism and dialectic work together to give us a single definition. C.D.C.
Reeve, *Substantial Knowledge: Aristotle's Metaphysics* (Indianapolis: Hackett Publishing
Company, Inc., 2000) 20-27.

   31. Although he later adds that in the case of physics, it is not necessary to consider all
possible aspects and instantiations of the infinite—for example, the number line—but "to
investigate whether there is a sensible magnitude which is infinite" (204a1-2).

32. This is most clear in *Top.* 100a25-30. Also see *Ph.* 208a31-35, where Aristotle complains that finding the definition in the case of 'place' will be more difficult than with the other definitions in physics because there are no extant *endoxa* about place.

33. In addition to *An. Pr.* I.30, central instances are *An. Post.* II.19, *Ph.* I.1, *An. Post.* II.5, II.16, *Meta.* VII.12.

34. Translation mine.

35. I have retained the Greek. Barnes has 'posit' and 'supposition,' respectively.

36. *Ph.* 185b5.

37. *An. Post.* 76b35-39, 81b10-16.

38. *Ph.* 253b6.

39. The Revised Oxford Translation has 'supposes' and 'supposition.'

40. Cf. *Meta.* 1064a6-9.

41. *Ph* 253b2-6.

42. In the same vein, some point to *Ph.* III.5, where Aristotle is talking about dialectic, and then says "If, on the other hand, we investigate the question more in accordance with principles appropriate to physics, we are led as follows to the same result" (204b10-11). This is a misreading, however. Aristotle is contrasting appropriate principles in physics not with dialectic, but with mathematical principles (204b1).

43. *Ph.* 202a35-203a4, quoted above. Cf. *Ph.* 213a13-14.

Chapter Four
Grasping the Principles: *Nous*

Introduction

Aristotle uses the word '*nous*' throughout his corpus. It has been variously translated into English as mind, thought, soul, intellect, intelligence, comprehension, and intuition, just to note the main renderings. At least part of the reason that it has been difficult to standardize a translation is that Aristotle uses the word in two distinct ways. It is most commonly an intellectual state (*hexis*) of capacity. Aristotle understands *nous* in this sense in comparison and contrast with *epistēmē*. We have *epistēmē* of demonstrated truths; but as noted, Aristotle commits himself to another kind of 'knowledge' of the principles, on pains of infinite regress.[1] Here, 'knowledge' cannot be *epistēmē*, but *nous*—a kind of knowledge that has been gained not through explanation, but what I will argue is intuition:

> Knowledge [*Epistēmē*] is belief about things that are universal and necessary, and there are principles of everything that is demonstrated and of all knowledge (for knowledge involves reasoning). This being so, the first principle of what is known cannot be an object of knowledge, of art, or of practical wisdom; for that which can be known can be demonstrated, and art and practical wisdom deal with things that can be otherwise...the remaining alternative is that it is comprehension [*nous*] that grasps the first principles (*EN* VI.3 1140b31-1141a8).

Nous, then, is an intellectual state (*hexis*) that describes our grasp of the first principles of demonstration.

Aristotle also (although less frequently) uses *nous* to mean a substance that is part of a person, such that a person is fully accounted for by accounting for composite substance (i.e., body and soul) *and* the substance of *nous*. I do not have a strong stand on the scholarly controversy about the proper translation of *nous* when *nous* is a substance, so I will leave it un-translated in this case.[2] When *nous* is meant as an intellectual state, I will argue that it is best translated as 'intuition,' or even 'intellectual intuition,' to distinguish it from the state on which it is modeled, sensible intuition. I will begin with the less complicated discussion of *nous* as substance.

Nous as Substance

In the *De Anima*, Aristotle gives an account of *nous* as substance while discussing the soul's capacities. Unlike many uses of the term 'soul' (*psuche*), Aristotle uses it simply as a way to pick out that which is alive; 'soul' functions as the mark of difference between natural bodies that are alive and those that are not: "of natural bodies some have life in them, others not; by life we mean self-nutrition and growth and decay. It follows that every natural body which has life in it is a substance in the sense of a composite" (*DA* II.1 412a12-15).

In this sense plants have a soul, for they are capable of growth and decay, and growth and decay are types of internally originating motion. All things that have soul have this capacity for self-nutrition, but there are other capacities which are part of some souls, namely "the appetitive, the sensory, the locomotive, and the power of thinking" (*DA* II.3 414a32). The sensory and appetitive capacities do not belong to plants, but to humans and non-human animals. And in addition to all these capacities, human beings are distinguished from all other species in that they also possess 'the power of thinking.'

It is easily shown that the capacities of soul besides thinking necessarily only exist enmattered: "if we consider the majority of [the capacities], there seems to be no case in which the soul can act or be acted upon without involving the body; e.g., anger, courage, appetite, and sensation generally" (*DA* I.1 403a6-7). Aristotle is pointing out the uncontroversial fact that it would not be possible to eat lunch or enjoy a subset without a body. But it is not immediately clear that all psychic capacities are like this: "are [the capacities] all affections of the complex body and soul, or is there any one among them peculiar to the soul itself? To determine this is indispensable but difficult" (*DA* I.1 403a3-5). Aristotle gives an immediate yet inconclusive answer: if there is one, it would be "thinking" (*DA* I.1 403a6). Aristotle chooses to leave this question unanswered at this point, but he does warn us that "if [thinking] too proves to be a form of imagination or to be impossible without imagination, it too requires a body as a condition of its existence" (*DA* I.1 403a8-10).

Aristotle begins a discussion of the possibility of a bodiless capacity in *DA* I.4: "*nous* seems to be some substance [*ousia*] born in us..." (*DA* I.4 408b18). His use of the word '*ousia*' is significant. Aristotle is clear that the body and soul are not two conjoined substances, since soul is the form or essence of a living body. They are rather one substance—a composite—related as the power of sight is to the eye: "every natural body which has life in it is a substance in the sense of a composite" (*DA* II.1 412a15-16). So any particular living thing is itself one substance composed of soul and body. Therefore, his belief that '*ousia*' is 'in us' signifies that he is speaking of a substance that inheres in the human composite.

Nous, therefore, is a substance distinct from the composite. One reason he distinguishes it as a separate substance is because *nous* differs from the rest of the composite with respect to its duration; the composite substance perishes, but *nous*-substance does not, nor do the activities of *nous*:

> if it could be destroyed at all, it would be under the blunting of old age. What really happens is, however, exactly parallel to what happens in the case of the sense organs; if the old man could recover the proper kind of eye, he would see

just as well as the young man... Thus it is that thinking [*to noein*] and reflecting [*to theōrein*] decline through the decay of some inward part and are themselves impassible [☐παθ☐ς]. Thinking [*to dianoeisthai*], loving, and hating are affections not of thought, but of that which has thought, so far as it has it. That is why, when this vehicle decays, memory and love cease; they were activities not of thought, but of the composite which has perished; *nous* is, no doubt, something more divine and impassible (*DA* I.4 408b18-31).

Aristotle has already said that all of our psychic capacities require a composite, although he has left the possibility that *nous* may not. One consequence of psychic powers being essentially part of the composite is that they would be corruptible, for all matter is corruptible. Therefore, if there is a capacity which is not necessarily enmattered, it may not be subject to decay. And indeed, Aristotle has just stated that "*nous* seems to be...incapable of being destroyed" (*DA* I.4 408b18).

This notion seems to contradict the appearances. We can observe the powers of mind declining with old age, and being entirely corrupted on the occasion of death along with all other psychic capacities. In this passage, Aristotle is acknowledging this obvious fact, but reconciling it with his notion that some mental activity is not corruptible. In the preceding paragraph, Aristotle has laid the groundwork for this insight: "...to say that it is the soul that is angry is as if we were to say that it is soul that weaves or builds houses. It is doubtless better...to say that it is the man who does this with his soul" (*DA* I.4 408b13-14). In the same way, the substantial change that we observe is not necessarily of the substance of *nous* itself, but of the substance in whom *nous* is born—this particular man. Since he is the possessor of *nous*, his substantial decay means that this particular substance which formerly carried *nous* is no longer capable of thinking. However, *nous* is not part of the substance which is this particular composite. With the phrase "in so far as it [i.e., the composite] has it [i.e., *nous*]," Aristotle seems to be reaffirming the existence of *nous* as an independent substance; it is something that the composite possesses, but its possession of it does not exhaust the substance of *nous*, since in this case, the composite only possesses it to a certain extent.

Aristotle thus believes that part of a human being is some kind of substance that is not reducible to body. Despite this, it is not always accepted that Aristotle is a dualist. For instance, Charles Kahn argues that Aristotle's doctrine stands outside of "the Cartesian curse of mind-body opposition with all the baffling paradoxes and philosophical blind alleys that this antithesis gives rise to."[3] Kahn admits that Aristotle's claim that "*nous* has no bodily organ and hence that the faculty of intellect...[because it] is not only logically distinct by essentially separable from the body...is an embarrassment to many of Aristotle's modern admirers, who fear that it commits him to some form of Cartesian dualism."[4] But Kahn believes that Aristotle's position is different because Descartes "conceives [the *cogito*] as carried out by a thinking being who might not have a body at all;

whereas Aristotle would have recognized such self-awareness…as an essentially embodied act."[5]

Kahn is right to notice that this is a genuine difference, but is this a relevant difference? Sympathizers of Aristotle's philosophy of mind[6] are understandably afraid of running into the 'baffling paradoxes' of Cartesian dualism. Kahn believes that noticing the aforementioned difference is supposed to bring relief to these sympathizers. But it does not seem to. The other parts of soul besides *nous* are related to the body as sight to the eye, but what is the relation of *nous* to the other parts of the soul and/or to the body? Aristotle's non-answer leads Kahn to say that he does "not see that there is any genuine resolution for this tension within Aristotle's account of the *psuche*," although we might gain some sympathy by chalking up this "lack of unity in Aristotle's account" to the "complex, paradoxical structure of the human condition."[7] And so while Kahn initially says that Aristotle is above the hopeless dualist paradoxes, only a page later he says very clearly that Aristotle is right in the middle of that fray. Although I am not here arguing for or against dualism, it does seem that Aristotle has the same challenges as any substance dualist, whatever nuances his doctrine of *nous* might have.[8]

So not only is *nous* a different substance than the composite, it is a different kind of substance. As noted, an essential characteristic of the composite is its corruptibility. Since *nous* is not perishable, but *apathes*, it belongs to a different genus. And since *to noein* and *to theōrein* are affections of *nous*, those functions in particular are incorruptible; since *to dianoeisthai* is an affection of the perishable composite possessing *nous*, it does in fact perish:

> We have no evidence as yet about thought [*tou nou*] or the power of reflexion [*tēs theōrētikēs*]; it seems to be a different kind [*genos heteron*] of soul, differing as what is eternal from what is perishable (*DA* II.2 413b25-26).

Nous—a substance—has activities that are proper to it. Aristotle is again contrasting these with the "powers of self-nutrition, sensation, thinking [*dianoētikōi*], and movement" (*DA* II.2 413b12), and so emphasizing his distinction between what is properly an affection of the composite and what is a function of eternal substance. I turn now to the first of these, namely *to noein*.

How *Nous* Becomes *Nous*: *To Noeiv*

Aristotle says that the substance *nous* only exists potentially and is actually nothing before it undergoes a process called *to noeiv*; its existence prior to this is a merely potential one, for *nous* "can have no nature of its own, other than having a certain capacity. Thus that in the soul which is called *nous*…is, before *noein*, not actually any real thing" (*DA* III.4 429a21-24). Of course there is the question of what *to noein* is, but there is the prior question of how *to noein* may begin; this is an issue that Aristotle predictably does not ignore, given his sensitivity to starting points. What, then, is the starting point for *to noein*?

Aristotle believes that the starting points are images: "to the thinking soul images [*phantasmata*] serve as if they were contents of perception...That is why the soul never *noei* without an image" (*DA* III.7 431a15-17). In chapter 3, I argued that *epagōgē*, which yields definitions of essences useful as first principles for demonstration, must be taken as a two-stage process. In the first stage, the soul comes to possess a kind of universal that is perceptible, and from that initial universal, we come to possess essences of things. One reason I coined the phrase 'perceptible universal' was that Aristotle called this first universal several things, none with any regularity, including 'experience,' the 'whole universal' 'primitive universal.' Here, I argue, Aristotle is referring to this process, which would mean that the perceptible universals are images, or at least a certain sort of image.

In one sense, images are of particulars, and so they may seem to be a poor candidate to be perceptible universals. However, they are universal in the sense that in an image, a (sensible) form is considered without its matter:

> The objects of thought [*ta noēta*] are *in* the sensible forms [*tois eidesi tois aisthētois*], viz., both the abstract objects and all the states and affections of sensible things. Hence no one can learn or understand anything in the absence of sense, and when the mind is actively aware of anything it is necessarily aware of it along with an image [*phantasma*]; for images are like sensuous contents except that they contain no matter (*DA* III.8 432a5-13, my emphasis).

In this passage, *phatasmata* are affirmed as having a central role in the process of acquiring *noēta*, for the *noēta* are in some sense acquired *from* sensible forms. (Aristotle notes that by sensible forms, he means 'the states (*hexeis*) and affections (*pathē*) of sensible things,' which we have only by the power of imagination). *Phantasmata* are thus starting points for *to noein*.

Aristotle models *to noein* on sensation (*to aisthanesthai*), which is an inherently passive process: "sensation depends, as we have said, on a process of movement or affection from without, for it is held to be some sort of change of quality" (*DA* II.4 416b32-34). Since our soul changes from a state of not-perceiving to perceiving, there is necessarily a movement. Movement, for Aristotle, is always from a potentiality to an actuality. And since our soul was brought to a state of actually perceiving, its potentiality must have been actualized by something external to it.

The two ends of the movement are the soul's power of sensation and the object of sensation. The potential end is the power of sensation, and the actual end is the object that is perceived: "what has the power of sensation is potentially like what the perceived object is actually" (*DA* II.5 418a3-4). Like any movement, before the movement starts the ends of the movement are in one sense dissimilar and in another similar. They are dissimilar because one side is potentially what the other is actually; they are similar because they are potentially identical: "while at the beginning of the process of its being acted upon the two interacting factors are dissimilar, at the end the one acted upon is assimilated to the other and is identical in quality with it" (*DA* II.5 418a4-5).

In sensation, unlike other kinds of movement, the movement that takes place is immaterial, for the form (*eidōn*) enters the soul without the matter (*aneu tēs hulēs*):

> Generally, about all perception, we can say that a sense is what has the power of receiving into itself the sensible forms of things [*tōn aisthētōn eidōn*] without the matter, in the way in which a piece of wax takes on the impress of sig-net-ring without the iron or gold;...in a similar way the sense is affected by what is colored or flavored or sounding not insofar as each is what it is, but insofar as it is of such and such a sort and according to its form [*logon*] (*DA* III.12 424a16-23).

This is despite the fact that what is affected is material, for "a primary sense-organ is that in which such a power is seated" (*DA* III.12 424a24). In the case of sense perception, the sense organs receive the sensible form, and so not only are they passive but also capable of receiving the form in an unenmattered state which previously only existed as enmattered. Sensation is therefore intuitive: it is taking in an object which in this case is a sensible form.

To Noein as Intellectual Intuiting

It is clear that Aristotle wants to model *to noein* on sensation (*to aisthanesthai*). But is he justified in doing so? If he is, then *to noein* is best understood as a kind of intuition, since perception is just the intuition of sensible objects; this, then, would be the intuition of intelligible objects. He makes his case for this in *De Anima* III.3 In that section, Aristotle considers whether the 'ancients,' who "go so far as to identify thinking and perceiving" (*DA* III.3 427a22) could be correct. He states their case as forcefully as he can:

> There are two distinctive particularities by reference to which we characterize the soul—(1) local movement and (2) thinking [*to noein*], understanding [*phronein*], and perceiving [*to aisthanesthai*]. Thinking and understanding are regarded as akin to a form of perceiving; for in the one as well as the other the soul discriminates and is cognizant of something which is (*DA* III.3 427a17-21).

An initial difficulty in considering whether *to noein* is a type of perception is that there are at least two possible meanings of *to noein* (to which a third will be added in the subsequent division): "[t]hinking is...held to be part imagination [*phantasia*], in part judgment [*hupolēpsis*]" (*DA* III.3 427b28).

Thinking in the sense of judging cannot be 'akin' to perceiving:

Thinking [*to noein*] is...distinct from perceiving—I mean that in which we find
rightness and wrongness—rightness in understanding, knowledge, true opinion,
wrongness in their opposites: for perception of special objects of sense is always free from truth and error...while it is possible to think [*dianoesthai*] falsely as well as truly, and thought is found only where there is discourse of reason
(*DA* III.3 427b9-14).

In this passage, Aristotle's words have implied much about his position on *to
noein*: *to noein* in *this* sense (whatever sense to which he is presently referring)
makes 'rightness and wrongness' possible, because it makes judgments (*DA*
III.3 427b15). Aristotle recognizes the uniqueness of this type of *to noein*
enough to give it its own name—*to dianoeisthai*. What we are witnessing, then,
is Aristotle making the decision to not use *to noein* as a general term for 'thinking' importantly, then, Aristotle's concept of *to dianoeisthai* just is *to noein* insofar as it judges.

Furthermore, it is also impossible that *to noein*, insofar as it is imagining,
can be like perceiving for three reasons:

Sense is either a faculty or an activity...: imagination takes place in the absence
of both, as e.g., in dreams. Again, sense is always present, imagination not. If
actual imagination and actual sensation were the same, imagination would be
found in all brutes: this is held not to be the case...Again, sensations are always
true, imaginations are for the most part false (*DA* III.3 428a5-13).

This last consideration, that sensations are incorrigible while imaginings are not,
also can be extended to exclude the possibility that understanding could be akin
to perceiving, since understanding often falls into error (*DA* III.3 427b7). The
common opinion of the ancients, then, that "thinking and understanding are regarded as akin to a form of perceiving" (*DA* III.3 427a20), is false.

Aristotle has thus used *DA* III.3 to prove that 'judging-*to noein*,' 'imagin-
ing-*to noein*,' and understanding are all unlike perceiving. In III.4, he now considers whether the opinions of the ancients might be true in another sense:

if *to noein* is like *to aisthanesthai*, it must be either a process in which the soul
is acted upon by that which is capable of being thought, or a process different
from but analogous to that (*DA* III.4 429a15-16).

Two features of Aristotle's analysis deserve attention here. First, the former uses
of *to noein* in III.3 are given specific names because of their unique functions,
and thus the locution '*to noein*' is no longer used in those cases. And second, his
current (and subsequent) use of *to noein* is something that *is* akin to perceiving.

Although *to noein* in the sense of judging and imagining could not be modeled on perception, this sense of *to noein* can:

If *to noein* is like perceiving *to aisthanesthai*, it must be either a process in
which the soul is acted upon by that which is capable of being thought, or a

process different from but analogous to that. The thinking part of the soul must therefore be, while impassible, capable of receiving the form of an object [*ta noēta*]; that is, must be potentially identical in character with its object without being the object. Thought must be related to what is thinkable, as sense is to what is sensible (*DA* III.4 429a12-18).

Nous in this function is passive in the same way as the soul is in sensation, for the movement that *nous* undergoes from potentiality to actuality is initiated by the object. The object in this case is not the sensible form (*tōn aisthētōn eidōn*), but the intelligible form (*ta noēta*). For Aristotle, both kinds of forms affect us by actualizing some potential in us. *To noein* is therefore intellectual intuiting, and 'thinking' is only an appropriate translation of '*to noein*' if 'thinking' can mean 'intuiting.' If one takes *DA* III.3 as proof that Aristotle takes *to noein* as a discursive capacity because *to noein* is a capacity for judging, one would be taking things quite out of context; *DA* III.3 presents a theory that Aristotle rejects, and *to dianoeisthai* is presented as a more appropriate term for the judging mind. Intuiting is a movement, but the actuality exists entirely in the object, for the mind is actually nothing before being actualized by the intelligible form.

Before any further defense of *to noein* as a kind of intuition, it is appropriate to define 'intuition' more directly because of the amount of baggage associated with the term. By 'intuition,' I believe that Aristotle just means something like 'immediate awareness,' where what we are immediately aware of are objects— whether sensible or intellectual; the objects actually exist, and we come to be aware of that existence. The reason why *nous*' awareness of intellectual objects is immediate is because it is passive with respect to those objects. And like sensible intuition, intellectual intuition is passive because *nous*, which is potential, is actualized by objects external to it. Besides the obvious difference between sensible and intellectual intuition (i.e., the objects are different), in sensible intuition, the *event* of sensation as well as the *process* is passive. Since the process of sense intuition is passive, it is of no great credit to the perceiver that she is in position to intuit sensible objects; any being endowed with perception and memory comes to have perceptible universals, and this is true of small children, non-human animals, and non-philosophical adult humans.

But even though the *event* of intuiting intellectual objects is also passive, the *process* is not passive at all; it requires hard work, and perhaps a copious amount of observation of perceptible particulars in the world and reflection and reasoning about those observations. But when the hard work is done, we are finally able to intuit the intellectual form, in the sense that the actual object actualizes *nous* in regard to that form. When commentators are concerned with ascribing intellectual intuition to Aristotle, they are fearful that intuition is purely passive, and therefore actual sense experience is irrelevant; perhaps 'meditation' will suffice as a translation.[9] But this is to miss the crucial distinction here: the event of coming to possess intellectual forms is indeed passive, but this kind of intuition is reserved for those willing to undergo the process of hard empirical investigation.

The Contact Metaphor: Intuiting Essences and Definitions

My argument that *to noein* should be translated as 'intuit' receives powerful support from a metaphor Aristotle uses in two passages in the *Metaphysics* that scholars widely agree are especially revealing of his position. In book XII, Aristotle says:

> And *nous noei* itself [*auton voei ho nous*] because it shares in the nature of the object of thought [*tou noētou*]; for it becomes an object of thought in coming into contact [*thigganōn*] with and thinking its objects, so that thought and the object of thought are the same (*Meta.* XII.7 1072b20-23).

I believe that Aristotle's main goal in this passage is to describe contemplation, which will be of interest elsewhere.[10] But what is relevant here is his description of how *nous* becomes what it is in the first place: *nous* 'makes contact' with objects of thought.

In an earlier passage in the *Metaphysics*, Aristotle gives more detail to this metaphor:

> With regard to incomposites [*asuntheta*] what is being or not being, and what is truth or falsity? A thing of this sort is not composite, so as to be when it is compounded…truth or falsity is as follows—contact [*thigein*] and assertion [*phanai*] are truth (assertion [*phasis*] not being the same as affirmation [*kataphasis*]), and ignorance is non-contact [*agnoein mē thigganein*]. For it is not possible to be in error regarding the question what a thing is, save in an accidental sense; and *the same is true* regarding non-composite substances [*tas mē sunthetas ousias*] (for it is not possible to be in error about them). And they all exist actually, not potentially; for otherwise they would come to be and cease to be; but, as it is, being itself does not come to be (or cease to be)…About the things, then, that are essences and exist in actuality, it is not possible to be in error, but only to *noein* them or not *noein* them (*Meta.* IX.10 1051b17-32, my emphasis).

I believe that this is one of the most revealing passages about Aristotle's theory of *epistēmē* in all of the corpus, although this is not always obvious from the present translation and dominant interpretations. Thus, several observations are in order.

First, Aristotle says that the truth about *asuntheta* is in *thigein* and *phanai* them; it is not immediately clear what '*asuntheta*' are, but his comments a few lines down indicate that they are expressions of the 'what it is' of a thing, i.e., a definition. So what does it mean to know *asuntheta*? First, he plainly states that we know them by *thigein* and *phanai*; but importantly, '*phasis*' does not mean 'affirmation' (*kataphasis*). Since an affirmation is an affirming of something concerning something else, it seems more appropriate to render *phasis* with the more generic 'saying' or 'expressing.' Another apparent difference—and one whose importance will be revealed—it that affirming something of something else essentially involves predicating. By drawing a distinction between *phasis* and *kataphasis*, then, Aristotle leaves open the possibility that *phasis* does not involve predicating, as *kataphasis* necessarily does. When it comes to incomposites, then, truth is contacting or expressing them, and expressing them without predicating them. To emphasize, this is in contrast to cases where "there is truth if the subject and the attribute are really combined, and falsity if they are not combined" (*Meta.* IX.10 1051b34-35). This leads to a second observation: a *phasis* is a kind of saying that does not combine a subject and a predication, since the more familiar kind of truth is not available to it. Third, it is an expression of the 'what it is' of something, which is to say that it is a definition.

Fourth, Aristotle stops talking about definitions and starts talking about substances at line 26: "*and the same is true* regarding non-composite substances." And line 31 makes it clear that these substances are the essences of which the definitions are expressions. About these, it is also "not possible to be in error" (line 27). The translation that it is only possible "to think or not think" (line 32) is misleading. It clearly fails to make sense of the contact metaphor being introduced here, since Aristotle clearly means to discuss a process that is much like touching, and not much like 'thinking.' Therefore it is better to say that it is only possible 'to intuit or not intuit' the essences. Thus, this passage is stating that both essences and definitions are intuited intellectually, where intellectual intuiting may be conceived of through the analogy with sense intuition—in this case, touch.

Intuiting Definitions: An Initial Problem

Aristotle variously uses two general terms for the objects of intellectual intuition—*noētos* and *noēma* (plural: *noēta*, *noēmata*)—and he probably does not mean any technical distinction between the terms. They appear to be general terms for that which falls within the domain of the thinkable; *noētos* is formed in contrast with '*opatos*'—the domain of the visible, so in a general sense, a *noētos* is any kind of concept. But what counts as a *noētos* or *noēma*? According to the observations drawn from *Meta.* IX.10, both definitions and essences are kinds of *noēmata*. This interpretation seems to be threatened by a complementary passage in *De Anima* III.6, where *noēmata* are explicitly under discussion:

> The *noēsis* of indivisibles [*tōn adiaipetōn*] is found in those cases where falsehood is impossible: where the alternative of true or false applies, there we always find a sort of combining of objects of thought [*noēmata*] in a quasiunity...objects of thought that were separate were combined, e.g., incommensurate and diagonal...falsehood always involves a combining...In each and every case that which unifies is thought [*nous*] (*DA* III.4 429b27-430a6).

Nous intuits objects that cannot be false because there is no combination of terms—that is, they are not assertions. Assertions are divisible; 'Cleon is white' is divisible into the terms 'Cleon' and 'white.' If there is to be truth, then there must be a combination of objects of thought, such as 'Cleon' and 'white,' or 'diagonal' and 'incommensurate.' This is so because "he who thinks the separated to be separated and the combined to be combined has the truth, while he whose thought is in a state contrary to that of the objects is in error" (*Meta.* IX.10 1051b3-5). The term 'Cleon,' however, cannot be true or false, since there is no possible separation of it, nor is it presently combined with another *noēma*. It is therefore only when *noēma* are put together that they may be true or false: "what is true or false involves a synthesis of thoughts [*noēmatōn*]" (*DA* III.8 432a10-11). This makes it seem likely that the objects of *nous* are single *noēma*, and these single *noēma* may then be combined with other *noēma*. The combined *noēma* then form an assertion, which may be true or false.

This indicates that a *noēma* is an object of thought prior to its use in an assertion. Some commentators believe that this is easily translated into the language of concepts and propositions.[11] These concepts cannot be true or false because they are indivisible. Taking concepts as the proper objects of *nous* seems to receive further support from Aristotle's examples, such as *An. Post.* II.19, when *nous* gets concepts such as 'man' and 'animal' (or 'circle,' 'shape') through *epagōgē*. After we possess the initial concepts, they can then be combined with other concepts ('shapes,' 'animals') in a proposition, such as 'All circles are shapes,' or 'All men are animals,' which is now a candidate to be true or false. And perhaps such propositions count as definitions. Thus, we intuit the concepts constituting the definition, but not the definition itself, because the definition is the result of a synthesis, not an intuition.

On this story, *nous* intuits concepts (*noēmata*) but not propositions (combinations of *noēmata*); I will call this the concept/proposition interpretation. This interpretation is perhaps natural, but it is, however, quite wrong, since it cannot account for all the texts. Of central importance is the question: is an assertion any kind of combination of terms (including combinations that are not connected by a state of being verb), or does it refer more specifically to a combination of a subject and predicate? I believe that both passages indicate the latter.

The concept/proposition interpretation of these passages is insightfully considered and rejected by Sorabji:

> [Aristotle] might be taken to mean [in *Meta.* IX 10 and *DA* III.6] that his subject is not propositional thought, but contemplation of concepts taken singly. However, it is an embarrassment for this interpretation that we should expect there to be *neither* truth *nor* falsehood, unless in *some* sense we are combining concepts.[12]

This criticism is devastating for the concept/proposition interpretation. In both passages, there is in fact a kind of truth available. In *Meta.* IX 10 this is more explicit, but also in the *DA* passage Aristotle more than once says that falsehood is not possible in this case, but he obviously believes that truth is. This rules out the possibility that Aristotle was *only* referring to concepts instead of propositions, since concepts are neither truth nor false: "every affirmation, it seems, is either true or false; but of things said without any combination none is either true or false (e.g., man, white, runs, wins)" (*Cat.* 4 2a8-10). Incomposite subjects as well as indivisibles, however, do have a kind of truth that attaches to them, for truth is contact.

One Kind of Definition as Non-Assertive *Logoi*

However astute the criticism, Sorabji himself ultimately fails to draw the correct conclusion. He believes that Aristotle was not referring to concepts but instead to definitions, of which an example is 'human is a two-legged animal.' This is a combination of concepts, and not a concept taken by itself. However, Sorabji does not count definitions as assertions because they are identity statements.[13] Therefore there is a kind of truth that expresses success in finding those definitions, but when one tries to assign 'four-legged animal' to 'human,' one has not made contact with the essence of 'human' after all. Hence falsity is impossible.

Sorabji is right to point out that Aristotle was referring to definitions when he talks about a kind of combination of concepts that is not the traditional combination in an assertion. But there is a consequential mistake here, for this interpretation fails to take into account that Aristotle equivocates on the word 'definition;' sometimes a definition is an assertion or proposition, such as 'human is a two-legged animal,' and sometimes, a definition is merely a complex of terms, such as 'two-legged animal.' In both *Meta.* IX.10 and *DA* III.6, I will show that Aristotle meant definition in the sense of 'two-legged animal.' If this is right, Sorabji believes correctly that a definition is a non-assertive *logos*, but he believes incorrectly that a non-assertive *logos* is a combination of terms that does not count as an assertion for the reason that it is an identity statement, such as 'human is a two-legged animal.' What else, then, could a non-assertive *logos* be?

Aristotle believes that we intuit essences of substances. But strictly speaking, acquiring an essence is somehow a private event, only intrinsically valuable; if it is to be of further philosophical use, it must be a *logos*, where *logos* means something like an expression or verbal formulation,[14] and the *logos* of an essence is a definition (*horismos*): "a definition is a *logos* signifying a thing's essence" (*Top.* I.3 101b35). On the concept/proposition model just considered, an essence would be a concept, like 'human,' while a definition would be a combination of concepts, like 'human is a two-legged animal,' which seems to be a true or false proposition. In the *De Anima*, however, definitions are not assertions:

Assertion [*phasis*] is the saying of something concerning something [*ti kata ti-nos*], as too is denial [*apophasis*], and is in every case either true or false: this is not always the case with *nous*: the thinking of the definition in the sense of what it is for something to be is never in error nor is it the assertion of something concerning something [*ti kata tinos*] (*DA* III.6 430b27-31).

A note on the translation: a '*phasis ti kata tinos*' is not Aristotle's general phrase for 'assertion' or 'statement' or 'predication,' as might be inferred from this translation. He more often uses *apophanesis*, where an *apophanesis* can either be an affirmation (*kataphasis*) or a denial (*apophasis*).[15] Furthermore, he contrasts *phasis to kata tinos* with *apophasis*. Therefore it is better to believe that Aristotle is saying in this passage that a definition is neither the kind of *phasis* that is *ti kata tinos*—an affirmation—nor a denial. This observation only emphasizes the symmetry with IX.10, where a definition is a *phasis*, although not a *kataphasis*. The point that must be taken is that it is linguistically possible that *phasis* is not meant as a species of *apophanesis*, but exactly the other way around.

The question, then, is how definitions could be neither affirmations nor denials, which in both cases require predication. Even Aristotle's remarks elsewhere clearly state that we cannot actually define a thing with a single term:

a definition is a phrase signifying a thing's essence...People whose rendering consists of a term [*onomati*] only, try it as they may, clearly do not render the definition of the thing in question, because a definition is always a phrase of a certain kind [*logos tis*] (*Top.* I.3 101b35-102a6).

Aristotle traditionally uses *onoma* to mean either a subject or a noun, depending on whether the context uses *logos* to mean a proposition or a sentence.[16] Here, it is tempting to interpret Aristotle as saying that a definition must also include a *rēma* (a predicate or verb), and the resulting *logoi* (in either case) will be assertive. But since a definition is a certain kind of *logos* (*logos tis*), Aristotle might actually be saying just the opposite: even though a *logos* usually needs a *rēma*, this special kind of *logos* does not, even though it needs more than one term. In what follows, this emerges as the better interpretation.[17]

It is from this perspective that we may observe Aristotle building his theory of definition, where a definition is a *logos* and must tell us what a thing is:

We should treat as predicates in what a thing is all such things as would be appropriate to mention is reply to the question, 'What is [*ti esti*] the object in question?'; as, for example, in the case of man, if asked that question, it is appropriate to say, 'He is an animal' (*Top.* I.3 102a31-35).

Aristotle calls this kind of term the genus, where "a genus is what is predicated in what a thing is [*ti esti*] of a number of things exhibiting differences in kind" (102a31). The thing we are defining—in this case, 'human'—thereby becomes the species. One part of a definition, therefore, is to state the genus of the definiendum, which is to specify what a thing is more generally—a human is an animal.

A genus, however, cannot by itself state the definition; definitions are expressions of essences, and a genus only gives the more general what-it-is. A true statement of the essence must distinguish the species from other kinds of beings in the genus; otherwise, a tiger and a human would share a definition. So human is an animal—but what kind of animal is he? This requires a second term that will function as an adjective. Aristotle immediately rejects two candidates for this second term in *Topics* I.5—a property (*idion*) and an accident (*sumbebēkos*). A property is a term that belongs to the species alone, and in this way will helpfully describe the species in many contexts. For example, man is an animal, and the only animal that is capable of learning grammar. 'Capable of leaning grammar' is the second term in this logos, and because man is the only animal capable of this, it is a controvertible term (i.e., animals capable of learning grammar are humans, and vice versa. A property, however, "does not indicate the essence of a thing" (*Top.* I.5 102a18). An accident more obviously does not define essence, since it is "something that may either belong or not belong to any one and the self-same thing" (*Top.* I.5 102b6-7).

Instead of these, Aristotle calls the term that is appropriate for the second term in a definition the differentia: "for the genus ought to divide the object from other things, and the differentia from any of the things contained in the same genus" (*Top.* VI.3 140a26-27). It appears, at least sometimes,[18] that a genus and a differentia have distinct tasks, despite the fact that they both divide. A genus signifies the what-it-is of a species, but a differentia identifies the important thing about the species: "a thing's differentia never signifies what it is [*ti estin*], but rather some quality [*poion ti*], as do walking and biped" (*Top.* IV.2 122b15-17). This yields a definition, such as 'human is a two-legged animal.' This is not all there is to human, of course, but it is a now a definition.

Does the differentia count as a '*rēma*'? It does not, for Aristotle is quite clear that definitions are the kind of *logoi* that lack a *rēma*:

> Every statement-making sentence [*logos apophantikos*] must contain a verb or an inflexion of a verb. For even the definition of man is not yet a statement-making sentence—unless 'is' or 'will be' or 'was' or something of this sort is added. (To explain why 'two-footed land animal' is one thing and not many belongs to a different inquiry; it will not be one simply through being said all together) (*DI* 5 17a10-15).

A statement-making sentence or *apophantic logos* is a sentence that has a verb, and statements are true or false if and only if they have verbs (*DI* 5 17a2-3). But a definition is not (or at least not in this context) a statement-making sentence. It follows that a definition cannot be either-true-or-false. However, since they are *logoi* of a certain kind, a kind of truth may attach to them. To confirm, Aristotle gives an example of a definition—'two-footed land animal—that is a concept and not an assertion.[19] Definitions of this kind, therefore, are indeed *noēmata*. It is therefore appropriate to say, like is said of all *noēmata* (the other kinds being essences and concepts of particulars), that they are intuited.

There is now good reason to believe that the incomposites (*asuntheta*) from *Meta.* IX.10 are the indivisibles (*adiaterōn*) from *DA* III.6. In both cases, Aristotle is discussing something that may be true (in a way) but not false. And since it may be true, he cannot be discussing concepts, because concepts are neither true nor false. Since they cannot be false, however, they cannot be assertions, because all assertions are always true or false. This is all perfectly consistent with Sorabji's remarks.

However, when this is combined with the observation that definitions are non-assertive *logoi* because lack a verb, it cannot be that they are identity statements, for identity statements contain a verb. The remaining alternative is the one I propose, which is that Aristotle sometimes means definitions is the sense of 'two-legged animal,' while sometime definitions are indeed assertions, such as 'humans are two-legged animals.'

Difficulties with Intuiting Non-Assertive *Logoi*

I take it that in the *Topics* passage, Aristotle has successfully articulated how a definition could be a *logos* but not an assertion. This allows us to make sense of his comments in *DA* III.6 when he takes definitions as non-assertive, even though they are a complex of terms. This at least shows that it is not obviously wrong to say that definitions are intuited. Still, however, Aristotle has given himself the task of explaining how a *logos* of any kind could be intuited. There are three problems created here, the first of which is quickly cleared up by Aristotle himself, namely, the problem of intuiting a complex unity. The second is how multiple terms (the genus and differentia) could even be a unity in the first place. Aristotle explicitly attempts to clear up this matter, although his solution leaves most contemporary scholars unsatisfied; I will argue that Aristotle's unsuccessful attempt to solve this difficulty is relatively unimportant. What is really important is the third problem, and it will require a radical re-thinking of Aristotle's contact metaphor.

The least difficult problem is this: if *nous* intuits *noēmata*, and a *noēma* is a definition, then the doctrine of the indivisibility of *noēmata* is pushed to the limits here. Intuition in the case of indivisible essence-concepts is plausible. But a definition like 'two-legged animal' is composed of multiple concepts or terms, and so it seems obvious that the concepts can be divided like the concepts in any assertion, even though 'two-legged' and 'animal' are not separated by a verb. Aristotle attempts to make sense of his doctrine that both essences and their definitions are indivisible objects of *nous* by introducing a technical distinction in the concept of indivisibility:

Since the word 'indivisible' has two senses, i.e., may mean either 'not capable of being divided' or 'not actually divided,' there is nothing to prevent thought from thinking of what is undivided, e.g., when it thinks of length (which is actually undivided) and that in an undivided time; for the time is divided or undivided in the same manner as the line...the object has no actual parts until it has been divided (*DA* III.6 430b7-12).

A particular length of line is actually undivided, but it is potentially divisible, as is the time in which it is thought. This makes it different than the concept 'diagonal' which is also actually undivided, but this is so because it is not even potentially divisible. 'Two-legged animal' is potentially divisible, of course, but it is actually undivided. But because it shares in indivisibility, it may be an object of intuition.

The second problem concerns why it is even possible to call the terms in a definition a unity at all. Aristotle was always well aware of this problem, as the *De Interpretatione* passage makes clear: "To explain why 'two-footed land animal' is one thing and not many belongs to a different inquiry; simply it will not be one simply through being said all together" (*DI* 5 17a13-15). In the *Metaphysics*, he explicitly attempts to solve this problem:

> Now let us treat of definition, in so far as we have not treated of it in the *Analytics*; for the problem stated in them is useful for our inquiries concerning substance. I mean this problem:—wherein consists the unity of that, the *logos* that we call a definition, as for instance in the case of man, two-footed animal; for let this be the formula of man. Why, then, is this one, and not many, namely, animal *and* two-footed...surely all the attributes in the definition must be one; for the definition is a single formula of substance, so that it must be a formula of some one thing; for substance means a 'one' and a 'this,' as we maintain (*Meta.* VII. 12 1037b9-28).

This passage makes it quite clear that Aristotle is not considering 'human is a two-legged animal' as a definition here, for he take his problem to be how 'two-legged animal' could count as a unity, which is exactly the same investigation into how a definition could count as a unity.[20]

As for the investigation itself, Aristotle suggests that the proper answer to this question may be found by first considering a case where there is not a unity, as in 'white man.' 'White' cannot be part of the definition of man, for in this case, "the same thing would share in contraries; for the differentiae by which the genus is divided are contrary [in the case of man and white]" (*Meta.* VII.12 1037b14-20). Aristotle apparently has in mind that a human's skin may be pigmented many ways, but being a human of a different color would not change one's humanness. So 'white' and 'human' have no essential unity. But the case is different with 'human' and 'two-footed,' for a being cannot be a human without also being a two-footed animal; conversely, being two-footed is one way of being an animal, but it is the only way that humans have by nature.[21] Aristotle wants to say that in order to grasp a *noēma* such as human, it is necessary to grasp 'two-legged animal.' Indeed, it would be impossible to understand the concept 'human' and not the concept 'animal.'

In any case, it is clear that at least in one sense of 'definition,' Aristotle had in mind an intuitable, non-assertive complex of terms, such as 'two-legged animal.' Since there is no verb, it is impossible to be in error about this definition, but only to make contact with it or not, as is true with any touchable object.

The Difference Between Intuiting and Grasping

As noted, there are three problems associated with the possibility of intuiting definitions, the first of which is the problem of intuiting a complex of terms, which Aristotle solves with his doctrine of potential indivisibility. The second is the problem of the unity of the genus and differentia, which Aristotle recognizes and attempts to solve, although the solution is less than convincing. But this is not yet the real problem. The real problem is that a definition must serve as a first principle, by which Aristotle means a first principle of demonstration, which in turn means that a definition in some sense must be an assertion after all. Aristotle clearly holds three theses: 1) first principles are grasped, 2) first principles are assertions, and 3) (some) first principles are definitions.[22] It follows that Aristotle believes that we can grasp assertive definitions such as 'humans are two-legged animals.'

From this perspective, it is clear that Aristotle equivocates on the word 'definition.' In one sense, a definition is merely a complex term that serves as a predicate in an assertion. Thus, what counts as a definition of 'human' in both the *De Anima* and *Metaphysics* is 'two-legged animal.' But obviously, 'two-legged animal' cannot serve as a premise in a demonstration, as is required for definitions by the *Posterior Analytics*. Thus, we are forced to admit that for Aristotle, there are two distinct kinds of definition. And so we must ask: in what meaningful sense could we intuit the definitions that are required to be assertions because they are principles of demonstration? It was not so difficult to believe that single concepts are intuited, and it required some explanation from Aristotle to help us understand how non-assertive *logoi* could be intuited. But it seems simply hopeless to think of how principles could be the objects of intuition.

Indeed, this is impossible, but this is not a real problem for Aristotle, given that he develops another metaphor for *nous* of principles. In the *De Anima*, *nous* is intellectual intuition of essences, and in the *Metaphysics*, he says that we 'make contact' (*thigganein*) with essences or definitions. He uses another metaphor in other contexts, for we 'grasp' (*labein*) definitions or principles.[23] Since Aristotle uses both 'grasping' and 'making contact' in similar contexts, it is natural to assume that these metaphors amount to the same thing—some kind of familiarity with essences or definitions that is quite unlike *epistēmē*. And indeed, they share a genus—'touch.' So perhaps Aristotle meant to develop the metaphor of 'touching' in general, which at least reverses the ubiquitous 'seeing' metaphor, where the objects of sight, like objects of knowledge, may be seen more or less clearly. But when something is touched, it is or is not touched. Indeed, the phrase 'intuitive grasp' makes its rounds in the secondary literature, showing that many scholars assume that the metaphors should be mixed.[24]

But when we examine these two metaphors more closely, we may wonder whether they are quite different kinds of touch. Indeed, Aristotle indicates that when the soul makes contacts with essences, the actuality exists all on the part of the essences, and it is *nous* that is brought to actuality. Indeed, this is why it was safe to translate *to noein* as 'intellectual intuition,' and this is why the contact metaphor worked in this context. Before *nous* is actual, it may be appropriate to say that the soul is acted upon by coming into contact and intuiting intellectual objects. But when *nous* has become a state, the person who possesses *nous* is then able to act upon intellectual objects by grasping them, and so the passivity exists all on the side of intellectual objects.[25] Thus, a person who possesses actualized *nous* "can reflect *when he wants to*, if nothing external prevents him" (*DA* II.5 417a27-28, my emphasis). That is to say, the possessor of *nous* becomes an agent:

> The expression 'to be acted upon' has more than one meaning; it may mean either the extinction of one of two contraries by the other, or the maintenance of what is potential by the agency of what is actual and already like what is acted upon, as actual to potential (*DA* II.5 417b1-8).

When a person is intuiting intellectual objects, it is being acted upon by intellectual objects. But after the intuition, the person acts upon intellectual objects.

Given this distinction, we should not only accept but expect the distinction between kinds of touch. Making contact is a 'being acted upon,' while grasping denotes acting upon something. My distinction between 'making contact' and 'grasping' has at least one important advantage, which is that it makes some sense of Aristotle's equivocation on the word 'definition.' On my interpretation, we intuit or make contact with essences and definitions as non-assertive *logoi*, but we grasp definitions as principles.

Nous as a State of Capacity to Grasp Principles

In one sense, *nous* is a substance, brought into actual existence through the intuitive process of *to noein*. Intellectual intuition is modeled closely on sense intuition, where the sensible objects do all the work, and the sense faculties are brought to actuality by the sensible objects. The same is true with intuition of intellectual objects: they are actual, and *nous* is potential, and *nous* becomes actual because a person makes contact with actual *noēmata*. But when this substance has been actualized by intellectual objects, a person is now in a certain intellectual state (*hexis*), namely, the state of having intellectual objects. This intellectual state is—confusingly enough—*also* called *nous*, such that *nous* describes the kind of knowledge we have of these particular intellectual objects, just as *epistēmē* is the word that describes our knowledge of demonstrated propositions.

It is true that in general, states only come into being through actualizations, although a state may be one of capacity or of activity. This is certainly true in the case of thinking since "there are two kinds of actuality corresponding to knowledge and to reflecting" (*DA* II.1 412a22-23). It is possible to have knowledge, of course, even when it is not being used. In this case, knowledge would be a capacity, rather than an activity. This is how things are when *nous* is actualized, but not active:

> When *nous* has become each thing in the way in which a man who actually knows is said to do so (this happens when he is able to exercise the power on his own initiative), its condition is still one of potentiality, but in a different sense from the potentiality that proceeded the acquisition of knowledge by learning or discovery; and *nous* is then able to *noein* of itself (*DA* III.4 429b6-9).

When *nous* has intellectual objects, it is actual in a way since it now exists as the form of forms, in the same way that a hand is a tool of tools (432a1-2). It is also potential in a different sense, since a person who previously made contact with intellectual objects is capable of grasping them when so desired, but is not currently doing so. This is why *nous* is a state of capacity.

In the *Nichomachean Ethics*, Aristotle clearly distinguishes this from other intellectual states of capacity, such as *technē*, "the reasoned state of capacity to make" (*EN* VI.4 1140a4-5), *phronēsis*, "a reasoned and true state of capacity to act with regard to human goods" (*EN* VI.5 1140b20-21), and of course, *epistēmē*, "a state of capacity to demonstrate" (*EN* VI.3 1139b31-32):

> *Epistēmē* is belief [*hypolēpsis*] about things that are universal and necessary, and there are principles of everything that is demonstrated and of all knowledge (for knowledge involves reasoning [*logos*]). This being so, the first principle of what is known cannot be the object of knowledge, of art, or of practical wisdom...the remaining alternative is that it is *nous* that grasps the first principles (*EN* VI.6 1141a32-1141b8).

In one sense, *nous* stands along these three states of capacities as a state "by virtue of which the soul possesses truth" (*EN* VI.3 1139l5-17). *Nous*, however, is different. For one thing, unlike the three former states, it is not arrived at by a process of reasoning (*logos*), but by intellectual intuition. The word '*logos*' obviously has a great many meanings, but here, Aristotle uses it to pick out reasoning that is *from* principles. This is so because *phronēsis*, *technē*, and *epistēmē* all have principles for their starting points, and then reason toward a conclusion. This is not the case with *nous*. It supplies the principles of demonstration, and so its starting point cannot be that kind of principle. Furthermore, it does not use *endoxa* (or something of the kind) as principles, as *technē* and *phronēsis* do.[26] In fact, its starting points are not principles at all, but actually existing intellectual objects.

The formula given by Aristotle is that *hypolēpsis* about necessary things results in *epistēmē*, and is reached through a process of reasoning. Aristotle means that we get *epistēmē* through a syllogism, which is always based on principles. All reasoning, in fact, is either away from (based on) principles or toward principles; *epistēmē* is a result of the former (*syllogismos*), *nous* is a result of the latter process (*epagōgē*). So the objects of *nous* are principles, and thus, they must be reached through *epagōgē*. But again, why does Aristotle have confidence that no object of *nous* is reached through syllogism?

The reason is that the principles *nous* grasps lack a middle term (i.e., are unmiddled),[27] which is Aristotle's way of saying that there is no explanation available for them. A demonstrative syllogism is an explanation (or at least an attempt at an explanation) of why Z belongs to X, where the belonging is explained by a third term. For example, 'Socrates is mortal' *is* middled since there is a middle term that would explain Socrates' mortality, namely 'man,' as in 'All *men* are mortal' and 'Socrates is a *man*.' The third term, then, is the one that connects the premises that explain (and hence justifies) the assertion in question. But Aristotle believes that principles have no middle term. As such, any kind of knowledge of them could never result from an explanation. But since knowledge as *epistēmē* only results from syllogisms that explain, and we have a kind of knowledge of the principles, this knowledge must be gained without syllogism. Since the objects of *nous* are unmiddled, they can only be reached through *epagōgē*, rather than through *logos* based on principles. If this picture is correct in general, then the contact metaphor is used as a way to describe the intellectual intuition of essences, which are non-assertive. The grasping metaphor is introduced in order to describe comprehension of unmiddled first principles.

Recent scholarship has pointed out that many commentators do not see it as problematic that Aristotle uses *nous* to mean a grasp of concepts *and* propositions, where essences are concepts and definitions are propositions.[28] This seems odd, given Aristotle's careful distinction between a single *noēma* and an assertion—a combination of *noēma*. The proposed solution is that Aristotle meant to say (or did say, implicitly) that we have an intuitive grasp of concepts (essences), while the cognitive state responsible for getting to know propositions that are definitions must be a third cognitive state—it is not *epistēmē*, because there is no demonstration of it, but it cannot be *nous*, because an intuitive grasp is not of propositions. Instead, Aristotle reserves the term 'non-demonstrative episteme' to refer to this third cognitive state.[29]

This would be a compelling criticism were it not resting on two interpretations that I have argued are mistakes. The first is that there is no simple association between concepts and essences on the one hand and propositions and definitions on the other. A *noēma* may be an essence, or any kind of single concept, or a definition such as 'two-legged animal.' But a principle of demonstration cannot be a *noēma*—it is a combination of *noēma*. One type of these are indeed definitions, but definitions in the form, 'human is a two-legged animal.' It is unclear why Aristotle gives two different descriptions of definitions, but it is clear that he does so.

The second mistake is to believe that there is such a thing as an 'intuitive grasp' of essences or anything else; but intuition is one thing, and grasping is another. It is indeed accurate to say that one cannot have an intuitive grasp of essences and definitions as principles, but there is no need to introduce a third cognitive state. It is better—both because it is simpler, and makes better sense of the texts—to say that *nous* is responsible for getting to know both essences and non-assertive definitions on the one hand, and definitions as principles on the other; it both cases, it touches them, but one kind of touch is passive and one is active.

Conclusion

Aristotle consistently states that *nous* grasps first principles, which are so-called because they are the fundamental premises of a demonstration. In the *De Anima*, it is clear that Aristotle wants to say that definitions are a kind of *noēmata*. Indeed, in this context Aristotle offers a telling locution that he uses only once: "*ta prōta noēmata*" (the primary objects of thought) (*DA* III.8 432a11). This is an unmistakable allusion to the *Posterior Analytics*, when he called first principles *prōtōn*, and even *ta prōta*.[30] Much confusion about this doctrine exists because of the tendency to treat Aristotle's intriguing reference to contact as another way to refer to the grasping metaphor. I think we should reject this possibility.

When Aristotle says that a *noēma* is 'touched,' he is thinking of an essence, or a non-assertive *logos* of the essence. When he says that it is not possible for these *noēmata* to be false, he is simply referring to the fact that they are not assertions. But in these contexts, he only speaks of contact and intuition; he never uses the Greek '*labein*.' I believe that this is because *nous* grasps definitions, but only the kind of definitions that are principles and therefore assertions. We grasp them only in the sense that there is no middle term capable of explaining why the predicate matches the subject. There is a sense in which we cannot be mistaken about these kind of definitions, but it is not the same sense that we cannot be mistaken about the objects of intuition.

Notes

1. See chapter 2, pp. 43-46.
2. I will do this even when quoting from the ROT, which usually translated *nous* as 'thought.'

3. Charles Kahn, "Aristotle on Thinking," 359.

4. Kahn, 360.

5. Kahn, 363.

6. See Deborah Modrak, "The Nous-Body Problem in Aristotle," *The Review of Metaphysics* 44, no. 4 (June 1991): 755-774.

7. Kahn, 361-362

8. Although there are well-known contemporary attempts to resurrect substance dualism that attempt to avoid the problem of a bodiless substance.

9. Enrico Berti has these sorts of fears in mind when he recommends rejecting the translation 'intuition' and instead speaking of the intellection of indivisibles. Intuiting could imply no mediation by sense experience, or even that discursive thinking is unnecessary (Enrico Berti, "The Intellection of Indivisibles According to Aristotle, *De Anima* III 6," in *Aristotle on Mind and the Senses*, ed. G.E.R. Lloyd and G.E.L. Owen (Cambridge: Cambridge University Press, 1978), 142). For a convincing attempt to resurrect the idea of intuition, see Victor Kal, *Intuitive and Discursive Reasoning in Aristotle*, (Leiden: E.J. Brill, 1988).

10. See pp. 95-102.

11. This kind of defense is given often. See Michael Wedin, *Aristotle's Theory of Substance* (New York: Oxford University Press, 2000).

12. Sorabji, 242.

13. This interpretation is developed by G.E.L. Owen

14. This is why Aristotle says in Zeta 10 in regard to definitions of essences that truth is making contact *and* expressing them.

15. *An. Post.* 72a11, *De Int.* 16b5-17a24.

16. *De Int.* 16b-17a24.

17. This is also Polansky's interpretation, as he reconciles the passage at xx by appealing to Aristotle's doctrine of non-assertive *logoi* in the DI.

18. See Granger for Aristotle's shifting views on the role of the genus and differentia. Herbert Granger, "Aristotle on Genus and Differentia," *Journal of the History of Philosophy* 22, no. 1 (1984): 1-23.

19. He gives this same example in the *Meta.* 1037b9-28

20. There seems to be a mistake in Reeve's analysis of this passage. He says that "if 'F is G' is a definition, both F and G must, in the appropriate way be "one"—one intrinsic being. But because a definition is a perforce complex, there is a problem here: 'that whose account we call a definition, why is it one? E.g., man is a two-footed animal—let this be the account. Why is this one and not many, animal *and* twofooted?' (*Met.* VII 12 1037b10-14." (70). But it seems as though Aristotle's issue here is how the G term *itself* could be unified, not how G could be united with the F term.

21. See Reeve, 70-79.

22. This is clear from *An. Post.* I.1-4.

23. *Ph.* 194b18-20, *Meta.* 1064a5, 1072b21, *An. Post* 71a7, 73a25, 74a7,76b37.

24. For instance, Irwin speaks this way. Irwin, pp. 134-136.

25. *DA* 417a22-417b8.

26. *EN* 1140a2-3. Cf. *An. Post.* 100a8.

27. See pages 43-46.

28. Zeev Perelmuter, "*Nous* and Two Kinds of *Epistēmē* in Aristotle's *Posterior Analytics*," *Phronesis* 55 (2010): 228-254.

29. Perelmuter, 250-1.

30. *An. Post.* 100b4.

Chapter Five
Using the Principles:
Demonstration and Contemplation

Introduction

The path to *epistēmē* requires *nous* of principles, for *epistēmē* only results from demonstration, and demonstration depends on possessing the truth of principles. I have on several occasions described the method of demonstration, although I have not described the object of demonstration. The present chapter begins with an account of what is demonstrated. But is demonstration the only kind of activity that begins with *nous*? It is if and only if *nous'* somewhat mysterious self-referential activity that Aristotle occasionally describes is identical with demonstration:

> When *nous* has become each thing in the way in which a man who actually knows is said to do so (this happens when he is able to exercise the power on his own initiative), it condition is still one of potentiality, but in a different sense from the potentiality that proceeded the acquisition of knowledge by learning or discovery; and *nous* is then able to *noein* of itself (*DA* III.4 429b6-9).

In this chapter, I present evidence in favor of the position that '*auton voei ho nous*' is not demonstration. This process is, rather, contemplation, and demonstration and contemplation are two distinct activities. The clearest way to understand the difference is in terms of what they yield: successful *epagōgē* results in *nous*, successful demonstration results in *epistēmē*, and successful contemplation—I contend—results in wisdom (*sophia*). Against my analysis, it may be argued that since wisdom is a virtuous intellectual state that is simply a combination of *epistēmē* and *nous*, contemplation is not a process distinct from demonstration: "the wise man must not only know what follows from first principles, but also must possess truth about first principles. Therefore wisdom must be *nous* combined with *epistēmē*" (*EN* VI.7 1141a17-19). This analysis, however, is too simplistic. It is true that contemplation cannot take place unless a person first has *epistēmē*, but the relationship is the same one as *nous* and demonstration have, for demonstration cannot take place unless a person first has *nous*. This of course does not mean that *epagōgē* and demonstration are the same kind of activities. I will argue that, like *epagōgē*, contemplation is essentially an intuitive process, while demonstration is essentially discursive. The full story is that contemplation is the intuition of the results of *epagōgē and also* the results of demonstration. These doctrines do not obviously belong to Aristotle, but I believe they result from the best interpretations of some of Aristotle's most difficult passages.

93

The Object of Demonstration

Aristotle has some complex rules for demonstration, which are discussed at length in the *Posterior Analytics*; in addition, there are other fine works that summarize this rules,[1] to which I have nothing more to add. The object of demonstration, however, should be discussed, for Aristotle is not at all clear on this point. This is an important missing detail in Aristotle's epistemology, because *epistēmē* is only of what is demonstrated. This is only complicated by the fact that Aristotle himself does not give an example of a demonstration in any of the works that are available to us. It is less difficult to affirm that *nous* is a kind of knowledge of the definition or essence. It is also accurate to describe the object of *nous* as the form or formal cause. I believe that Aristotle's understanding of proper scientific method is that we grasp the formal cause (which will include the final cause in living things), and then use the definition to get *epistēmē* of the material cause and efficient cause through demonstration. On my account, then, when it comes living substances, we have *nous* of the formal cause, which implies the final cause, and we have *epistēmē* of the material and efficient causes. Aristotle occasionally bestows moments of clarity on his readers that allows for such an interpretation:

> The fittest mode, then, of treatment is to say, a man has such and such parts because the essence of man is such and such, and because they are necessary conditions of his existence, or, if we cannot quite say this then the next thing to it, namely, that it is either quite impossible for a man to exist without them, or, at any rate, that it is good that they should be there. And this follows: because man is such and such the process of his development is necessarily such and such; and therefore this part is formed first, that next; and after a like fashion should we *explain* the generation of all works of nature (*PA* I.1 640a33-640b4, my italics).

Aristotle begins with his most consistent epistemological doctrine, which is that the path to *epistēmē* begins with knowledge of the essence. Using knowledge of the essence as a principle, the investigator then goes on to conclude that man has 'such and such parts' because of the particular essence that man has. Also, knowledge of the essence allows us to conclude that 'the process of development is necessarily such as it is.' The latter two features are succinct descriptions of the material and efficient causes, respectively, and knowledge of them is based on our previous knowledge of the essence. And importantly, the knowledge of the material and efficient cause comes via an explanation, which is exactly what we should expect Aristotle to say if we believe that he is discussing demonstration.

I think that my interpretation of this passage is as close to an accurate summary of Aristotle's method in natural science as possible, but even this summary is only vaguely true, for there is an important complicating factor. It will be use-

ful for me to say something about this from the outset, because to an uncharita-
ble observer they might seem to make Aristotle's scientific method absurd. The
two difficulties stem from these truths: first, even though in some sense
knowledge of the essence precedes knowledge of the material and efficient
causes, one cannot in fact have a full account of what something is unless one
already knows the material and efficient causes. And second, one cannot get
knowledge of any kind of essence of something without beginning by examining
the parts.

It may be thought that either of these complications are vicious circles that
effectively undermine Aristotle's method in natural science. I draw a different
moral from these observations. I believe that the complexity of these doctrines
only mirrors the complexity of real scientific discovery. This is despite the fact
the process of scientific discovery often beings with a rigid plan: one is supposed to start with a question, then do some research, then formulate a hypothesis, then gather data, then organize that data, then analyze it, and only then reach
a conclusion. Any scientist, sophisticated or school-age, would be able to appreciate the logical order of these steps. And yet I doubt that very many—if any—
scientific discoveries actually follow these steps exactly in order. After the scientist has made the discovery, she may *present* the order of discovery in the appropriate order, but it is hardly likely she followed this method rigidly. Any real
scientist will admit that in actual science, the order of data gathering, question-
ing, hypothesizing, researching, and concluding is rather a jumbled mess that
results in truth with any luck.

It is with this in mind that such statements should be appreciated:

> It seems not only useful for the discovery of the causes of the incidental proper-
> ties of substances to be acquainted with the essential nature of those substances
> (as in mathematics it is useful for the understanding of the property of equality
> of the interior angles of a triangle to two right angles to know the essential na-
> ture of the straight and the curved or of the line and the plane) but also con-
> versely, for the knowledge of the essential nature of a substance is largely pro-
> moted by an acquaintance of its properties; for, when we are able to give an
> account conformable to experience of all or most of the properties of a sub-
> stance, we shall be in the most favorable position to say something worth say-
> ing about the essential nature of that subject; in all demonstration a definition
> of the essence is required as a starting point, so that definitions that do not ena-
> ble us to discover the incidental properties, or which fail to facilitate even a
> conjecture about them, must obviously, one and all, be dialectical and futile
> (*DA* I.1 402b17-403a2).

Aristotle refers to the 'causes of the incidental properties of substances;' in order
to distinguish the incidental properties (*ta sumbebēkota*) from the essential ones,
one must already be acquainted with the essential nature of the substance in
question. The problem is that "the knowledge of the essential nature of a substance is largely promoted by an acquaintance of its properties" (*DA* I.1

402b22). How, then, could knowledge of the formal cause or essence come before knowledge of the material cause?

In the context of the *Parts of Animals*, the problem is much the same. We have to go about observing the parts, and only then are we in a good position to state the essence of the substance:

> The best course appears to be that we should follow the method already mentioned—begin with the phenomena presented by each group of animals and, when this is done, proceed afterward to state the causes of those phenomena—in the case of generation too (*PA* I.1 640a14-16).

So does the natural scientist begin by observing the parts, or by stating the essence, and then demonstrating the material cause? In the *De Anima*, Aristotle expresses this problem by saying that 'we shall be in the most favorable position to say something worth saying about the essential nature of that subject' only after we have observed the parts.

The key to resolving this problem is to note that 'observing the parts' is ambiguous. In one sense, of course we must observe the parts of animals in order to get to get *nous* of the essence. This is merely a necessary ingredient in Aristotle's insistence elsewhere that having images are essential to human knowing.[2] But this is different from demonstrating the material cause of a substance; to demonstrate the material cause is to demonstrate the hypothetical necessary of a substance. It is one thing to observe that in fact giraffes have long necks; you have to make such an observation in order to state the 'what it is to be' of a giraffe. But such knowledge is not *epistēmē*, for there is no demonstration of the why. This is merely nous of the essence of giraffe. But once the evolutionary biologist possesses the essence, he can then demonstrate why a giraffe *must* have the neck length that it does. After such a demonstration, he has *epistēmē* of the material cause. And I think this completely vindicates Aristotle, for in one sense, knowledge of the essence of giraffe had to proceed knowledge of the material cause, but it is also perfectly true that knowing of the material cause put us in an even better position to know what a giraffe is.

How Could 'Thought Think Itself'?

Demonstration is one activity that depends on having *nous* of essences. But Aristotle also believes that *nous* is able to engage in some kind of self-referential activity which is not obviously part of demonstration; he says that '*auton voei ho nous.*' The common English translation is 'thought thinks itself.' Leaving *nous* un-translated, should we believe that *nous* thinks itself? If so, what could that mean? Sometimes Aristotle uses this curious phrase to describe an activity of divine cognition,[3] and sometimes it is of human cognition[4;] in both cases, Aristotle calls this 'contemplation' (*theoria*).[5] The relevant question here is whether *theoria* is simply another word for demonstration, and thus '*nous* thinking itself' is a description of demonstrating, or at least discursive activity in general, of which demonstration is a kind. I will argue that the answer is 'no,' for Aristotle's description of contemplative knowledge in the *De Anima* and the *Metaphysics* shows that contemplation is essentially intuitive.

Aristotle says that after "*nous* has become each thing"—i.e., after its passive intuition of the forms—"*nous* is then able to *noein* of itself" (*DA* III.4 429b9). This is clearly an activity: "In every case the *nous* that is actively thinking is the objects that it thinks" (*DA* III.6 431b16). Since contemplation is the mind's activity, *noein* in this case must not be passive as it was in the case of intuition of the intellectual forms. I want to suggest that the phrase sometimes translated as 'thought thinks itself' is still describing an intuitive act of *nous*, but it is no longer *passive* intuition, for there are no external, enmattered forms actualizing it. The difference is that *nous* is intuiting unenmattered intelligible forms that are the complete constitution of itself. It is now *active* intuition because it is actualizing *itself*; that is to say, the source of its actualization is not external to it.[6] Indeed, Aristotle even worries why this sort of actualizing is not always happening, because this actualization comes from the mind itself rather than being dependent on the occasion of encountering an enmattered form.[7] Therefore, the meaning of '*auton noei ho nous*' when considered in context should be, according to my claim, '*nous* intuits itself'; rendering '*noei*' as 'thinking' is misleading, for thinking normally implies judging and inferring, which are not present here.

Before encountering *ta noēta*, *nous* was purely potential. It had no existence to speak of, and only became actualized by *ta noēta*:

> *Nous* is in a sense potentially whatever is thinkable [*ta noēta*], though actually it is nothing until it has *noē*. What it thinks must be in it just as characters may be said to be on a writing-table on which as yet nothing actually stands written: this is exactly what happens with *tou nou. Nous* is itself thinkable in exactly the same way as its objects are. For in the case of objects that involve no matter, what thinks and what is thought are identical; for speculative knowledge and its object are identical [*ē gar epistēmē ē theōrētikē kai to houtōs epistētov to auto estin*] (*DA* III.4 429b30-430a5).

After the intelligible forms 'write' on *nous*, it is in a sense actualized, but it remains potential in another sense, for at times when it is not being used, it is not fully actualized: "its condition is still one of potentiality, but in a different sense from the potentiality which preceded the acquisition of knowledge by learning or discovery" (*DA* III.3 429b7-9). *Nous* at this stage thus admits of both actuality and potentiality. It is actual because the mind that has received intelligible forms actually becomes those forms. It remains potential, however, insofar as the forms constituting the mind are not currently being intuited. A person that knows "is now able to exercise the power on his own initiative" (*DA* III.3 429b7), which of course in no way implies that he is currently doing so; he simply may do so whenever he chooses.

Aristotle re-affirms his notion that *nous* only has potential existence before its reception of the forms at least twice: "thus that in the soul that is called *nous*…is, before it *noeiv*, not actually any real thing…It was a good idea to call the soul 'the place of forms'…" (*DA* III.4 429a22-28). The point is that before the intuition, *nous* was purely potential; its present actuality, insofar as it is actual, is due entirely to the intuition of the forms. Aristotle makes the same point in the *Metaphysics*:

> And *nous* thinks itself because it shares the nature of the object of thought [*tou noētou*]; for it becomes an object of thought in coming into contact with and *noōn* its objects, so that thought and object of thought are the same. For that which is capable of receiving the object of thought, i.e., the substance [*ousias*], is *nous* (*Meta.* XII.7 1072b20-22).

After *nous* has received the intelligible forms and thus has become them, it can actively intuit those forms that it 'knows' or 'possesses' without depending on encountering them in their material instantiation. This is why "there are two kinds of actuality corresponding to knowledge and contemplating [*to theōrein*]" (*DA* II.1 412a22)[8]; what Aristotle means is that knowledge is a certain actuality because *nous* has now become (and thus, in a sense possesses) the intelligible forms which it was potentially. But when we contemplate, we have them in front of us, so to speak, in a way that we do not when we are sleeping. Contemplation, then, is the mind's active possession of the forms, as Aristotle makes clear in the remainder of the *Metaphysics* passage:

> that which is capable of receiving the object of thought…is *nous*. And it is *active* when it *possesses* [*hechōn*] this object. Therefore the latter rather than the former is the divine element which mind seems to contain, and the act of contemplation [*theōria*] is what is most pleasant and best (*Meta.* XII.7 1072b22-24).

Aristotle seems to deny that *nous*, in its passive employment —*to noein*— is divine. This sort of intuition of the intelligible form is passive because its change is actualized by a form that is external to it. In this sense, its intuition is a reception. All intuition is affection by something simple. This is obviously true in the sensible and intelligible intuition of the enmattered forms, but this also seems to be true in the case of contemplation. The mind is still being affected by intelligible forms, although now the mind *just is* those forms, and so this affection is a self-affection. What makes intuition passive, therefore, is receptivity, not affection. While contemplation is divine because it is the activity of a divine substance, *nous*, *to theōrein* is divine in that sense and also in a much more important sense; it is intuition that is no longer passive but active, and it is active because its actualization is internal to it; *ē theōria* does not depend on encountering a particular in the world in which the form resides. It is therefore *nous'* intuition *of itself*.

De Anima III.5, With Reference to Polansky

I believe that my analysis of the difference between *to noein* and *to theōrein* has the great benefit of making sense of the infamous 'maker mind' passage in *De Anima* III.5. In an earlier discussion of human cognition, Aristotle had said that the mind's change from being potentially all the forms to intuiting itself requires not one but two actualizations:

> But we must now distinguish different senses in which things can be said to be potential or actual; at the moment we are speaking as if each of these phrases had only one sense. We can speak of something as a knower either as when we say that man is a knower...And there is a man who is already reflecting—he is a knower in actuality and in the most proper sense is knowing, e.g., this A (*DA* II.5 417a22-30).

Aristotle is simply re-describing this process in III.5. There he says that there is

> a cause which is productive in the sense that it makes [all the particulars included in the class]...And in fact *nous*, as we have described it, is what it is by virtue of becoming all things, while there is another which is what it is by virtue of making all things (*DA* III.5 430a12, my insertions).[9]

Aristotle's reference to *nous* in the first sense is by now familiar as a central theme of Aristotle's philosophy of mind, for the mind becomes what it is by becoming the intellectual forms that it intuits. But what exactly is this 'making mind'? Aristotle says that it is a state (*hexis*), and suggests an analogy to the state of light because making mind and light do the same job, "for in a sense light makes potential colors actual colors" (*DA* III.5 430a16-7). Aristotle, by analogy, is saying that the intellectual forms constituting the mind are like colors in the dark; in one sense they are there, of course, but in another sense, they are not, because light is an essential part of color. The same is true when a knower is asleep; in one sense the intellectual forms are there, constituting the mind, but in another sense they are merely potentially there because we are not aware of them. So making is this sense is certainly not creation *ex nihilo*, nor can it be thought of as a shaping or reformation. The making mind is simply a description for the mind that is actualizing what is already there as the constitution of itself.

Furthermore, *nous* "in this sense of it is separable, impassible, unmixed, since it is in its essential nature activity" (*DA* III.5 430a17). Previously, Aristotle had said that *nous* is a substance "born in us" — that is, in the composite substance (*DA* I.4 408b18). In this, he is in accord with any traditional substance dualist[10] who argues that the mind and the body are distinct. But Aristotle is not saying that the making mind is merely conceptually separable from the composite, but actually has different persistence conditions; it keeps existing even when the composite's mind perishes: "when separated it is alone just what it is, and this…is immortal and eternal (we do not remember because, while this is impassible, passive *nous* is perishable)" (*DA* III.5 430a24-5).

So in III.5, is Aristotle describing God's cognition, human cognition, or both? I argue that the remainder of the passage indicates the last possibility. Aristotle has just described mind insofar as it makes, which he also calls actual knowledge. Now he turns his attention to potential knowledge:

> Actual knowledge [*ē kat'energeian epistēmē*] is identical with its object; *in the individual*, potential knowledge is in time prior to actual knowledge, but *absolutely* [*holōs*] it is not prior even in time….When separated, it is alone just what it is, and this…is immortal and eternal…" (*DA* III.5 430a20-24, my italics).

Aristotle therefore considers potential knowledge (*ē kata dunamin epistēmē*) in two senses: in the individual, and absolutely (i.e., in itself).

We may note that Aristotle here does not describe actual knowledge—that is, contemplation—in two senses. Since it is pure activity, it is simply 'separable, impassible, unmixed.' But does Aristotle really mean to imply that actual knowledge never really exists in the individual? It doesn't seem like it, at least not if we read III.5 as giving a clue to his earlier statements about cognitive function:

> Thus it is that intuiting [*to noein*] and contemplating [*to theōrein*] decline through the decay of some inward part and are *themselves* impassible. *To dianoeisthai*, loving, and hating are affections not of mind, but of that which has mind, so far as it has it. That is why, when this vehicle decays, memory and love cease; they were activities not of mind, but of *the composite* which has perished; *nous* is, no doubt, something more divine and impassible (*DA* I.4 408b18-31, my italics).

Here, Aristotle explicitly considers *nous* both insofar as it becomes all things (*to noein*) and *nous* insofar as it makes actual the things that it has become (*to theōrein*); and importantly, he considers both of them in two senses: in the individual *and* in themselves. Specifically, in the individual they both perish along with *to dianoeisthai*; and this is a complete end to *to dianoeisthai*, because it *only* exists in the individual and not at all in itself. But in themselves, *to noein* and *to theōrein* do actually exist; furthermore, their existence is *apathes*.

Aristotle is describing *to noein* in precisely the same way in *DA* III.5:

> in the individual, potential knowledge is in time prior to actual knowledge, but absolutely [*holōs*] it is not prior even in time. It does not sometimes *voein* and sometimes not *voein*. When separated, it is alone just what it is, and this…is immortal and eternal…" (*DA* III.5 430a20-24).

It is therefore uncontroversial that Aristotle believes that potential knowledge exists in the individual and in itself. Its former mode of existence is temporary, but its latter existence is eternal. The same appears to be true for actual knowledge, which is simply described as 'contemplation' in *DA* 408b. According to my earlier claim, *to dianoeisthai* is un-described in III.5; if so, it is neither 'becoming mind' nor is it 'making mind.'

My own interpretation may be understood as a response to Ronald Polansky's recent work. Polansky's most distinctive position on III.5 is that when Aristotle describes actual knowledge, he is not describing contemplative activity: "the actuality intended here need only be the sort appropriate to possessed knowledge, that is, first actuality or developed potentiality, that accords with its being called a kind of *hexis*..." (464).[11] He also points out that in 429b6-7 Aristotle has referred to dispositional knowledge as 'actual knowledge.' While there is much to commend about Polansky's recent work on the *De Anima*, I will argue that his analysis *De Anima* III.5 is not sustainable.

The claim that orients his interpretation is his identification of agent mind and knowledgeable mind, which would mean that "possessed knowledge serves as unmoved mover of mind's capacity for thinking."[12] I will show that possessed or dispositional knowledge could never serve this role; it is instead absolute, actual knowledge that is the unmoved mover of iii.5. The claim that possessed knowledge can be the mover of the capacity for thinking obligates Polansky to believe that the 'actual knowledge' described in the latter half of the passage (lines a17-25) is referring to possessed knowledge, or knowledge at first actuality. This claim might seem to be jeopardized by Aristotle's claim that actual knowledge is "in its essential nature *energeia*" (*tē ousia ōn energeia*, *DA* III.5 430a17). If Aristotle were describing second actuality, then translating '*energeia*' as 'activity'[13] would have been appropriate. But Polansky regards it as a mere temptation to suppose that Aristotle is describing second actuality. He translates it as 'actuality,' noting that

> Many commentators take this to be the highest sort of actuality, activity (*energeia*) opposed to motion (*kinesis*)...Nothing has prepared us to suppose this distinction enters here. The actuality intended need only be the sort appropriate to possessed knowledge, that is, first actuality or developed potentiality...Nothing too surprising or extraordinary has to be evoked either within or without our mind to get us thinking. Possessed knowledge serves as unmoved mover for thinking.[14]

It is difficult to understand how possessed knowledge could be thought of as unmoved, although that worry seems trivial compared to more important task of determining whether possessed knowledge could be a mover. An answer to this question will tell us whether Aristotle is here describing knowledge at first actuality (possessed knowledge), or second actuality (contemplating), and thus whether '*energia*' is here 'actuality' or 'activity.' Let us agree for the sake of argument that either interpretation could be reconciled with III.5. What else does Aristotle say about actual knowledge that would help?

Aristotle has been insisting that there are two epistemological actualities throughout the *De Anima*. The most straightforward discussions occur in II.1

(412a6-26), II.5 (417a22-417b16), and III.4 (429b6-9). In II.1, possessed knowledge is an actuality analogous to the sleeping soul, and contemplating to waking:

> Now there are two kinds of actuality corresponding to knowledge and to *to theōrein*. It is obvious that the soul is an actuality like knowledge; for both sleeping and waking presuppose the existence of soul, and of these waking corresponds to *to theōrein*, sleeping to knowledge possessed but not employed, and knowledge of something is temporally prior (*DA* II.1 412a22-26).

Here Aristotle says that possessed knowledge may be 'not employed' and when not, it is analogous to sleeping. When employed, it is *not* called 'possessed, employed knowledge,' because it is more appropriately described simply as knowledge at second actuality. Aristotle's point is that the essence of possessed knowledge is non-activity, while the essence of contemplation is activity. The passages in II.5 and III.4 only reinforce this point. In order for Polansky to be right that possessed knowledge is a mover, he does not need to say that it is 'in essence activity,' but he does need to avoid concluding that it is essentially passive. Aristotle doesn't appear to consider the possibility of active, possessed knowledge elsewhere in the *De Anima*, and so we should wonder why he would here.

But the most problematic part of Polansky's thesis ironically comes in the context of his most penetrating insight into III.5. He observes that in the *De Anima* generally, "knowledge does not itself undergo any transition from its dispositional condition to some activity of knowing. Instead it is the soul or person who engages in thinking because of the possession of knowledge."[15] As evidence, Polansky references a passage in I.4 that seems to offer strong support for this thesis,[16] for there Aristotle says that "thinking, loving, and hating are affections not of *nous*, but of that which has *nous*, so far as it has it" (*DA* I.4 408b25-27). And indeed, if Aristotle's account of 'thinking' were as uncomplicated as it is sometimes presented, Polansky would have been correct to cite this passage.

The passage in question, however, is making precisely the opposite point. Polansky correctly says that it is the soul proper that 'thinks,' but he has assumed that 'thinks' is simply a general word to describe knowledge at second actuality. In the passage at *DA* 408b18-31, *to noein* and *to dianoeisthai* were both translated as 'thinking' by the ROT, and Polansky apparently believes that 'to theōrein' could be as well. Unless we believe that Aristotle is using these terms in non-technical ways, it must be the case that there are at least some differences between *to noein*, *to dianoeisthai*, and *to theōrein*.

Why did Aristotle write III.5? He begins by noting that

> Since in every class of things, as in nature as a whole, we find two factors involved, a matter which is potentially all the particulars included in the class, a cause which is productive in the sense that it makes them all (the latter standing to the former, as e.g. an art to its material), these distinct elements must likewise be found within the soul (*DA* III.5 430a10-15).

Polansky says that Aristotle's reference to matter must be metaphorical since "it was urged that mind and the intelligible are unenmattered."[17] However, Aristotle means 'matter' literally, not metaphorically. This is the case because for Aristotle, 'matter' does not to pick out some certain, fixed kind of thing, but is a relative concept that simply means whatever underlies a change (*Meta.* VIII.4 1044a15-32). The term 'matter' is particularly well-suited to describe knowledge at first actuality, which is merely made actual in the way a color is by light; that is, there is a change, but dispositional knowledge survives the change.[18] The other principle or factor in a change is the cause, the understanding of which allows us to give an explanation of the change. Of course, since there is a movement from potentiality to actuality, there must be something already actual to account for this movement. There is no reason to suppose that this sentence is making a more subtle point.

But why is it necessary (*anagkē*) that these elements (i.e., a matter and a cause) be found within the soul? For what if there is no strong similarity between *nous*[19] and other natures? If there is none, then it is not necessary to believe that similar elements will be found in the mind. Aristotle, however, in iii.4, has already indicated that such a division is *anagkē*:

> When *nous* has become each thing in the way in which a man who actually knows is said to do so (this happens when he is now able to exercise the power on his own initiative), its condition is still one of potentiality, but in a different sense from the potentiality which proceeded the acquisition of knowledge by learning or discovery; and *nous* is then able to think of itself (*DA.* III.4 429b6-9).

When '*nous* has become each thing,' Aristotle is referring to the process when *nous* becomes actualized at the first level, and this happens when it becomes the (unenmattered) intellectual forms that are intuited. This change is accounted for by the enmattered intellectual forms, for they are actual. Therefore, the explanation for how *nous* can become all the things in that particular class (i.e., the class of intellectual objects) is the intellectual objects themselves. Therefore no further explanation of 'becoming *nous*'—the movement from first potentiality to first actuality—is necessary.

But there is the account of second actuality to worry about, that is, when "*nous* is able to think of itself" (*DA* III.4 429b9). We know that *nous* becomes actual in this second sense, but *how*? Enmattered intellectual objects explain the soul's acquisition of dispositional knowledge, but they can't explain this second transition. In this latter transition, 'becoming *nous*' will serve as the matter, while 'making *nous*' will be the cause; III.5 is written to offer this explanation, as Aristotle's words imply in the first sentence.

It is important to note that Aristotle speaks of actual knowledge in two senses. *In the individual*, "potential knowledge is in time prior to actual knowledge" which contrasts with how it exists *absolutely* (*holōs*); when considered *holōs*, it never exists in a state of potentiality, for it "does not sometimes think and sometimes not think" (*DA* III.4 430a22). Aristotle is here simply high-lighting the fact that actual knowledge in the individual must be actualized by something that is already actual, because in individuals, actual knowledge comes to be from potential knowledge. What this means is that actual knowledge in the individual must be actualized by something that is already actual, and this could only be actual knowledge that was never in a state of potentiality; this is why "without this nothing thinks" (*DA* III.4 430a25). Aristotle clearly emphasizes this in III.7 when he delivers the exact same line about absolute knowledge, but then adds that "for all things that come into being arise from what actually is" (*DA* III.4 431a1), as if to remind us why he needed to reference absolute, actual knowledge. And of course, because absolute, actual knowledge never comes to be from a state of potentiality, this is no further mover needed to account for its actualization. This sort of actual knowledge is immortal, eternal, and separated, and its existence is the only thing that could explain how dispositional knowledge could become contemplative knowledge in the individual. Knowledge at second actuality in the individual is a mover, but it is not un-moved; what it moves is knowledge at first actuality, which is not only moved by enmattered forms, but cannot be a mover. Only absolute, actual knowledge could be the unmoved mover of III.5.

To Dianoeisthai in the *De Anima*

Nous has a passive function (*to noein*) in intuiting the intelligible forms, and an active one (*to theōrein*) in possessing them. I have characterized both pro-cesses as essentially intuitive. But it is obvious that the human mind is active in another way, for we have discursive mental powers: we can make judgments, analyze arguments, connect or separate premises, make inferences, and change our conclusions in the face of new data. It is possible to believe, because con-templation is an activity of the mind, and discursive reasoning is a type of cogni-tive activity, that discursive reasoning must be identical with or at least a form of contemplation. I will reject that possibility; *to dianoeisthai* is the term that Aristotle reserved to refer to discursive as opposed to intuitive processes. Ac-cordingly, I will argue that *to dianoeisthai* is not identical with *to theōrein*, nor a species of it; it follows that the activity of demonstration but not contemplation is *to dianoeisthai*.

I have argued that Aristotle uses several phrases to describe the activity of contemplation (*to theōrien*); it is speculative knowledge (*ē epistēmē ē theōrētikē DA* III.5 430a5), it is actual knowledge (*ē kat'energeian epistēmē, DA* III.5 430a20, II.5 417a29-30), it is *nous* insofar as *nous* makes all things (*DA* III.5 430a15), and it is *nous'* active possession of intellectual objects (*Meta.* XII.7 1072b22-24). And as noted in chapter 4, *to noein* should be translated as 'intel-lectual intuiting' rather than 'thinking'; I now establish that 'thinking' should be reserved only for *to dianoeisthai*, since Aristotle uses it to pick out the discur-sive function of *nous*; in English, the phrase 'discursive thinking' is redundant, since thinking already indicates judging and inferring. This distinction is important because the failure to distinguish them leads some commentators to conflate contemplating (*to theōrein*) and thinking (*to dianoeisthai*), and this conflation leads to the false belief that human contemplation is discursive.

Aristotle contrasts *to dianoeisthai* with the other functions of mind in several other passages in the *De Anima*. One particularly helpful passage is at 429a23-24: "that in the soul which is called *nous* (by *nous* I mean that whereby the soul thinks [*dianoeitai*] and judges [*hypolambanei*]) is, before it *noein*, not any real thing." *Nous* is 'in' the soul as a separate substance; however, it is nothing actual before it intuits forms in the external world. That is consistent with what we know about Aristotle's doctrine of intellectual intuiting. Now, in addition to intellectual intuiting, Aristotle mentions a distinct function of mind that is dependent on a previous act of intuition, for the mind also '*dianoeitai* and *hypolambanei*.' Later in that passage, Aristotle makes indicates that these words are meant to be understood as synonymous:

> Thinking is...distinct from perceiving—I mean that in which we find rightness and wrongness—rightness in understanding, knowledge, true opinion, wrongness in their opposites: for perception of special objects of sense is always free from truth and error...while it is possible to think [*dianoeisthai*] falsely as well as truly, and thought is found only where there is discourse of reason [*logos*]. For imagination is different from either perceiving or discursive thinking [*dianoias*], though it is not found without sensation, or judgment [*hypolēpsis*] without it (*DA* III.3 427b9-14).

The mental function *to dianoeisthai* is therefore unique because it judges (*hypolēpsis*), which is to say that it gives rise to the possibility of truth and error. This is simply the mind insofar as it engages in an explicit or implicit syllogism, a process which Aristotle analyzes at length, and often simply picks out with '*logos*':

> Further, every opinion is accompanied by belief, belief by conviction, and conviction by discourse of reason, while there are some of the brutes in which we find imagination, without discourse of reason [*logos*] (*DA* III.4 428a24).

Furthermore, when Aristotle mentions some of the capacities of soul, he names "the appetitive, the sensory, the locomotive, and the power of thinking [*dianoētikon*]" (*DA* II.3 414a32). But when he considers the possibility that some mental activity may be not an actuality of the body, he does not use the articular infinitive of *dianoētikon*—'*to dianoeisthai*'—but '*to noein*' (*DA* I.1 403a3-5). The significance of this line of reasoning is clarified in an earlier passage:

> But *nous* seems to be an independent substance [*ousia*] implanted within us and to be incapable of being destroyed. If it could be destroyed at all, it would be

under the blunting of old age. What really happens is, however, exactly parallel to what happens in the case of the sense organs; if the old man could recover the proper kind of eye, he would see just as well as the young man... Thus it is that thinking [*to noein*] and reflecting [*to theōrein*] decline through the decay of some other inward part and are themselves impassible [*apathes*]. Thinking [*to dianoeisthai*], loving, and hating are affections not of thought [*nous*], but of that which has thought, so far as it has it. That is why, when this vehicle decays, memory and love cease; they were activities not of thought *nous*, but of the composite which has perished; *nous* is, no doubt, something more divine and impassible (*DA* I.4 408b18-31).

There are several relevant observations about this passage. First, and most obviously, Aristotle uses *to noein, to dianoesthai*, and *to theorein* is a single passage, already indicating that there is a noteworthy difference. The three activities at least have in common that they all belong to a single person, although there is an important difference here: they differ with respect to their duration, for *to noein* and *to theōrein* are *apathes*. In what sense?

What is important in this context is *to noein* and *to theōrein* are affections of *nous*, which means those functions are incorruptible; since *to dianoeisthai* is an affection of the corruptible composite possessing *nous*, it does in fact perish. It is at least obvious that it is not helpful to translate both *to dianoeisthai* and *to noein* as 'thinking,' and it is equally clear that Aristotle does not use *to theōrein* and *to dianoesthai* interchangeably to mean a general kind of mental activity. Even without an analysis of their philosophical uses in other contexts, this passage already announces a difference, namely, that one is perishable while two are not. It is no doubt better to believe that Aristotle *purposely* used different words because he was attempting to pick out *distinct* processes. There are many ways to think discursively, but demonstration certainly is such a way. Contemplation, however, is not.

Human and Divine Contemplation

Another helpful way to explore the nature of human contemplation is to compare and contrast it with divine contemplation, for both kinds of cognition exist for Aristotle. The question is whether—given that divine contemplation is not discursive—human contemplation distinct in kind from divine contemplation. I think that it is not. I do not mean that there are no noteworthy differences between God's cognition and human cognition, but only that a limited, human intellect can become more or less like the divine intellect depending on the quality of one's contemplative life.[20] For Aristotle, a person may live one of two lives. In the ethical life, *nous* has the task of controlling the appetites. In itself, however, its activity will be something else: 'contemplation' (*theōrētikē*) is Aristotle's word for "the activity of the mind" (*EN* X.7 1177a16), and a life devoted to this activity is a divine life (*EN* X.7 1177b30-31). But what makes this life divine? There are at least three (non-exclusive) possibilities: human contemplation would be divine if 1) *nous* is a divine substance, 2) our contemplative life is our attempt to imitate the activity of God's life, in the same way that animals imitate God's activity through reproduction, or 3) humans are engaged in the same sort of activity as divine contemplation when we contemplate. It is not very controversial that Aristotle affirms the former two possibilities,[21] but his acknowledgment of the third is not widely recognized.

It seems obvious that Aristotle should argue for the third possibility since he says in reference to contemplation that "God is always in that good state in which we sometimes are" (*Meta.* XII.7 1072b24). This seems to be a straight-forward indication that he sees a continuum between human and divine contemplation: human contemplation is divine contemplation, writ small. However, this is a difficult claim to accept because the fact that God's cognition does not involve sensation seems to exclude the possibility that God uses *phantasms*—images derived from sense experience—to contemplate. And human contemplation can only take place in images: "when one contemplates something, one necessarily contemplates it along with an image" (*DA* III.8 432a8-9).[22] This difference is significant, but it does not yet eliminate the possibility that human cognition can be more or less similar to divine cognition. But if this is true, then it will turn out that human contemplation is active intuition, after all.

Kosman is one who does not draw a distinction between human contemplating and discursive reasoning. His position may be observed when he describes what divine contemplation is not:

> Aristotle's god is not a scientist, nor a philosopher, and divine thought is not a cosmic form of ratiocination or brilliantly articulated scientific theory. For *theoria* is not theory; it is simply the principle of *awareness*..., the divine full self-manifesting and self-capturing of consciousness, of which scientific activity and philosophical speculation are to be sure particularly subtle forms, but of which the ruder and more incorporate activities of perception and nutrition are equally images...."[23]

Although Kosman is not explicitly characterizing human contemplation, his comments about divine contemplation indicate his position. He is right, of course, that Aristotle's God does not reason discursively in contemplation. But Kosman's position a contrast that is not sustainable: divine contemplation is not discursive, but human contemplation is. When God contemplates, God is not a scientist, but human contemplation *is* scientific. This presents a difficulty for Kosman, because Aristotle has said that contemplation is divine, even for human contemplators. This is why he is forced to argue that human contemplation is divine in another way, for when humans engage in "scientific activity and philosophical speculation," we are attempting to imitate God's contemplation through a shared "principle of awareness."[24]

God is aware when God is contemplating, and when humans contemplate, even though it is discursive, it is *also* a manifestation of awareness. This then, is the connection between human and divine contemplation for Kosman. This is to deny the uniqueness of human contemplation, for there are many ways besides thinking to share the divine principle of awareness. Indeed, this principle of awareness that we have in discursivity is echoed throughout all of biology, for the "activities of perception and nutrition are equally images"[25] of the divine's principle of self-awareness. Discursivity is not different in this sense from reproduction; both are vague reflections of perfect, divine awareness.

It therefore appears that Kosman conceives of *to theōrein* and *to dianoeisthai* as identical in humans, and he considers this identification to be unproblematic. This conception, however, is simply not faithful to the texts, and specifically *DA* I.4 408b18-31. It is true that God's contemplation is intuitive, but it is false that human contemplation is discursive. Aristotle has made this clear by drawing an important distinction between *to theōrein*, which is simply the mind's active possession of the forms, and *to dianoeisthai*, which is the mind insofar as it engages in discursive activity. They differ to the same degree as that which is temporal and destructible differs from that which is eternal and impassible, for contemplation is a property of *nous*, while discursive reasoning is a property of the composite; although the composite contemplates, contemplation in the individual will perish, while contemplation in itself is impassible. This text does not indicate how discursivity is related to contemplation, but it does make it clear that they are not identical.

But how could human contemplation and divine contemplation be the same sort of activity when human contemplation relies on images? I have been arguing that both human and divine contemplation are active intellectual intuition, and thus non-discursive, but Aristotle does make it clear that there is a difference between human and divine contemplation: "when one contemplates something, one necessarily contemplates it along with an image" (*DA* III.8 432a8-9). This is so because "in all cases, when *nous* is active, it is its objects. Whether it is possible for the mind to contemplate its objects apart from spatial magnitude while the mind does not exist this way, must be considered later" (*DA* III.7 431b17-19).[26] And indeed, Aristotle does conclude that nothing exists for us outside of a spatial magnitude, which is why contemplation must take place in images.[27]

But importantly, it is clear that this is not the nature of contemplation itself, but a result of the finite structure of human cognition: "one would not learn or understand anything if it were not for sense-perception...for images are like sense-perceptions, except without matter" (*DA* III.8 432a7-10).[28] Aristotle's point is that human cognition in general is dependent on sense-perception, because without initial sense-perception, *nous* would be nothing. And equally as obviously, we are not always standing in front of a tree (e.g.) and perceiving it, but the mind is able to have it before itself in the form of an image. In this way, contemplation, and cognition is general, cannot taken place unless one is in possession of a stock of images.

But this does not yet show that human and divine contemplation are different kinds of activities. I follow Charles Kahn, who explains Aristotle's reasoning about the role of images in contemplation as a logical consequence of his analysis of the conditions of a composite existence:

> In order for [any minimally rational train of thought] to take place the first condition—call it Condition A—is empirical consciousness or sentience, what human beings share with animals...Sentience in the subjective side of *aisthesis*...The second condition, Condition B, is the specific capacity of *nous*, access to the noetic domain...The requirement of phantasms is a direct consequence of Condition A, our existence as sentient animals. As sentient, embodied beings, we cannot think even of *noeta*, intelligible objects, except by way of phantasms, the hylomorphic basis of our thought..."[29]

Kahn correctly recognizes that *nous* is of divine origin, and that contemplating itself is not essentially tied to images. This means that God, who is not bound by Condition A, does not need images in order to contemplate. So while human contemplation is necessarily tied to phantasms, it is not because of the nature of intelligible objects. Rather, it is because as hylomorphic beings, our having of intelligible objects is necessarily dependent on specific acts of passive intuition. Therefore, the way that humans have intelligible objects in phantasms is a consequence of our embodiment.

This appears to be yet another reference to contemplation as it exists in the individual, as opposed to how it exists in itself: "intuiting [*to noein*] and contemplating [*to theōrein*] decline through the decay of some inward part and are themselves impassible [*apathes*]" (*DA* I.4 408b28-31). It is necessary that contemplation in the individual perishes, for it can only take place in images. Thus, in III.8, when Aristotle tells us that 'when one contemplates something, one necessarily contemplates it along with an image,' he is answering a question that he first raised in the very first section of the *De Anima*: "...to *noein*[30] looks most like what is peculiar to the soul. But if this too is a form of imagination or does not exist apart from imagination, it would not be possible even for this to exist apart from the body" (*DA* I.1 403a6-7). Contemplation in the individual is not possible apart from imagination; thus, it perishes, although contemplation in itself does not perish. This is apparently what Aristotle means when he distinguishes the intelligible forms as they exist in themselves from images: "what is the difference between the primary intelligible forms [*prōta noēmata*] and images? They are not images, although we cannot have them without images" (*DA* III.8 432a10-12).[31]

The Philosophical Life

Aristotle says that "the states of virtue by which we possess truth by way of affirmation and denial are five in number, i.e., art [*technē*], knowledge [*epistēmē*], practical wisdom [*phronēsis*], philosophic wisdom [*sophia*], comprehension [*nous*]" (*EN* VI.3 1139b15-16). I have by now discussed all of these virtues except *sophia*. Aristotle has much praise for the life that cultivates *phronēsis*. However, a life devoted to *phronēsis* is only the second-best kind of life:

> This activity [i.e., contemplation] is the best (since not only is intellect the best thing in us, but the objects of intellect are the best of knowable objects); and secondly, it is the most continuous, since we can contemplate truth more continuously than we can do anything. And we think happiness has pleasure mingled with it, but the activity of wisdom is admittedly the pleasantest of excellent activities (*EN* X.7 1177a20-24).

Just as *epagōgē* leads to *nous*, and demonstration to *epistēmē*, so contemplation leads to *sophia*. But *sophia*, like *phronēsis*, is a different kind of intellectual virtue because it is possible to devote a life to it. For various reasons, *technē*, *nous*, and *epistēmē* could not be someone's greatest happiness. But someone can lead a life fundamentally devoted to *sophia*.

This is not surprising, given Aristotle's comments about *sophia* earlier in the *Nicomachean Ethics*, for *sophia* is of *nous* and *epistēmē*: "wisdom must be *nous* combined with *epistēmē*—knowledge of the highest objects which had received as it were its proper completion" (*EN* VI.7 1141a18-19). If my interpretation of contemplation is correct, this makes great sense. If *nous* is only for the purpose of demonstration, then *epistēmē* would already imply the existence of *sophia*, because it is not possible to have epistēmē without nous. But clearly, Aristotle intends that sophia is something above and beyond *epistēmē*. This is because one may gain *nous* and then *epistēmē*, but a person does not really possess wisdom until she reflects or contemplates or intuits the results of his own attempts to gain knowledge. A person who devotes his life to this is a lover of wisdom in the fullest possible sense.

Notes

1. See, for example, Jonathan Barnes, *Aristotle's Posterior Analytics* (Oxford: Oxford University Press, 1975), and Orna Harari, *Knowledge and Demonstration: Aristotle's Posterior Analytics* (Dordrecht, The Netherlands: Kluwer Academic Publishers, 2004).
2. *DA* 432a8-9.
3. *Meta.* 1072b14-29.
4. *DA* 429b9.
5. He does this explicitly at 1072b23. Also, see *EN* X.7-8. Although there Aristotle does not use the phrase 'thought thinks itself,' it seems unproblematic to make this identification, especially given his remarks that 'thought thinking itself' and 'contemplation' (1177b17, 1178b8) are both ways to describe a human activity that is divine.
6. Cf. *DA* 417b18-20.
7. Cf. *DA* 430a5-6.

8. This is my own translation of *"autē de legetai dichōs, ē men ōs epistēmē, ē d'ōs to theōrein."*

9. It is first worth nothing that when the mind in one sense 'becomes all things' (*tō panta ginesthai*) and in another 'makes all things' (*tō panta poiein*), the reference to 'all things' cannot be simply everything that exists. As Kosman notes, "the phrase is prefaced by the qualification *hekastō genei*, which makes clear that what we are talking about is what makes things be of a particular sort" (344). And in particular, we are talking about things that are potentially thought, and the only candidate here is the intellectual forms. So Kosman proposes that Aristotle meant that the making mind "makes everything that is potentially thought actually thought" (344). L.A. Kosman, "What Does the Maker Mind Make?," in *Essays on Aristotle's* De Anima, ed. Martha Nussbaum and Amelie Rorty (Oxford: Claredon Press, 1992).

10. See chapter 4, pp. 70-72.

11. Ronald Polansky, *Aristotle's* De Anima: *A Critical Commentary* (Cambridge: Cambridge University Press, 2007), 464.

12. Polansky, 465.

13. Smith does this in the ROT, as do Hamelyn and Ross.

14. Polansky, 464-5.

15. Polansky, 459

16. Besides the passage from I.4, there is 414a32 and 429a22, among others. They at first appear to and then fail to support Polansky's thesis for precisely the same reason as I.4.

17. Polansky, 460.

18. And indeed, contemplating supposes the continued existence of possessed knowledge. Cf. 412a22-26.

19. *Nous* is the substance that is born in the soul, which is what is clearly under discussion in this passage.

20. This would be quite different from the position of Kant, for example, for whom the activities of human and divine cognition are different in *kind*, rather than *degree*, such that a human cognition cannot be closer to or farther from divine cognition.

21. The first is stated straightforwardly in *EN* 1177a15-16. The second is advanced in *DA* 415a26-415b8.

22. This is my translation of: *"otan te theōrē, anagke hama phantasma ti theōrein."*

23. Kosman, 356.

24. Kosman, 356.

25. Kosman 356.

26. This is my translation of: *"holōs de ho nous estiv, ho kat.energeian, ta pragmata. Ara d'endechetai tōn kechōpismenōn ti noein onta auton mē kechōrismenon megethous, ē ou, skepteon hysteron."*

27. *DA* 432a3.

28. This is my translation of: *"oute mē aisthanomenos mēthen outhen an mathoi oude xunein...ta gar phantasmata hōper aisthēmata esti, plēn aneu hulēs."*

29. Charles Kahn, "Aristotle on Thinking," in *Essays on Aristotle's* De Anima, ed. Martha Nussbaum and Amelie Rorty (Oxford: Claredon Press, 1992), 362.

30. It will be recalled that is not until DA III.4 that Aristotle distinguishes the senses of *to noein*; here he is apparently using it as a general term for the cognitive processes.

31. This is my translation of: *"ta de prōta noēmata ti dioisei tou mē phantasmata einai; ē oude tauta phantasmata, all'ouk aneu phantasmatōn."*

Part Two:

Aristotle and Modern Skepticism

Chapter 6
Hume and Kant on the Problem of Objective Validity

Introduction

One way to approach Kantian epistemology is to see his initial problem as with the problem concerning the objective validity of concepts. He believes not just that no Western philosopher before him has sufficiently addressed the question of objective validity, but that no one has even thought to address it.[1] In the introduction to the transcendental deduction (TD) of the *Critique of Pure Reason*, Kant evokes a legal image in order to help us understand his project:

> Jurists, when they speak of entitlements and claims, distinguish in a legal matter between the questions about what is lawful (*quid juris*) and that which concerns the fact (*quid facti*), and since they demand proof of both, they call the first, that which is to establish the entitlement or the legal claim, the deduction (A84/B116).[2]

In certain legal cases, a lawyer has to prove not only that *this* crime was committed, but that *this* sort of thing should count as a crime given the current law. And the second proof may be characterized as a deduction because the lawyer must show how the established law necessarily applies to the act in question, thus making clear why the act is an illegal act. In an epistemological context, it is possible merely to assume that the categories of thought apply to objects; but with what right (*quid juris*) do we make this assumption? If we wish to deduce the right, we must show that our conceptual representations necessarily apply to objects; this is objective validity. This is the goal of the deduction that Kant has set out to give.

I believe that this is another version of the question that Kant earlier asked in a letter to Marcus Herz (henceforth, LH), although with different emphasis: "What is the ground of the relation of that in us which we call 'representation' to the object?" (*PC* 71).[3] The similarity of those two questions is demonstrated because the questions may be elided without changing the meaning of either. The new form may be this: "*With what right do we believe that the relation between our representation and its putative object is grounded by necessity?*" In other words, do we have a right to assume that our representation is necessarily of its putative object? I will henceforth refer to this as the *quid juris* question.

Kant sees this question as undermining ordinary knowledge claims within the two great epistemological traditions. He believes that Hume has shown sufficiently that empiricism cannot demonstrate objective validity, and so it ends in skepticism. Kant himself shows that rationalism relies on the doctrine of subjective necessity, and so it also ends in skepticism. But Kant—who rivals Aristotle

115

in his incurable epistemological optimism—refuses to accept either of these dismal alternatives. His solution, famously, it to show that the choice between empiricism and rationalism is a false dichotomy, for they are both versions of transcendental realism. The path forward is to reject transcendental realism itself for a position that Kant calls 'transcendental idealism.' Only the doctrine of transcendental idealism shows how human thought might attain objective validity, and therefore shows that skepticism is false. In the present chapter, I wish to explore the nature of the problem, and then compare and contrast Kant's and Aristotle's answers in chapter 7.

The Empiricists and the *Quid Juris* Question

At first glance, it seems odd that Kant frames the TD with the *quid juris* question, for the deduction is apparently directed at least partly at the empiricists, and Kant seems to imply both in the letter to Herz and in the TD that the empiricist is not obligated to answer this question:

> If a representation comprises only the manner in which the subject is affected' by the object, then it is easy to see how it is in conformity with this object, namely, as an effect accords with its cause, and it is easy to see how this modification of our mind can represent something, that is, have an object. Thus the passive or sensuous representations have an understandable relation to objects, and the principles that are derived from the nature of the soul have an understandable validity for all things... (*PC* 71).

> We may make use of a multitude of empirical concepts without objection from anyone, and take ourselves to be justified in granting them a sense and a supposed signification even without any deduction, because we always have experience ready at hand to prove their objective reality (A84/B116).

For the empiricist, the object is the cause and our representation of it is the effect. This is the sort of relation that Kant believes that our intuition has to objects, and since Kant is clear that no transcendental deduction is necessary if the object is the cause and the representation is the effect (A93/B125), it is possible to believe that the empiricist is required merely to give an empirical deduction. An empirical deduction is simply a *quid facti* question: 'From which of our particular experiences did this concept arise?' (A85/B117).

But empiricism is not thereby a live option. Kant also notes in both places that this is the relation with which the empiricist accounts for *all* representations, not just the sensible representations that Kant allows:

> the object [is not] the cause of our intellectual representations in the real sense (*in sensu reali*). Therefore the pure concepts of the understanding must not be abstracted from sense perceptions, nor must

they express the reception of representations through the senses...
(*PC* 71).

> Among the many concepts, however, that constitute the very mixed
> fabric of human cognition, there are some that are also destined for
> pure use *a priori* (completely independently of all experience), and
> these always require a deduction of their entitlement, since...one
> must know how...concepts can be related to objects that they do not
> derive from any experience (A85/B117).

These quotes are both outlines of the Metaphysical Deduction, which is supposed to show that it is simply false that all of our ideas could be *a posteriori*;
hence, an empirical deduction will only account for some of our representations,
but not the *a priori* ones.

Specifically, Kant mentions how both Locke and then Hume stand with regard to the *quid juris* question:

> the famous Locke, from neglect of this consideration, and because he
> encountered pure concepts of the understanding in experience, also
> derived them from this experience, and thus proceeded so inconsist-
> ently that he thereby dared to make attempts at cognitions that go far
> beyond experience (A95/B127).

Although it may be that Locke cannot account for how we acquire representations, Kant is concerned with a very different problem here. The problem is that
even if Locke could explain how all concepts can be derived from experience,
he still would not be able to explain how these concepts could be applied beyond
experience. Locke assumes this, but *with what right*?

Hume shares a general commitment to empiricism with Locke, but Hume's
empiricism is, according to Kant, more reflective; indeed, it is not stretching
matters to say that Humean epistemology anticipated Kantian epistemology in
an important way. It will be useful to recall that in the LH, dated 1772, Kant said
that "...I, as well as others, had failed to consider...this question: What is the
ground of the relation of that in us which we call "representation" to the object?"
(*CK* 10:130). Somewhere between 1772 and 1783 (the publication date of the
Prolegomena), Kant must have realized that he hadn't said that quite right, because Hume before him *had* addressed something like the *quid juris* question:

> the question was not, whether the concept of cause is right, useful,
> and, with respect to all cognition of nature, indispensable, for this
> Hume had never put in doubt; it was rather whether it is thought
> through reason *a priori*, and in this way has an inner truth independ-
> ent of all experience, and therefore also a much more widely extend-
> ed use which is not limited merely to objects of experience...The dis-
> cussion was only about the origin of this concept, not its
> indispensability in use; if the former were only discovered, the condi-

tions of its use and the sphere in which it can be valid would already
be given (*Pro.* 4:258-259).[4]

Hume asks: 'With what right do we utilize the concept of cause and effect to
explain experience, since we did not get this concept from experience?' Locke
before him thought it unproblematic to call the idea of cause and effect an *a posteriori* idea; thus, its objective validity is unproblematic in the same measure.

Hume, however, realized that we never actually observe causation, but
merely the conjunction of two events; hence, cause and effect are not *a posteriori* concepts in the sense that they were not directly observed, but neither are they
a priori concepts. Instead,

> he concluded that reason completely and fully deceives herself with
> this concept, falsely taking it for her own child, when it is really noth-
> ing but a bastard of the imagination, which, impregnated by experi-
> ence, and having brought certain representations under the law of as-
> sociation, passes off the resulting subjective necessity (i.e., habit) for
> an objective necessity (from insight). From which he concluded that
> reason has no power to think such connections, not even merely in
> general, because its concepts would be mere fictions (*Pro.* 4:257-8).

Because Hume posed this critical question to himself, he "subsequently pro-
ceeded quite consistently in declaring it to be impossible to go beyond the
boundary of experience with these concepts and the principle that they occasion" (A95/B127). Of course, Hume did not need to go this far according to
Kant because "it never occurred to him that perhaps the understanding itself...could be the originator of the experience in which it is encountered..."
(A95/B127). But given Hume's assumptions about the nature of mind and
world, he was right to advance the skepticism that he did; and if the term 'critical philosophy' may be extended to describe any philosophy that confronted the
quid juris question, then Hume was a critical philosopher before Kant.

The Rationalists and the *Quid Juris* Question

Kant's acceptance of Hume's accusation that empiricism could not demonstrate objective validity is rather well known. What is far less well known is
Kant's scorching criticism of other previous epistemologies with regard to the
quid juris problem. In the *LH*, Kant complains about a certain tradition within
epistemology that will remain unnamed for the moment:

> Plato assumed a previous intuition of divinity as the primary source
> of the pure concepts of the understanding and of first principles.
> Malebranche [*sic*] believed in a still-continuing perennial intuition of
> this primary being...Crusius believed in certain implanted rules for
> the purpose of forming judgments and ready-made concepts that God

implanted in the human soul just as they had to be in order to harmonize with things...However, the *deus ex machina* is the greatest absurdity one could hit upon in the determination of the origin and validity of our cognitions... (*PC* 72).

According to Kant, the epistemologies of Plato, Malebranche, and Crusius rely
on explanations *deus ex machina*. This criticism is apparently analogous to the
one given of a scientist, who when confronted with a problem that he cannot
solve at the moment, concludes, 'God must have done this.' Kant has in mind,
no doubt, the sort of explanation of the origin of innate ideas that Plato gives in
the *Meno*: "...the divine among our poets...say...this...: As the soul is immortal, has been born often and has seen all things here and in the underworld, there
is nothing which it has not learned; so it is in no way surprising that it can recol-
lect the things it knew before..." (*Meno* 81b-c).[5] Although it is true that Plato is
not committed to this particular explanation, he does not give an alternate one,
thus leaving himself open to Kant's charges. Instead of a deduction, there is an
appeal to an unknown, and more significantly, unknowable, origin of our ideas.
But if this origin is unknowable, then why do we have a right to conclude that
the ideas gained in this way before birth apply necessarily to objects? Kant believes that Plato cannot answer this question.

   I believe that Kant is here criticizing not just these three named thinkers, but
rationalism in general, although this is not apparent from the LH itself; it is helpful, then, that he takes up this criticism again in the final section of the second
edition of the TD. Kant imagines one who defends the view that the categories
are

subjective predispositions for thinking, implanted in us along with
our existence by our author in such a way that their use would agree
exactly with the laws of nature along which experience runs (a kind
of pre-formation system of pure reason)...[I]n such a case the categories would lack the necessity that is essential to their concept. For
e.g., the concept of cause...would be false if it rested only on a subjective necessity, arbitrarily implanted in us... (B167).

It at first seems that this passage must be taken as a reference to Hume's epistemology, since Hume directly confronts the issues of subjective necessity and
causation. But a closer examination yields a different conclusion. First, Kant's
language of an 'author' of our existence who 'arbitrarily implanted' concepts in
us is an echo of the references to 'God' and explanations '*deus ex machina*' in
the LH. Second, the subjective necessity of the TD passage is a 'predisposition,'
by which Kant indicates something that arrived *before* experience. In contrast,
Hume referred to subjectively necessary ideas such as causation as bastards implanted *by* experience. These considerations make it unlikely that Kant was addressing Hume here.

The best evidence, however, that Kant is not addressing any empiricist in the 'implantation passage' is gained by examining Kant's biological analogues in that same section (§27):

> either the experience makes these concepts possible or these concepts make the experience possible. The first is not the case with the categories (nor with the pure sensible intuition); for they are *a priori* concepts, hence independent of experience (the assertion of an empirical origin would be a sort of *generatio aequivoca*) (B167).

Kant therefore encourages us to think of the first possibility, that the objects make the concepts possible, on analogy with the biological theory of *generatio aequivoca*. This is simply the theory of "spontaneous generation," and holds that "generation is the process by which the material takes the form of the living organism... without the agency of other living organisms."[6] The Guyer/Wood translation of the *Critique* calls this "the generation of one sort of thing out of something essentially different, e.g., the supposed generation of flies from rotting meat" (264fn). In epistemology, this is what the empiricists propose, for elements of perception (one thing) are said to generate experiences and concepts in the mind (something essentially different). As a blank slate, the mind contributes nothing to this generation.

Kant's swift dismissal of the *generatio aequivoca* model is explained by recalling his reasoning elsewhere concerning the empirical unity of consciousness, namely that "no cognitions can occur in us, no connection and unity among them, without that unity of consciousness that precedes all data of the intuitions..." (A107). Empiricism characterizes human cognition as purely receptive. But as Kant points out, if the powers of the mind are merely receptive, then there is no feature of the mind capable of the power of synthesis, for synthesis requires spontaneity. Without synthesis, however, even the weakest of experiences would not be possible:

> If every individual representation were entirely foreign to the other, as it were isolated and separated from it, then there would never arise anything like cognition, which is a whole of compared and connected representations. If I therefore ascribe a synopsis to sense, because it contains a manifold in its intuition, a synthesis must always correspond to this, and receptivity can make cognitions possible only if combined with spontaneity (A97).

By not attributing any kind of spontaneity to human cognition, Kant points out, the empiricists cannot explain how raw sensation can even become the kind of intuition that be conceptualized; "the appearance would lack connection in accordance with universal and necessary laws, and would thus be intuition without thought..." (A111). According to Kant, spontaneous generation and empiricism suffer for the same reason; they are partners in absurdity.

Importantly, spontaneous generation is incompatible with something he calls 'preformation theory.' Preformation theory is then analogized with whatever Kant is talking about in the 'implantation passage'; hence, the implantation passage is not referring to empiricism. But what is preformation theory? Like *generatio aequivoca*, preformation theory is a model of evolutionary development. This model, however, is more complicated, and was even accepted by some in Kant's day. This theory holds that "the supreme world-cause...would only have placed in the initial products of its wisdom the initial predisposition by means of which an organic being produces more of its kind and constantly preserves the species itself" (*CJ* 5:422).[7] God did not create the world in its current form, but God did create the elements necessary for evolutionary development along pre-determined patterns. For example, the preformationist would give this analysis of reproduction:

> Preformation assumed that all livings things had been formed by God at the beginning of time and then encased in seeds or germs, either in the ovaries...or in the sperm...Conception merely awakened one of these sleeping forms..."[8]

Kant explicitly contrasts preformation theory with the evolutionary theory which he actually prefers, namely epigenesis.[9] The theories differ because in epigenesis, any given living thing is a product generated by some other living being; in contrast, preformation theory characterizes any given living being as an educt (*CJ* 5:423).[10] The difference between products and educts can be characterized by speaking of the opposite modes of forces, *formative* and *motive*, that arose when speaking of the difference between things with natural purposes and those without; formative forces yield products, while motive forces yield educts. Kant says that the preformationists deny "every individual from the formative power or nature in order to allow it to come immediately from the hand of the creator" (*CJ* 5:423). In that case, purposes are not natural but supernatural. The beings that are generated have already been given formative force by God and therefore do not need the capacity for self-formation; if this were true, the term 'formative force' would no longer be appropriate when describing organisms. Among other things, this implies "that the paternal contribution in generation is miniscule, merely setting in motion the development of structures already present in the egg..."[11] If this is how the force required to produce the organism is analyzed, then it is a motive force producing an educt.

If, on the other hand, we do attribute a formative impulse to organisms, the "*receptivity* of the organism to external stimuli and the interconnected ability to set its organs in motion" is taken seriously.[12] In contrast to the educt theory, on which there were "severe limits placed on this adaptive power by the original organization..."[13,] the organisms could form *themselves* by adapting to external stimuli; because they form themselves, their mode of force is formative. In the end, Kant rejects preformation theory specifically because it does not respect the formative force that he attributes to nature:

> Kant is saying that organic nature must be construed not merely as evolutionary—as self-evolving according to the preformation theory—but also exhibiting a certain creative activity—as self-evolving and relatively autonomous in its overall developmental process.[14]

If preformation were an epistemological theory, sense experience would be the paternal contribution and innate ideas the maternal contribution. This is, then, to attribute passivity to our conceptual capacity, which for Kant would mean that the categories are purely passive; in that case, the categories would be nothing by 'subjective predispositions...implanted in us.' In terms of force, the categories would have motive as opposed to formative force. That this is an analogue to rationalism is made by clear by noting two Leibnizian theories of which Kant would have been aware:

> Since Leibniz believed that souls are immortal, his theory is that all thoughts a mind will ever think were preformed at the Creation, when all souls were created. He also held a preformation theory of biology. He thought it analogous to his theory of mind and important for his theory of pre-established harmony, since it provided for the parallel between activities of living bodies and mind.[15]

Since Leibniz championed preformation theory both in epistemology and biology, and since Kant would have been familiar with both of Leibniz' positions, Kant must have had Leibniz at least partly in mind in the TD passage. And since I have demonstrated the continuity between the LH passage and the TD passage, we now can observe that Kant believes that his criticism caught up both Plato and Leibniz. It is not stretching things, therefore, to believe that Kant was attempting to characterize rationalism in general in those passages.

Rationalism, then, undermines objective validity according to Kant. His concern about objective validity may be illustrated by another analogy suggested in the LH but not carried through: "Various moralists have accepted precisely this view with respect to basic moral laws. Crusius believed in certain implanted rules for the purpose of forming judgments..." (*PC* 10:131). Kant is implicitly critical of this kind of moral theory because if the rules for moral judgments are implanted, then we have no right to characterize those judgments as *our* moral judgments. We are, so to speak, a conduit, a moral robot programmed by our maker who at best judges and subsequently acts in accordance with the moral law. The important point is that we are not justified in concluding anything about the judgment because we cannot explain *why* the judgment is the right one. It turns out that we are not the moral knowers who deserve the moral praise (or blame) for our knowledge; if God ordered our moral judgments, then God is responsible for the origin of the judgment. We simply cannot be held responsible for our judgments and subsequent actions if we could not have judged otherwise.

A similar story can be told about implanted innate ideas. It may be that the judgments springing forth from our innate ideas 'harmonize' with the world perfectly. Perhaps, but whether they do or do not is necessarily unknown to us. The most I can say is that "I am so constituted that I cannot think of this representation otherwise than as so connected..." (B168). Karl Ameriks puts the matter this way: "Kant stresses that even for God to put a thought into us, there must be a ground within us, a capacity to receive and have the thought; otherwise, there would be no point to say that it is we rather than God who have the thought."[16]

For a theory that considers the categories as a subjective predisposition, the most optimistic case is that our implanted representations of objects do indeed map onto the world perfectly. In that case, there would be a causal story to be told about my knowledge: experience causes my representations, but it does so by activating latent, implanted capacities, which are themselves effects, for God causes their existence. And *that* is the best case; there is still the possibility that our implanter is Descartes' evil genius, purposely causing mismatches between our implanted representations and the world. Rationalism, as an analogue to preformation theory, lacks objective validity, and in this way fails to extend our cognition of objects.

Conclusion

According to Kant, rationalism correctly rejects empiricism's belief that "the object alone makes the representation possible" (A92/B124-5). However, rationalism must go further by abandoning the assumption shared with empiricism that our cognition must conform to the objects, because this model has failed to extend our cognition of objects. When applied to empiricism, this point had already been made by Hume, but it is often not sufficiently understood why rationalism fails this test. I have argued that what Kant finds objectionable in rationalism is its reliance on what he calls a 'subjective predisposition'; because of this, Kant believes that rationalism can never achieve objective validity. The search for knowledge that attains objective validity lead Kant all the way to a version of idealism, although it will strike some that this is too high a price to pay for knowledge. While that question is outside the scope of this work, I turn to another question that may be relevant here: does Aristotle also see the problem of objective validity, and formulate an epistemology that can attain objective validity? If so, then we would have an instance of objective validity within the realist tradition, a possibility that Kant believed he had ruled out. This is the question of chapter 7.

Notes

1. Although as will be noted, sometimes Kant seems to count Hume as a striking exception. If Hume is included, then, the statement should be amended to say that no one has confronted the problem and yet avoided skepticism.

2. Immanuel Kant, *Critique of Pure Reason*, tr. and ed. Paul Guyer and Allen W. Wood. *The Cambridge Edition to the Works of Immanuel Kant* (Cambridge: Cambridge University Press, 1998). All citations of Kant that include no reference to the title of the book are from the *Critique of the Pure Reason.*

3. Immanuel Kant, *Philosophical Correspondence: 1759-99*, ed. and tr. Arnulf Zweig (Chicago: The University of Chicago Press, 1967).

4. Immanuel Kant, *Theoretical Works After 1781*, eds. Henry Allison and Peter Heath. *Prolegomena* Translated and Edited by Gary Hatfield. *The Cambridge Companion to the Works of Immanuel Kant* (Cambridge: Cambridge University Press, 2002).

5. Plato, *Plato: Complete Works*, ed. John M. Cooper, assoc. ed. D.S. Hutchinson. *Meno* translated by G.M.A. Grube (Indianapolis: Hackett Publishing Company, 1997).

6. J. Wubnig, "The Epigenesis of Pure Reason," *Kant-Studien* 60 (1969), 148.

7. Immanuel Kant. *Critique of the Power of Judgment,* ed. Paul Guyer, tr. Paul Guyer and Eric Matthews. *The Cambridge Edition to the Works of Immanuel Kant* (Cambridge: Cambridge University Press, 1998).

8. Peter Reill, "Between Preformation and Epigenesis: Kant, Physiotherapy, and Natural History," in *New Essays on the Precritical Kant*, ed. Tom Rockmore (New York: Humanity Books, 2001), 170.

9. He first mentions it as an epistemological theory at B167.

10. Kant does not associate spontaneous generation with any particular mode of force.

11. Timothy Lenoir, "Kant, Blumenbach, and Vital Materialism in German Biology," *Isis* 74, no. 1 (March 1980): 77-108, and 81.

12. Lenoir, 85.

13. Lenoir, 85.

14. A.C. Genova, *"Kant's Epigenesis of Pure Reason,"* Kant-Studien 65 (1974): 259-273, 265.

15. Wubnig 150.

16. Karl Ameriks, "The critique of metaphysics: Kant and traditional ontology," in *The Cambridge Companion to Kant,* ed. Paul Guyer (Cambridge: Cambridge University Press, 1992), 263.

Chapter 7
Kant and Aristotle on Spontaneity

Introduction

In chapter 6, I laid out a problem that Kant describes as the problem of objective validity. While I want to describe the general contours of Kant's own answer to the *quid juris* question—transcendental idealism—I do not plan to give a formal assessment of it, nor do I wish to disagree with Kant's belief that rationalism and the kind of empiricism that he is familiar with end in skepticism. My task, rather, is to compare and contrast Kant and Aristotle's positions on objective validity with the goal of demonstrating that Aristotle does in fact at least attempt to answer the *quid juris* question. He does not use any phrase that can be reasonably translated as 'objective validity' or '*quid juris*,' but I think the basis for the idea is there. If it is true that Aristotle answers the *quid juris* problem while remaining optimistic about the possibility of knowledge, then this is something that Kant skipped over on his way to idealism. There is an obvious historical drawback to this: even if Kant accepted my argument, it is not at all clear what he would have done with it, or how and to what extent it might have changed the subsequent debates about idealism. But it would at least show that he was unjustified in believing that any transcendentally realistic epistemology necessarily lacks objective validity and thus ends in skepticism.

Objective Validity for the *Intellectus Archetypus*

Kant believes that empiricism and rationalism, despite their differences, share a general model of cognition; he proposes a system that attains objective validity by re-imagining human cognition itself. For him, a human cognizer is an *intellectus ectypus*, a term he defines negatively through his thought experiment of a divine cognizer—the *intellectus archetypus*. In his introductory remarks to the transcendental deduction, Kant says that

> only two cases are possible where synthetic presentation and its objects can concur, can necessarily refer to each other, and can,—as it were—meet each other: viz., either if the object makes the presentation possible, or if the presentation alone makes the object possible (A92/B125).[1]

Kant explicitly states that the former possibility is empiricism's model of cognition, while the second possibility is his own.[2] So does rationalism not figure in to this seemingly pithy dilemma? It does not, because Kant is talking about the

two cases where objects and representations '*necessarily* refer to each other'—
the necessity, of course, must not be subjective necessity. In rationalism, objects
do not necessarily refer to each other; they may refer to each other, but even a
perfect match between the object and our representation of it falls short of objective validity. Such a coincidental fit is about which the "skeptic most longs [to
hear]" (B168).[3]

There is an objectively valid match between sensible objects and sensible
representations, but according to Kant, that does not account for very much of
our cognition. Objective validity, however, does obtain of a cognition that
'makes the object possible.' 'Making possible' can be interpreted in two ways;
Kant mentions one way in the LH. There, he describes a problem that

> I, as well as others, had failed to consider and which in fact constitutes the key
> to the whole secret of metaphysics, hitherto still hidden from itself. I asked my-
> self this question: What is the ground of the relation of that in us which we call
> representation to the object? (*PC* 71).

He had previously addressed this topic without the rigor required by the complexity of the task: "in my dissertation I was content to explain the nature of the
intellectual representations in a merely negative way, namely, to state that they
were not modifications of the soul brought about by the object" (*PC* 72). This
was a problematic position, however, because a representation can only have
objective validity if there is a causal relationship between it and its object.[4] For
example, the sensible representations are caused by certain sensible objects, and
thus "the passive or sensuous representations have an understandable relationship to objects" (*PC* 72). But since intellectual representations are not caused by
intellectual objects (as Kant asserts), they lack objective validity: "[since intellectual representations cannot be] given to us...whence comes the agreement
that they are supposed to have with objects...?" (*PC* 72). Kant is confident that
this observation undermined his own pre-critical philosophy as well as the rationalist tradition generally, because in rationalism, there is no such simple
causal relationship between the object and our intellectual representation of it.

It is here that Kant mentions one way cognition could make its objects possible, and thus, obtain objective validity:

> If that in us which we call "representation" were active with regard to the ob-
> ject, that is, if the object itself were created by the representation (as when di-
> vine cognitions are conceived as the archetypes of things), the conformity of
> these representations to their objects could also be understood (*PC* 72).

Kant considers the nature of this creational cognition in only a few places: here
in the letter to Herz, after the discussion of the mechanism/teleology antinomy
in the third *Critique*,[5] and at various places in the first *Critique*.[6] Perhaps the
most obvious feature uniting all of these references is that this alternate cognition is posited explicitly for the sake of better understanding human cognition.

For example, after examining the nature of human understanding in the third *Critique*, Kant asks us to consider "a possible understanding other than the human one (as in the *Critique of Pure Reason* we had to have in mind another possible intuition if we were to hold our own to be a special kind, namely one that is valid of objects merely as appearance)" (*CJ* 5:405). Kant refers to this possible being in 1790 as an "*intellectus archetypus*" (*CJ* 5:408), a term he had already used in his 1772 letter to Herz. And while he did not use the term '*intellectus archetypus*' in either edition of the first *Critique* (1781 and 1787)—there he focuses on intuition and prefers the term "*intuitus originarius*" (B72)—he does say that this type of intuition already implies a unique type of understanding: "an understanding, in which through self-consciousness of all the manifold would at the same time be given, would intuit; ours can only think and must seek the intuition in the senses" (B135). So even though the first *Critique* is most concerned with imagining a possible non-human intuition, it is clear that Kant never meant to separate this non-human intuition from the non-human understanding that he mentions in the LH and develops in the third *Critique*. I will thus refer to a possible being with a non-human mode of cognition as the *intellectus archetypus*.

The intuition of a finite being, *intuitus derivativus*, is an intuition that "is dependent on the existence of the object..." (B72); that is to say, there must already be an object for it to be affected. Kant emphasizes that the human intuition is called '*intuitus derivatus*' and the non-human intuition is '*intuitius originarius*' specifically because of how they stand with respect to the existence of objects. In addition to its dependence on the existence of its object, human intuition is also different because it is only part of human cognition: "there are two stems of human cognition...namely sensibility and understanding," which can be analyzed separately because they have distinct tasks: "through [sensibility] objects are given to us, but through [understanding] they are thought" (A15/B29). Human cognition is thus made up of two distinct yet mutually dependent elements: "thoughts without content are empty, intuitions without concepts are blind" (A51/B75). The understanding thinks or judges, but it must have intuited objects lying before it about which to make judgments: "...all thought...must...ultimately be related to intuitions...since there is no other way in which objects can be given to us" (A19/B33).

This, however, is only one possible conception of intuition: "...I cannot presuppose that in every such being thinking and intuiting...are two different conditions for the exercise of its cognitive faculties" (*CJ* 5:403). For finite beings, knowledge of an object requires the work of two different faculties: intuition and understanding. In contrast, the intuition that Kant imagines that an infinite being would have is already intellectual. For an infinite mind, intellectual intuition (B68) and intuitive understanding (B145) would be synonyms. This "original being" (B72) therefore does not think in the sense that humans think, where thinking is a process separate from and dependent on intuition. Human thinking requires an understanding that is not intuitive; it is, rather, a discursive understanding that cannot judge without the intuited manifold. And this intuitive understanding is non-discursive not because it lacks this capacity, but because it has no need for it:

> For if I wanted to think of an understanding that itself intuited (as, say, a divine understanding, which would not represent given objects, but through whose representation the objects would themselves at the same time be given, or produced), then the categories would have no significance at all with regard to such a cognition. They are only rules for an understanding whose entire capacity consists in thinking, i.e., in the action of bringing the synthesis of the manifold that is given in intuition from elsewhere to the unity of apperception... (B145).

Kant also gives this analysis in terms of receptivity and spontaneity. Our intuition is dependent on objects being given to it; but since it is possible to imagine "a complete spontaneity of intuition...and thus an understanding in the most general sense of the term, one can thus also conceive of an intuitive understanding (negatively, namely merely as not discursive)..." (*CJ* 5:406). Kant has pointed out that our understanding is discursive because it is limited by whatever manifold is intuited. This is how the understanding of an *intellectus ectypus* (a cognition with human intuition) is constrained to operate. Thus, the spontaneous power of the understanding is first dependent on an act of receptivity by the intuition. This type of intuition gives rise to a type of self-consciousness that is distinguished from the self-consciousness that would accompany an intellectual intuition:

> Consciousness of itself (apperception) is the simple representation of the I, and if the manifold in the subject were given self-actively through that alone, then the inner intuition would be intellectual. In human beings this consciousness requires inner perception of the manifold that is antecedently given in the subject, and the manner in which this is given in the mind *without spontaneity* must be called sensibility on account of this difference (B68, my italics).

In the case of the *intellectus archetypus*, "the object itself [is] created by the representation," and so "the conformity of these representations to their objects could also be understood" (*CK* 10:130). The representations of the intellectual intuition of the *intellectus archetypus*, then, are objectively valid.

What Would Count as Objective Validity for the *Intellectus Ectypus*?

Intuition, an element of human cognition, is not passive, although it is receptive; this is simply because it allows for the possibility of its own objects. For intuitions, "despite being *a priori* cognitions, must yet refer necessarily to objects... For only by means of such pure forms of sensibility can an object appear to us... and the synthesis in space and time has objective validity" (B121).[7] Because of this, there is no need for a justification of the objective validity of the intuition like there is for the categories, because objects can never be given to us without the forms of space and time. Therefore, the metaphysical deduction of space and time also entails its transcendental deduction. There is no worry of the subjective conditions of intuition not having objective validity.[8]

This is not the case, however, for the categories; they

> do not at all present to us the conditions under which objects are given in intuition. Therefore objects can indeed appear to us without having to refer necessarily to functions of understanding, and hence without the understanding's containing a priori the conditions of these objects. Thus we find here a difficulty that we did not encounter in the realm of sensibility: viz., how subjective conditions of thought could have objective validity, i.e., how they could yield conditions for the possibility of all cognition of objects (A89/B122).[9]

As is clear from Kant's reference to evolutionary theories,[10] what is required in order to support the claim that the categories are objectively valid would be the epistemological analogue to the theory of epigenesis, which is markedly different from *generatio aequivoca* or preformation theory: "...the understanding itself, by means of [the categories], could be the originator of the experience in which its objects are encountered..." (A95/B127). The key to understanding this possibility is understanding Kant's insistence that "the representation alone makes the object possible" (A92/B124-5). Making possible, however, must be distinguished the kind of creating done by the *intellectus archetypus*: "representation in itself (for we are not here talking about its causality by means of the will) does not produce its object as far as its existence is concerned..." (A92/B125). Kant's desiderata are now clear. If he is going to show that the intellectual representations of the *intellectus ectypus* are objectively valid, he must show that they are simultaneously spontaneous and non-creational.

Kant summarizes his own answer to the *quid juris* question in a famous passage to the introduction to the second edition of the *Critique of Pure Reason*:

> up to now it has been assumed that all our cognition must conform to the objects; but all attempts to find out something about them *a priori* through concepts that would extend our cognition have, on this presupposition, come to nothing. Hence let us once try whether we do not get farther with the problems of metaphysics by assuming that the objects must conform to our cognition... (Bxvi).

Kant believes that objects must conform to our cognition because space and time are not features of things as they are in themselves, but the pure forms of intuition. Later in the *Critique*, he refers to this the doctrine as "transcendental idealism," while the presupposition that cognition must conform to objects is "transcendental realism" (A369). Transcendental idealism answers the *quid juris* question because in that case, "the object...conforms to the constitution of our faculty of intuition, [therefore] I can very well represent this possibility to myself" (Bxvii). But in transcendental realism, "intuition has to conform to the constitution of the objects, [therefore] I do not see how we can know anything of them *a priori*" (Bxvii).

It turns out then that Kant's notion that "the representation makes the object possible" (A92/B124-5) cannot mean that the representation creates its own object, nor can it be a reference to any kind of theory of innate ideas. It would be inaccurate to say that the cognition of the *intellectus ectypus* is completely spontaneous, but it is also false to believe that it is passive. Rather,

> Our cognition arises from two fundamental sources in the mind, the first of which is the reception of representations (the receptivity of impressions), the second the faculty for cognizing an object by means of the representations (spontaneity of concepts) (A50/B74).

Divine cognition is spontaneous, creative intuition; therefore thinking (i.e., spontaneous intellectual activity) is superfluous for divine cognition, and so there is nothing receptive in this cognition. Human cognition, however, involves both spontaneity and receptivity; thought is spontaneous, while sensibility is receptive.[11] Both elements are necessary for cognition.

So Kant believes that his insight that "receptivity can make cognitions possible only if combined with spontaneity" (A97) rules out rigorous 'blank slate' empiricism.[12] By itself, the rationalist may agree with this statement. However, the mind that has been implanted with 'innate ideas' is just as passive as the model of mind proposed by the empiricist. Kant would say that the rationalists had the good sense to posit *a priori* ideas, and thus do not have to rely on the unexplained (because unexplainable) determinateness of sense-data, but they believe that the spontaneity which necessarily exists when *a priori* ideas apply to experience does not spring from the *a priori* ideas themselves. Rather, the spontaneity of implanted innate ideas belongs to their author. Again, the evolutionary analogy rings true; in the preformation theory of evolutionary development, nature is inert, while God is active; the ideas that come to exist are therefore analogous to educts and not products. What appears to be the activity of nature is simply an 'awakening' or what God had already encased. But for Kant, in order for objective validity to obtain of *human* cognitions, the spontaneity must be *human* spontaneity. If the spontaneity belongs to the implanter, it could not be ours.

What Kant has done, therefore, is to formulate a new model of spontaneity: the empiricists do not recognize spontaneity, the rationalists are forced to attribute spontaneity to the implanter, and the (non-transcendental) idealist must posit a type of spontaneous intuition that Kant believed that humans do not have.[13] Objects must conform to the mind and not vice-versa because the condition for the possibility of having objects at all is that they conform to the mind. But since they conform to the mind's epistemic conditions, what the human mind cognizes are appearances of objects, not the objects as they are in themselves. This is the inevitable consequence of making "...that in us which we call 'representation'...active with regard to the object" (*PC* 72). Furthermore, we simply have no basis for assuming that the object as it appears to us is the object as it is in itself, "for if the senses merely represent something to us as it appears, then this something must also be a thing in itself and an object of non-sensible intuition, i.e., of the understanding" (A249). Therefore, while it is accurate to say that the epistemic conditions of the mind are constitutive of the appearance of the object, Kant does not believe it is possible that the human mind causes its objects to exist.

Kant has made two important claims about objective validity. First, he has said that a representation has objective validity only if it has causal relationship with its object. This happens when the object causes our representation of it, as in the case of sensuous representations. However, intellectual representations cannot be caused in the same way, as an empiricist such as Locke believes; empiricism fails for this reason. Rationalism does not even propose a cause and effect model between objects and our representations of them; instead, the originator is the cause of our innate ideas, and one simply hopes that they correctly map onto the world. Whether they happen actually to do so or not is irrelevant, because in either case intellectual representations do not have objective validity. Spontaneity, then, is the key for objective validity of intellectual representations. Thus, if such as being as the *intellectus archetypus* existed, its cognitions would be objectively valid because they cause the existence of their objects. But Kant believes that this cognition is quite unlike human cognition, which creates form, but not content.

Transcendental Idealism

Kant has therefore proposed a kind of formal answer to the *quid juris* question. If there is to be objective validity for human beings, then humans must have an understanding that is simultaneously spontaneous and non-creational. How does Kant explain how this could be so? It is possible to locate Kant's radical redefinition of the limits of human thinking in Kant's theory of transcendental idealism, which he opposes to transcendental realism:

> I understand by the transcendental idealism of all appearances the doctrine that they are all together to be regarded as mere representations and not as things in themselves...To this idealism is opposed transcendental realism, which regards space and time as something given in themselves (independent of our sensibility). The transcendental realist therefore represents outer appearances...as things in themselves (A369).[14]

Transcendental realism is simply a general label for any ontology that does not recognize a distinction between things as they appear and things as they are in themselves. According to Kant, therefore, all epistemology is either transcendentally idealistic or transcendentally realistic, for any epistemology either recognizes this distinction or it does not. Kant, apparently for the first time in Western philosophy, recognizes such a distinction; as Henry Allison says, "only the 'critical philosophy' has succeeded in getting this distinction right."[15] This is to say that Kant believes that all non-critical philosophies are, at bottom, varieties of transcendental realism; this is true of thinkers as widely varied as Descartes, Newton, Berkley and Hume.[16]

It is in this context that Allison argues that Kant, for the first time, articulates a conception of the human mind that is genuinely human. Allison takes Kant's description of the Copernican Revolution as a straightforward statement of transcendental idealism:

> Up to now it has been assumed that all our cognition must conform to the objects; but all attempts to find out something about them *a priori* through concepts that would extend our cognition have, on this presupposition, come to nothing. Hence let us once try whether we do not get farther with the problems of metaphysics by assuming that the objects must conform to our cognition... (Bxvi).

This is a statement against transcendental realism because "the 'objects' to which our knowledge presumably conforms must be characterized as things in themselves in the transcendental sense."[17] Furthermore, Allison detects in this formula a different way to understand the nature of transcendental realism: "we can be said to know objects just to the extent to which our thought conforms to their real nature, or equivalently, to God's thought of these same objects."[18] Allison thus introduces another name for transcendental realism: the theocentric view of knowledge. An epistemology is theocentric if it presupposes a "hypothetical "God's eye view" of things [that] is used as a standard in terms of which the "objectivity" of human knowledge is analyzed."[19]

Symmetrically, Allison re-describes transcendental idealism as an 'anthropocentric view of knowledge,' "the defining characteristic of which is that the cognitive structure of the human mind is viewed as the source of certain conditions which must be met by anything that is to be represented as an object by such a mind."[20] The connection is that if one uncritically presupposes that that the mind conforms to objects, then one assumes that there are no conditions to which the object must conform if it is to be an object for us. And if there are no such *a priori* conditions for human knowledge, then the object that appears is the object as it is in itself. Similarly, if there are no conditions which make the appearance a uniquely human appearance, then there is no qualitative difference between human and divine knowledge. As Allison says, "to say that objects conform to our knowledge is just to say that they conform to the conditions under which we alone can present them as objects."[21] Allison gives these conditions a special name: 'epistemic conditions.' Allison therefore believes that transcendental idealism implies a doctrine of epistemic conditions; transcendental realism implies no such thing.

Objective Validity and Transcendental Idealism

How does transcendental idealism deliver objective validity and avoid the pitfalls of subjective necessity? It is possible to say that, in general, Kant rethinks the very notions of 'objectivity' and 'subjectivity.' This is most clear from his in his discussion of the reflective power of judgment in the *Critique of Judgment*. It is in this context that he returns to the *intellectus archetypus*:

> a complete spontaneity of intuition would be a cognitive faculty distinct and completely independent from sensibility, and thus an understanding in the most general sense of the term[;] one can thus also conceive of an intuitive understanding (negatively, namely merely as not discursive), which does not go from the universal to the particular and thus to the individual (through concepts) (*CJ* 5:407).

For the *intellectus archetypus*, intuition is not receptive and understanding is not discursive. Indeed, for such an understanding, concepts would be useless:

> since it is not discursive like ours but is intuitive, [it] goes from the synthetically universal (of the intuition of a whole as such) to the particular, i.e., from whole to the parts, in which, therefore, and in whose representation of the whole, there is no contingency in the combination of the parts (*CJ* 5:407).

For human beings, however, there are two functions of the power of judgment, distinguished by how they stand in regard to principles. One type of judgment is determinative judgment: "[t]he determining power of judgment by itself has no principles that ground concepts of objects. It is no autonomy, for it merely subsumes under given laws or concepts as principle" (*CJ* 5:385). Since the determining power of judgment uses laws or principles that are *not* of its own making, Kant says that it is *not* 'nomothetic.' Kant anticipates the coming sections by pointing out an advantage that comes from merely following (and not creating) laws, namely, that the determining power of judgment "could never fall into disunity with itself..." (*CJ* 5:386).

Since principles (or laws) that ground concepts are *given to* the determining power of judgment, we may ask, 'from where are they given?' The answer from the transcendental realist would be 'from the world as it is in itself.' Kant is here testing this presupposition. Here in the third *Critique* he considers in particular the principles of mechanism and teleology:

If one were to transform these…into constitutive principles of the possibility of the objects themselves, they would run: Thesis: All generation of material things is possible in accordance with merely mechanical laws. Antithesis: Some generation of such things is not possible in accordance with merely mechanical laws (*CJ* 5:387).

According to Kant, this contradiction can be resolved only by abandoning the presupposition that these are "objective principles for the determining power of judgment" (*CJ* 5:387). So if these are not objective principles gleaned from our observation of the operation of world as it is in itself, where else could they have come from?

It is not possible to believe that the principles do not exist. The mere fact that we are judging rules this out, for "no use of the cognitive faculties can be permitted without principles" (*CJ* 5:385). The last possibility, then, is that the principles are features of the power of judgment itself, although not in its determinative capacity, for the determining power of judgment "merely subsumes under given laws or concepts as principles" (*CJ* 5:385). This points to a special power of judgment: "…the reflecting power of judgment must serve as a principle itself…" (*CJ* 5:385). To return to his example, both mechanism and teleology are principles. It is less controversial that the principle of mechanism is necessary for judging natural objects, but Kant argues that the principle of teleology is also necessary for judging: "…we must…apply this maxim of judgment to the whole of nature…given the limitations of our insights into the inner mechanisms of nature, which otherwise remain hidden from us" (*CJ* 5:398).

Therefore the principles of teleology and mechanism are necessary, but only "necessary…for the sake of cognition of natural laws in experience…" (*CJ* 5:385). This has the effect of removing the contradiction between the principles of mechanism and teleology because "it is only asserted that human reason, in the pursuit of this reflection and in this manner" must use these principles for reflecting on nature, and "reflection in accordance with the first maxim is not thereby suspended, rather one is required to pursue it as far as one can" (*CJ* 5:387-8). Kant's point is that conceiving ends in nature is not anti-scientific, nor a relic from a religiously-motivated physics. Rather, it is a necessary presupposition of human cognition, which understands nature through the power of judgment. In the end, the mistake "rests on confusing a fundamental principle of the reflecting with that of the determining power of judgment…" (*CJ* 5:389). Mechanism and teleology are principles, but for the realist, they are both rival principles of nature in itself, and we must choose which of the two principles are true. For Kant, they are both principles of the reflective judgment that exist at all for the sake of understanding nature.

The investigation into the powers of judgment has identified "a special character of our (human) understanding with regard to the power of judgment in its reflection upon things in nature" (*CJ* 5:406). Our species of understanding is distinguished in part because of the way we are constrained to view the relationship between the particular and the universal:

this contingency [in the constitution of our understanding] is quite naturally found in the particular, which the power of judgment is to subsume under the universal of the concepts of the understanding; for through the universal of our (human) understanding the particular is not determined... (*CJ* 5:406)

This is so because "it is contingent in how many different ways distinct things that nevertheless coincide in a common characteristic can be presented to our perception" (*CJ* 5:406). This contingency is due to the fact that our intuition is receptive, and thus our concepts depend on an act of receptivity in order to have objects.

There are two ways that the *intellectus ectypus* may proceed in judging nature; one way is from the parts of nature to the whole of nature. In this case, "a real whole of nature is to be regarded only as the effect of the concurrent moving forces of the parts" (*CJ* 5:407). If we proceed in the opposite manner, from whole to parts, we are confined to "go from the analytical universal (of concepts) to the particular (of the given empirical intuition), in which it *determines* nothing of the latter, but *must expect* this determination for the power of judgment..." (*CJ* 5:407, my italics). Béatrice Longuenesse notes that these two ways represent the principles of mechanism and teleology, known by now as subjectively necessary principles of reflective judgment:

> the rule of mechanism is imposed upon our reflective power of judgment by the understanding in its distributive use, which proceeds from parts to whole. The rule of teleology is imposed upon our power of judgment by consideration of particular objects, which have to be understood from whole to parts. Both depend upon the discursive nature of our understanding.[22]

As Longuenesse notes, both ways of proceeding (whole to parts, parts to whole) "depend upon the discursive nature of our understanding. *Both would be useless for an intuitive understanding, which would reveal their common ground.*"[23]

It is obvious that Kant believes that judgments of mechanism and teleology are legitimate ones, provided that they are categorized as reflective (and hence subjective) and not determinative (and hence objective). While this is certainly true, Longuenesse is pointing to a more profound subjectivity:

> The very fact that determinative and reflective uses have to be distinguished in this way is a characteristic of our own finite, discursive understanding. In this sense...*both* determinative and reflective uses of our power of judgment are "subjective."[24]

Thus, mechanism and teleology are both different reflective principles specifically because they are both necessary 'from the point of view of man' (this is the title of her chapter). The truth is that the human condition forces us to consider objects both from whole to parts and from parts to whole. Specifically, the culprit is receptivity:

If we suppose an intellect for which concept and intuition are not distinct, an intellect which unlike ours does not depend on receptivity for the reference of its concepts to objects, then neither determinative judgment (which has to find the particular objects for a given general concept) nor reflective (which has to find universal concepts for given particular objects) have any use at all.[25]

Longuenesse emphasizes Kant's point that this antinomy is generated specifically because of the conditions of our cognition. They simultaneously require us to recognize our human limits and that there is another possible cognition that is of a *different kind*: "the supposition of an intuitive understanding which escapes the distinctions of our own understanding…is itself a supposition proper to an understanding such as ours."[26]

For Kant, concepts such as teleology and mechanism are objectively valid in the sense that they are the real conditions for understanding nature, generated by our own reflective judgment. But in a sense, they are deeply subjective, since they are not concepts that represent the world as it is in itself. And of course, anyone who is accustomed to presuppose transcendental realism will find this kind of objectivity quite dissatisfying. The price for the objective validity of concepts is that we must give up the idea that the principles we think about are principles are principles of the world in itself, but Kant is willing to pay this price. After all, he would emphasize, the price of insisting that we cognize the world as it is in itself is ultimately skepticism.

Objective Validity Without Transcendental Idealism: Aristotle and the *Quid Juris* Question

We have seen that for Kant, spontaneity is the key to the *quid juris* question, although it is spontaneity that is akin to the spontaneity of the evolutionary theory of epigenesis, and nothing like that of spontaneous generation. The problem is that traditional empiricism does not recognize spontaneity at all on the side of the mind, since the mind a purely passive blank slate. As such, an empiricist theory of mind could never explain why we cognize anything more than a bare manifold of intuition for Kant. Thus there is a sense in which he is more closely aligned with the rationalist tradition, although on this particular point the rationalists come out worse, as they posit no spontaneity at all, but mere implanted the innate ideas. In this case, there is nothing that guarantees the connections between objects and *our* concepts of them. A third position, and the one to which Kant believes both empiricism and rationalism inevitably lead, is skepticism, which insists that there is no way to answer the *quid juris* question. Objective validity, then, requires a certain kind of spontaneity that transcendental realism cannot provide in the case of human cognizers. I believe that Aristotle implicitly recognizes this problem, but is able to remain optimistic about the possibility of knowledge, even though he believes that what we cognize is the world as it is in itself. If this is true, then this would be significant exception to Kant's analysis, because he believed that all varieties of transcendental realism were doomed to subjective necessity and hence to skepticism.

The beginning of a proper analysis of Aristotle's view begins by observing a striking similarity between Kant and Aristotle. With regard to concept acquisition, both think of themselves as carving out a middle ground between the theory of innate ideas on the one hand, and the model of the mind as a blank slate on the other. Kant's version of this maneuver is better known (or rather, it is usually thought that this move is properly *Kantian*), but this is precisely how Aristotle characterizes the roots of his own insights in the *Posterior Analytics*:

> consider whether the states [of knowledge] are not present in us but come about in us, or whether they are present but escape notice. Well, if we have them, it is absurd; for it results that we have pieces of knowledge more precise than demonstration and yet escapes notice. But if we get them without having them earlier, how might we become familiar with them and learn them from no pre-existing knowledge? For that is impossible...It is evidently impossible, then, both for us to have them and for them to come about in us when we are ignorant and in no such state at all (*An. Post.* II.19 99b24-b31).

The dilemma Aristotle describes here has to do with concept acquisition. We have concepts, but from where did they arise? Aristotle dismisses a theory of innate ideas, because any kind of 'innatism' must insist that we already have our knowledge even though we are unaware that we have it; according to Aristotle, this possibility is 'absurd.'

Innate ideas are out, but this quote makes it seem as though the possibility that our concepts come 'from no pre-existing knowledge' is out also. So is Aristotle after a third way? Jonathan Barnes complains that this passage is misleading, and Aristotle is not proposing a middle way at all, as it might seem.[27] This is because Aristotle's explicit solution in the remaining text of II.19 is *epagōgē*, where *epagōgē* is a process that instills a kind of universal via perception; these perceptible universals then become the starting points for acquiring real concepts and definitions—*ta noeta*. Hence Aristotle's solution to this dilemma is just straightforwardly empiricist according to Barnes.

I do not wish to enter into the debate about whether Aristotle was an empiricist, for that would require us to get the exact definition of 'empiricism,' which I am not optimistic can be done without real controversy. Instead I will examine the more specific question of whether Aristotle's alleged empiricistic answer to this dilemma is sufficiently like Kant's in its use of spontaneity. Aristotle's doctrine is that *noeta*—real concepts—come to us from the contents of perception. A truly empiricist interpretation would require us to suppose that this process is a kind of abstraction. What must happen is that certain properties must be isolated and abstracted from the sensible objects that are best suited to be the concepts with which our mind is stocked. At this point, it will be useful to call to attention

Kant's criticism of the inability of empiricism to explain cognition, on account of the lack of anything that could give synthesis to the intuited manifold:

> If every individual representation were entirely foreign to the other, as it were isolated and separated from it, then there would never arise anything like cognition, which is a whole of compared and connected representations. If I therefore ascribe a synopsis to sense, because it contains a manifold in its intuition, a synthesis must always correspond to this, and receptivity can make cognitions possible only if combined with spontaneity (A97).

This amounts to a criticism of 'abstraction' since the concepts cannot be abstracted from the sensible perceptions, but must arise spontaneously from the mind's activity and interaction with the sensible manifold. Returning to evolutionary analogies, Kant's criticism is that theories of abstraction are like spontaneous generation, where one thing is supposed to come from something completely different.

I believe that Kant's concern with abstraction is quite similar to Aristotle's. Charles Kahn offers a convincing warning to those who suppose they will find abstraction in Aristotle:

> Such theories miss the point of the Aristotelian claim of a radical difference in kind between concepts (*noēta*) and the information provided in sense perception (*aisthēta*); hence they imagine that the former are presented to us a particular features of the latter and need only be separated out by selective attention. But for Aristotle sense perception can instruct us in conceptual matters only if we already possess, or can *spontaneously supply*, the relevant concepts. This spontaneity is the work of the intellect as an active principle, and is at least notionally different from the act of abstracting and subtracting some properties [in] order to conceive others as separate and distinct.[28]

Nor does Aristotle's rejection of abstraction place him in the rationalist camp. As noted in the passage from the introduction of *An. Post.* II.19, Aristotle does not believe that we 'already possess' the 'relevant concepts.' Again, Kahn:

> The rationalist model simply does not fit [Aristotle's epistemology], since our potential intellect is not stocked at birth with noetic principles and does not acquire them by any act of direct intuition that we can perform. One may...speak of the active intellect as continuously intuiting the forms and essences of the natural world. But we can enjoy such an intuition only to the extent that we succeed in realizing its activity *in our own thought and knowledge*. And this process of learning and exercising science...must be achieved *in our own experience* by the ordinary process of induction and hard work (411, my emphasis).

Because there is nothing like innate ideas, Aristotle's theory cannot be classified as a kind of rationalism. What we discover instead is that Aristotle's epistemology is not at all analogous to spontaneous generation or preformation theory, but rather to epigenesis.

Making a point that anticipated Kant's insights by some 2,500 years, Aristotle insists that we do not simply find our minds stocked with concepts; rather, those concepts arise from our own experience with the world, although they do not come about via abstraction. Kant points out that this makes our possession of them legitimate, not simply subjectively necessary. Aristotle never used the word 'epigenesis,' of course, (not to mention the fact that he considered and rejected any possibility of evolutionary development),[29] but Kant and Aristotle share this model of concept development. Therefore Aristotle comes up with a kind of cognition that is like epigenesis, and very much unlike spontaneous generation or preformation theory. By Kant's own standards, then, Aristotle has come up with an epistemological theory that attains objective validity. This fact is apparently not recognized by Kant.

Notes

1. This translation is Pluhar's. Immanual Kant, *Critique of Pure Reason*, tr. Werner S. Pluhar (Indianapolis: Hackett Publishing Company Inc., 1996). I will indicate when the Pluhar tranlstion is used. When there is no particular translation indicated, it is the Guyer/Wood translation.

2. Cf. B166-7.

3. Tr. Pluhar.

4. This is true only of the varieties of transcendental realism. Kant's system of transcendental idealism does not rely on a causal model for objective validity.

5. 5:401-5:410

6. A27/B43, A42/B59, B68, B71-2, B135, B145, A255/B310.

7. Tr. Pluhar.

8. Merold Westphal suggests understanding this principle via analogy: "the definitions, axioms, and demonstrations which are possible in mathematics result from a direct insight we have into mathematical objects. One might say that we simply read off their properties. But this is possible only because in mathematics we have first constructed or created our objects in spatial or temporal intuition which is pure…a knower whose intuition was creative would have a knowledge of nature like our knowledge of mathematical objects" Merold Westphal, "In Defense of the Thing in Itself, " *Kant-Studien* 59, no.1 (1968): 118-41, 123. Our intuition is creational in mathematics, although there is form without content in this case. So although we don't know what it might be like to create content, at least we know what it is like to create form, and so this analogy may be useful.

9. Tr. Pluhar.

10. See pp. 118-121.

11. In a footnote, Kant adds that 'intuition' could be taken in two ways, for the "form of intuition merely gives the manifold" (B160fn.). This, however, is still not sufficient to account for experience, for the manifold must already be unified in order to be thought. Thus, Kant has recourse to a formal intuition, which "gives unity of the representation" (B160fn.). This means that while sensibility is passive, intuition is not, for "the unity of

this a priori intuition belongs to space and time, and not to the concept of the understanding" (B160fn).

12. This does necessarily rule out any doctrine that can go by the name 'empiricism.' Depending on how one defines empiricism, the empiricist may attribute some kind of spontaneity to the mind.

13. Indeed, that fact that humans do not have the type of intuition that creates its own objects is central to his distinction between the *intellecus archetypi* and the *intellectus ectypi*.

14. And elsewhere Kant makes clear that this is a confusion of representations in general, not merely 'outer appearances': "[t]he realist, in the transcendental signification, makes the modifications of our sensibility into things subsisting in themselves, and hence makes mere representations into things in themselves" (A491/B519).

15. Henry Allison, Henry. *Kant's Transcendental Idealism: An Interpretation and Defense* (New Haven:Yale University Press, 1983), 16.

16. See Allison, pp. 16-25.

17. Allison, 29.

18. Allison, 29.

19. Allison, 29.

20. Allison, 29.

21. Allison, 29.

22. Béatrice Longuenesse, *Hegel's Critique of Metaphysics*, tr. Nicole J. Simek (Cambridge: Cambridge University Press, 2007), 174.

23. Longuenesse, 174, my italics.

24. Longuenesse, 173.

25. Longuenesse ,173.

26. Longuenese, 174.

27. Jonathan Barnes, *Aristotle's Posterior Analytics* (Oxford: Oxford University Press, 1975). See especially pages 259-265.

28. Kahn, 410fn, my emphasis.

29. This is explicitly argued in *Ph.* II.7.

Chapter 8
Gettier and the Problem of Justification

The Gettier Problem and Its Reception

Gettier famously argues that a belief might be true and justified, and yet fail to be an instance of knowledge. This presents an obvious problem for anyone who defines knowledge simply as 'true, justified, belief' (TJB). Gettier makes his argument via two examples, the first of which features a putative knower named Smith who has "strong evidence"[1] for the proposition 'Jones is the man who will get the job,' and also for the proposition 'Jones has 10 coins in his pocket.' In the first case, the strong evidence is that the boss told him that Jones would get the job. In the second case, the evidence is perceptual in nature, as Smith has counted the coins in Jones' pocket. According to Gettier, this strong evidence makes Smith justified in his beliefs, whether or not those beliefs are true; Gettier insists that "it is possible to be justified in believing a proposition that is in fact false."[2] Thus, for Gettier, 'justified' means 'has strong evidence for.' As the example has it, the first proposition is false since Smith, and not Jones, gets the job. The second—the perceptual belief—turns out to be true.

This part of the analysis is not particularly relevant for Aristotle, because as we have seen, Aristotle's *epistēmē* is only gained as a result of a deduction (*syllogismos*). *Epistēmē* cannot be a direct result of perceptual awareness or testimony.[3] So for the sake of comparing Gettier and Aristotle, it is important that Gettier adds a layer to his analysis with the principle of logical entailment. According to the example, Smith sees the entailment from the first two propositions (Ps) to a conclusion (Q), 'The man with 10 coins in his pocket will get the job.' This is another case of true, justified, belief, because entailment preserves justification. In this case, Smith (S) "is justified in believing P, and P entails Q, and S deduces Q from P and accepts Q as a result of this deduction...[and so] S is justified in believing Q."[4] Smith, then, has strong evidence for two propositions, which entail 'The man with 10 coins in his pocket will get the job.' However, in a surprise twist, Smith himself gets the job, and Q is true because unknown to Smith, his pockets contain 10 coins. If knowledge is defined as 'true, justified, belief,' then it may seem that Smith knows that Q. But most people would agree Smith does not know that Q, since Smith was quite surprised to learn *why* the statement 'the man with 10 coins in his pocket will get the job' was true.

Gettier does not mention Aristotle, although he does pin Plato with the TJB analysis. He also cites two contemporary sources that give the TJB analysis, implying that nothing noteworthy had happened to the basic definition of knowledge since Plato, which further implies that Aristotle did not have anything to add to the TJB formula that would necessitate a change in Gettier's examples. Gettier published this paper in 1963, and fifty years of epistemological chaos ensued in the English speaking philosophy world. It was as if the very foundations of epistemology had been overturned, and the world was waking up to a new problem. Apparently, most mainstream philosophers accepted both that the traditional definition of knowledge had been 'true, justified, belief,' and that the Gettier examples present a compelling case that the TJB formula "does not state a *sufficient* condition for someone's knowing a given proposition."[5] I think that the latter statement is true, but the former statement is quite false. This is because 2,500 years earlier, Aristotle had given some Gettier-type examples, specified why these are not examples of knowledge, and then proposed a compelling solution. I will begin, however, with an account of why the Gettier problem, as stated, does not even apply to Aristotle at all.

The Aristotelian Dissolution of the Gettier Problem

The Gettier problem, as stated, is actually quite easy to dissolve. In the first place, many people would not think that Smith knows that 'The man with 10 coins in his pocket will get the job' because this conclusion is based on the false premise 'Jones will get the job.' It does not really matter that Smith accurately saw the entailment from 'Jones will get the job' and 'Jones has 10 coins in his pocket' to 'The man with 10 coins in his pocket will get the job.' In more basic terms, this argument is indeed valid but it is not sound because one of the premises is false. Of course there are many cases where an unsound argument yields a true conclusion, but not many philosophers would expect an unsound argument to deliver something as coveted as knowledge.

This observation is a real problem for Gettier's actual examples. However, it does not require much work to think of Gettier-type examples that have no false premises that still do not yield knowledge. Alvin Goldman thinks of one:

> Henry is driving in the country-side with his son. For the boy's edification Henry identifies various objects on the landscape as they come into view. "That's a cow," says Henry, "That's a tractor," "That's a silo," "That's a barn," etc. Henry has no doubt about the identity of these objects; in particular, he has no doubt that the last-mentioned object is a barn, which indeed it is. Each of the identified objects has features characteristic of its type. Moreover, each object is fully in view, Henry has excellent eyesight, and he has enough time to look at them reasonably carefully, since there is little traffic to distract him.[6]

In this example, Henry identifies the object to which he is pointing as a barn, and in fact, it is. So it is true that it is a barn, Henry believes that it is a barn, and in Gettier's language, Henry has 'strong evidence' for his belief that it is a barn. If we accept the insistence that 'strong evidence' is identical to 'justification,' then this is a case of TJB. But as it turns out in this story, this town has a curious tradition of erecting paper-maché barns. Now, the barn that Henry saw was not one of those fake barns, and so it is true that Henry saw a real barn. However, the strong possibility that he very well could have been looking at a paper-maché barn and was only lucky that he was not is enough to make most people withdraw our conclusion that Henry has knowledge that the thing in front of his is a barn.

We are getting closer, but this still does not state a Gettier-style example that is relevant for Aristotle, as it is fairly simple for Aristotle to dissolve this problem. Given his restrictions on *epistēmē*, it is easy to explain how a knowledge claim could result from a sound, deductive argument and neverthe-less fail to be an instance of *epistēmē*. This is because for Aristotle, only a demonstration (*apodeixis*) yields *epistēmē*, and a deduction (*syllogismos*) is not necessarily a demonstration[7]; in the first case, a deduction is not a demonstration it if is not based on appropriate principles. Aristotle makes this doctrine clear after giving certain criteria for demonstration: "there will be deduction [*syllogismos*] even without these conditions, but there will not be demonstration [*apodeixis*]; for it will not produce *epistēmē*" (*Post. An.* 71b23-24). By 'these conditions,' Aristotle is referring to the requirement that the deduction must be based on appropriate principles:

> If, then, *epistēmē* is as we posited, it is necessary for demonstrative knowledge in particular to depend on things which are true and primitive and immediate and more familiar than and prior to and explanatory of the conclusion (for in this way the principles will also be appropriate to what is being proved (*An. Post.* I.2 71b20-23).

These criteria for principles—that they must be true, primitive, immediate, prior to the conclusion, etc., have been explored at length elsewhere.[8] The point here is that any argument that is not based on these principles will not yield *epistēmē* for the very reason that it is not based on these principles. Aristotle warns about the folly of ignoring this important feature of *epistēmē*:

> It is clear too that those people are silly who think they get their principles cor-rectly if the proposition is reputable and true (e.g., the sophists who assume that to understand is to have understanding). For it is not what is reputable or not that is a principle, but what is primitive in the genus about which the proof is; and not every truth is appropriate (*An. Post.* I.6 74b22-26).

This is an obvious reference to the two possibilities for premises—*archē* and *endoxa*. Many arguments appropriately begin with *endoxa*, but these are dialec-tical arguments that end in a sort of knowledge,[9] but they do not end in *epistēmē*. As such, a person who expects *epistēmē* to issue from arguments that rely on *endoxa* is 'silly.'

It is this sort of thinking that gives rise to the general Aristotelian critique of the Gettier problem. The way to dissolve the Gettier problem from Aristotle's perspective is to argue that in his examples, Gettier deduces the fact, but he does not demonstrate the reason why, simply because his examples do not begin with *archē*:

Knowing [*epistathai*] the fact [*to oti*] and the reason why [*to dioti*] differ, first in the same science—and in that in two ways: in one way, if the deduction [*sullogismos*] does not come about through immediates [*di' ameson*] (for the primitive explanation is not assumed, but knowledge of the reason why occurs in virtue of the primitive explanation [*proton aition*]) (*An. Post.* I.13 78a23-26)

For Aristotle, a deduction that is not based on the immediate principles cannot yield *epistēmē*, even if the deduction in question is sound. If it did not start in the right place, it cannot end in the right place. Gettier clearly does not even attempt to make his premises anything like the first principles that Aristotle requires for a demonstration of the reason why, and hence for *epistēmē*. Hence, if we allow Aristotle to be the one giving the conditions, Gettier's examples do *not* in fact satisfy all the conditions for knowledge and yet fail to yield knowledge, as his article claims.

'That It Is,' 'Why It Is'

I think it is true that Aristotle's epistemology dissolves the Gettier problem because Gettier does not try to use first principles. But perhaps all this talk of principles is distracting; perhaps it is not fair to Gettier simply to point out that Aristotle restricts *epistēmē* to claims made on the basis of principles. This makes it seem as though Aristotle is talking about apples and Gettier is talking about oranges, and thus comparison is not appropriate here. I think this is a worthwhile complaint, but one that has a clear response, for in I.13 of the *Posterior Analytics*, Aristotle actually gives two examples of arguments that do not have principles, but their lack of principles is not what accounts for their failure to yield *epistēmē*. This allows us to compare Aristotle and Gettier directly, since they would be talking about the same thing in this case.

I will take a circuitous route to explain that observation, because the full explanation begins elsewhere in the *Posterior Analytics*; Aristotle begins its second book by announcing that "the things we seek are equal in number to those we know [*epistametha*]. We seek four things: the fact [*to hoti*], the reason why [*to dioti*], if it is [*ei esti*], what it is [*ti estin*]" (*An. Post.* II.1 89b23-24).[10] Aristotle attempts to clarify these remarks by giving an example of each of the four. In the course of these examples, we also learn that Aristotle intends that there are two pairs of knowledge claims here, and each pair has an initial part and a latter part:

For when we seek whether it is this or this...(e.g., whether the sun is eclipsed or not), we seek the fact [*to hoti*]. Evidence for this: on finding that it is eclipsed we stop; and if from the start we know that it is eclipsed, we do not seek whether it is. When we know the fact we seek the reason why (e.g., knowing that it is eclipsed and that the earth moves, we seek the reason why it is eclipsed or why it moves). Now while we seek these things in this way, we seek some things in another way—e.g., if a centaur or a god is or is not (I mean if one is or is not simpliciter and not if one is white or not). And knowing that it is, we seek what it is [*ti estin*] (e.g., so what is a god? Or what is a man?) (*An. Post.* II.1 89b25-35).

The fact and the reason why are related because only when we are aware of a fact may we seek the reason why it is the way it is. Of course, there is no requirement that we must go on. In fact, most people would not care to. This may be the very difference between a philosopher and a non-philosopher ('philosopher' understood in the broadest sense, to include all those who practice theoretical and/or certain practical disciplines). A philosopher would be the sort of person who would go on to ask, "What explains this state of affairs?," whereas a non-philosopher would just accept the state of affairs as given.

Similarly, the 'if it is' and the 'what it is' are related because when we are aware that something is, then we may seek to know what it is. The most important difference between these two pairs is the 'the that' and 'the reason why' are different ways to cognize some state of affairs, such as that the sun is eclipsed. The 'if it is' and the 'what it is' are two ways to cognize substances; Aristotle here uses stranger examples than usual, as 'centaur' and 'god' replace his standard 'horse' and 'man' (perhaps centaurs and gods are fancier versions of horses and men). But the relation between the two kinds of cognitions are the same in both cases—if we know that a horse is, then we are in position to seek what it is. I will here submit but not argue that this maps on very closely to what I have elsewhere called a 'perceptible universal' and a 'definitional universal,' respectively, where knowledge of a perceptible universal is the knowledge that this *is* a substance in its own right and *has* some definition; now, at least, we know that there is something to seek. As such, we cannot seek the definitional universal without knowing the perceptible universal. And knowledge of a definitional universal is knowledge of what it is to be that substance.

There is strong evidence that this passage (II.1) is referred to implicitly when Aristotle addresses the topic of definition a few sections later in II.10. Aristotle's theory of definition has been discussed elsewhere,[11] but these remarks at II.10 do not seem to fit in with his more well-developed theory of definition. For Aristotle elsewhere has carefully used the word '*horismos*' as a specific word to indicate the 'what it is to be' of a substance, and reserves '*ti estin*' for a more general kind of definition. As I argued, these two kinds of definitions will often be used simultaneously as first principles for demonstrations in natural science. But in this passage, Aristotle says that there are at least three kinds of *horismoi*, and only one of them is a definition of a substance, appropriate for use as a first principle of demonstration: "the definition of immediates [*ho ameson horismos*] is an undemonstrable [*anapodeiktos*] positing of what they are. One definition, therefore, is an undemonstrable account [*anapodeiktos logos*] of what a thing is..." (*An. Post.* II.10 94a10-13). This is an unambiguous reference to the first principles that are gained by *epagōgē* and apprehended by *nous*, and what Aristotle throughout his corpus simply calls *horismos*.

In these lines of II.10 and throughout the corpus, a *horsimos* just is an 'undemonstrable account' of what it is to be a substance. Here, however, there are at least two other kinds of *horismoi*, the first of which has been traditionally called a 'nominal definition,' and reasonably so, given Aristotle's description:[12]

> Since a definition [*horismos*] is said to be an account [*logos*] of what a thing is [*ti esti*], it is evident that one type will be an account of what the name [*to onoma*], or a different name-like account [*logos onomatōdēs*], signifies [*sēmainei*]—e.g., what triangle signifies. And when we grasp that this is [*hoti esti*], we seek why it is [*dia ti estin*]; but it is difficult to grasp in this way why a thing is if we do not know that it is. The explanation of the difficulty has been stated already—that we do not even know whether it is or not, except accidentally [*kata sumbebēkos*]. (An account is a unity in two ways—either by connection, like the *Illiad*, or by making one thing clear of one thing non-accidentally. Thus one definition of definition is the one stated...[this] type of definition signifies [*sēmainei*] but does not prove [*deiknusi*] (*An. Post.* I.10 93b29-94a1).

The first definition of definition discussed in both II.1 and II.10 is the 'that it is.' A central feature of II.1 was that there were two pairs of knowledge claims—one pair for states of affairs and one pair for substances. Now, Aristotle appears to be loosening that distinction, as the 'that is it' is a precursor not to 'what it is,' but more generally 'why it is.' Thus, the distinction between methods regarding states of affairs and substances does not persist. In II.1, Aristotle's example is being aware 'that the sun is eclipsed.' In II.10, Aristotle says that this is a 'name-like account;' and this account 'signifies but does not prove.' The question is whether Aristotle develops this distinction between the nominal definition (the fact) and the reason why in a way that would be useful for solving the Gettier problem. When put this way, it is now possible to see that this is the very distinction that Aristotle has already developed in A.13.

Demonstrations Based on Principles, but Lacking Explanations

Aristotle goes on in *Posterior Analytics* I.13 to explain why the difference between 'the fact' and 'why it is' is epistemologically important:

> Knowing [*epistathai*] the fact [*to oti*] and the reason why [*to dioti*] differ, first in the same science—and in that in two ways: in one way, if the deduction [*sullogismos*] does not come about through immediates [*di' ameson*] (for the primitive explanation is not assumed, but knowledge of the reason why occurs in virtue of the primitive explanation [*proton aition*]); another if it is through immediates but not through the explanation but through the more familiar of the converting terms. For nothing prevents the nonexplanatory one of the

counterpredicated terms from being more familiar, *so that demonstration will occur through this* (*An. Post.* I.13 78a23-29, my italics).

It is important to note that there are three kinds of sound deduction implied in this passage: 1) a deduction that is not a demonstration at all, 2) a demonstration that issues in an explanation, and 3) a demonstration that does not issue in an explanation. The first possibility results in a deduction of the fact, and is what happens when the deduction is not based on principles, as has been discussed. The second is a demonstration of the reason why, and the third is a demonstration of the fact. It is not very controversial that 2) results in *epistēmē*.[13] *Epistēmē* is usually a direct result of demonstration, but as we learn in this passage, there is an important subtlety: it is possible to have a demonstration that does something less than deliver true knowledge. This is a somewhat of a surprise, since Aristotle does not hint at this possibility anywhere else in his corpus, but he is sufficiently clear about it here. Specifically, the possibility he introduces is that a demonstration may be of the fact and not a demonstration of the reason why. Furthermore, this third kind of sound deduction can be sub-divided into 3a) and 3b), where we have 3a) a demonstration that does not issue in an explanation *even though it is based on principles*, and 3b) a demonstration that does not issue in an explanation, *whether or not it is based on principles*. In the present section, I focus on 3a); 3b) deserves its own section, since it has direct relevance to the solution of the Gettier problem.

If it is true that there are three kinds of sound deductions referred to in I.13, then there are two kinds of pseudo-explanations—merely apparent demonstrations that are actually deductions of the fact, and non-explanatory demonstrations, i.e. demonstrations of the fact. The first kind of pseudo-explanation does not come through 'the immediates,'[14] i.e., is not based on first principles. In the second part of the passage at 78a, Aristotle mentions the second kind: a fact is demonstrated, but the demonstration fails to deliver the reason why, i.e., the explanation. This is possible because the demonstration may come about "through immediates but not through the explanation but through the more familiar of the converting terms" (*An. Post.* 78a26-27). In this case, there *is* demonstration, since the deduction comes through principles (although as we will see, there is another version of this same problem that does not involve principles). And because there is demonstration of the fact, there is 'knowledge' of the fact in a certain sense, but lacking explanation, it is not *epistēmē*.[15]

The first example of demonstration through immediates but without explanation that Aristotle gives concerns twinkling heavenly bodies:

E.g., that the planets are near, through their not twinkling: let C be the planets, B not twinkling, A being near. Thus it is true to say B of C; for the planets do not twinkle. But also to say A of B; for what does not twinkle is near (let this be got through induction or through perception). So it is necessary that A belongs to C; so that it has been demonstrated that the planets are near. Now this deduction is not of the reason why but of the fact; for it is not because they do

not twinkle that they are near, but because they are near they do not twinkle
(*An. Post.* I.13 78a30-a37.

The demonstration of the fact is based on a principle gained through induction:
"All things that do not twinkle are near." Based on this principle, if it is observed that planets do not twinkle, then it is demonstrated that the plants are
near. This is a fact, and it is deduced by taking 'non-twinkling' as the middle
term.

There is, however, no explanation here (at least according to Aristotle), and
this is because 'it is not because they do not twinkle that they are near, but because they are near they do not twinkle.' This means that the principle of
knowledge here should be "Things do not twinkle because they are near," which
implies that "All things that are near do not twinkle." This yields the conclusion
"Planets do not twinkle," which is explained by the principle and also by the
premise that "The planets are near." Thus, 'being near' is the middle-term. This
is the sense in which the explanation of "The planets are non-twinkling things"
comes through the proper middle term:

> But it is also possible for the latter to be proved through the former, and the
> demonstration will be of the reason why—e.g., let C be the planets, B being
> near, A not twinkling. Thus B belongs to C and A to B; so that A belongs to C.
> And the deduction is of the reason why; for the primitive explanation has been
> assumed (*An. Post.* I.13 78a30-78b2).

Even if Aristotle's particular example is distracting, his intent is clear: it is possible to demonstrate a fact without thereby giving an explanation of it. And significantly, this demonstration of the fact can be turned into a demonstration of
the reason why simply by reversing the conclusion and one of the premises, all
while retaining the first principle of the demonstration.

Aristotle's Solution to the Gettier Problem

This still does not get us to Gettier's problem, because thus far in *Posterior
Analytics* I.13, Aristotle is still describing arguments based on principles gained
by *egagōgē*. But there are other demonstrations that fail to deliver knowledge
owing to the inappropriateness of the middle term exclusively: "again, in cases
in which the middle is positioned outside—for in these too the demonstration is
of the fact and not of the reason why; for the explanation is not mentioned" (*An.
Post.* I.13 78b14-15). This is a problem that might affect an argument regardless
of whether that argument is based on principles, since the problem has nothing
to do with principles. In these cases, the explanation is not forthcoming because
the middle term—the term that is supposed to disappear by the conclusion, is
somehow positioned too far away.

To the examples themselves: the important feature of them that makes them directly comparable to Gettier-type examples is that they are epistemologically problematic, but not because they are not based on principles. Like the twinkling planet example, Aristotle says that this still counts as demonstration, because the fact is still *proved* or *demonstrated*, but "the reason why is not" (I.13 78b12). This is so because the demonstration occurs through 'the nonexplanatory one of the counterpredicated terms' (I.13 78a28-29). The first example is:

> Why does the wall not breathe? Because it is not an animal...The deduction of such an explanation comes about in the middle figure. E.g., let A be animal, B breathing, C wall: then A belongs to every B (for everything breathing is an animal), but to no C, so that B belongs to C—therefore the wall does not breathe. Explanations of this sort resemble those that are extravagantly stated (that consists in arguing by setting the middle term too far away) (*An. Post.* I.13 78b15-30).

The problem here is not that the terms in the principle are converted, as in the first case, for the principle is "All breathing things are animals," but it is false that "All animals are breathing things."[16] So converting the terms in the principles would give a false premise, and it is not a consideration that an unsound argument may produce *epistēmē*. Nor is it a problem that this is a deduction and not a demonstration, for this argument is based in principles. Rather, the problem is that the middle term is set 'too far away.' Here, the middle term is 'animal,' since the second premise is that 'No walls are animals.' The image of being too far away has to do with the connection between 'walls' and 'animals;' more premises need to be added in order to make this connection. Aristotle's second example makes this clearer.

Another instance of this problem occurs in an argument that Aristotle attributes to Anacharsis: "there are no flute-girls in Scyths, for there are no vines" (*An. Post.* I.13 78b31). Here again, the argument is not based on principles, but that is not the problem Aristotle instead, highlights the fact that "explanations of this sort...are extravagantly stated (that consists in arguing by setting the middle term too far away)" (*An. Post.* I.13 78b29-30). The argument, informally reconstructed, would apparently be that 'there are no vines in Scyths; there are no flute-girls where there are no vines; therefore there are no flute-girls in Scyths.' This is a valid argument, and let's pretend that the premises are true. That makes this a sound argument with a middle term "vines." There is thus a deduction of 'there are no flute-girls in Scyths,' and if someone believes it for the stated reasons, then that person has true, justified, belief that 'there are no flute-girls in Scyths.'

According to Aristotle's epistemology, however, a proposition must not simply be justified; the question of justification is a question of deduction, and deduction is a necessary but not sufficient condition for knowledge. What Aristotelian *epistēmē* demands is an appropriate middle term, for the explanation is supposed to come through it. So does the term 'vines' in any way explain how the facts entail the conclusion? Aristotle correctly says 'no,' because this argument does not offer an explanation of the reason why there are no flute-girls in Scyths; in his terminology, this is a demonstration of the fact but not a demonstration of the reason why; here, the reason is that the middle term is positioned 'too far away' from the other terms in the sense that the connection between terms as it is does not explain anything. A person could be justified in believing the facts, could see the entailment of the conclusion, but might still lack knowledge according to Aristotle. The real explanation would involve quite a few more premises, such as where there are no vines there is no wine, where there is no wine there are no drunken parties, and where there are no drunken parties there are no flute-girls, for that is sort of entertainment requested by the inebriated. It would take all of those facts before we had any kind of explanation of why there are no flute-girls in Scyths.

Conclusion

What is noteworthy is that 2,500 years before Gettier shook the analytical world by pointing out the truth, justification, and belief are not sufficient conditions for knowledge, Aristotle insisted on precisely the same point. Aristotle makes two distinctions—between the fact and the reason why, and between a demonstration and a deduction. There are then three sorts of sound deductions— a deduction of the fact, a demonstration of the reason why, and a demonstration of the fact (there is no deduction of the fact). The first type of deduction is not based on principles, so it cannot be a demonstration, and hence, cannot yield knowledge. The third does yield the reason why, regardless of whether it is based on principles, and when Aristotle points to examples of these arguments that are not based on principles, they are reminiscent of Gettier's problem, in that there is true, justified belief, but not *epistēmē*. Gettier merely recognizes this problem; Aristotle recognizes this problem, and also solves it. It is quite difficult to critique an essay from all directions two and a half millennia before its publication. Given that Aristotle was able to do that to Gettier, there are at least two lessons here: first, at least some of Aristotle's theoretical doctrines have contemporary relevance, and second, that relevance is at least sometimes dramatically under-appreciated. It is my hope that this work leaves no question about this.

Notes

1. Edmund Gettier, "Is Justified True Belief Knowledge?" *Analysis* 23, no. 6 (June 1963): 121-132, 121.
2. Gettier, 121.
3. See pp. 20-24.
4. Gettier,121.
5. Gettier, 123.

6. Alvin Goldman, "Discrimination and Perceptual Knowledge," *The Journal of Philosophy* 73, no. 20 (November 1976): 771-791, 772.

7. See pp. 24-26.

8. See chapter 2.

9. See pp. 21-24.

10. Given the rest of the corpus, we cannot have 'knowledge' (*epistēmē*) of these four things, for *epistēmē* is carefully reserved to refer to the material, efficient, and sometimes final causes of substances However, I think we should not make too much of this wording, for Aristotle elsewhere draws a sharp distinction between 'to know' (*epistathai*) and actually 'to have knowledge' (*to epistēmēn echein*)—that is, genuinely to possess *epistēmē*—such that Aristotle can speak of a person 'knowing' without committing to say that the person has real *epistēmē*.

11. See pp. 81-83.

12. There is at least one notable exception, namely W.D. Ross, although Barnes has a convincing explanation of why Ross should fall in with the tradition on this point (222).

13. This is just Aristotle's definition of *epistēmē*.

14. See pp. 43-46 for why the principles of demonstration can also be called immediates.

15. Again, given Aristotle's other uses of *doxa*, it would have been an acceptable word here, although Aristotle does not opt for it.

16. *An. Post.* 78b22.

Chapter 9
Descartes and the Problem of External World Skepticism

Descartes' Argument

Descartes is concerned that there is no logical way to eliminate the possibility that what he assumes to be experience had while awake is actually dreaming experience, entirely conjured up by one's own mind. In itself, dreams are not deceptive, but they are deceptive to us if we believe that the dream we are currently having is taking place external to our mind.[1]

> How often have I dreamt that I was in these familiar circumstance, - that I was dressed, and occupied this place by the fire, when I was lying undressed in bed? At the present moment, however, I certainly look upon this paper with eyes wide awake; the head which I now move is not asleep; I extend this hand consciously and with express purpose, and I perceive it; the occurrences in sleep are not distinct as all this (23).[2]

This passage introduced two relevant observations. The first is that it is possible to make systematic assumptions about the character of our experiences, yet be completely mistaken about this. This, at least, occurs when we are dreaming. The second observation is that we usually do not have (or even entertain) the concern that we are currently undergoing such a systematic deception. However, this lack of concern is philosophically unimportant, because we also have this same lack of concern while we actually are dreaming; that is, we are unconcerned about this possibility at the very moment when are in fact undergoing systematic deception.

What follows from these observations is a conclusion about discrimination:

> But I cannot forget that, at other times, I have been deceived in sleep by similar illusions; and, attentively considering those cases, I perceive so clearly that there exist no certain marks by which the state of waking can ever be distinguished from sleep, that I feel greatly astonished; and in amazement I almost I almost persuade myself that I am now dreaming (23-24).

This is importantly different than seeing a straight stick in the water (e.g.) and believing it to be bent. The relevant difference is that this deception is not systematic. That is, we are deceived about this, but this is only one part of our experience. Since there are other features of our experience, it is very well possible that I may be able to use other features of my experience to give me clues about the deception. For instance, I may observe that the things around the stick are not bent, or my judgment may conflict with other beliefs I have, or with the judgments of those around me, etc. The point is that there are any number of ways to draw my attention to this optical illusion.

This is quite unlike the scenario of Descartes' thought experiment. In the dreaming case, all the features of my experience are caught in this deception to an equal degree. The implication is that I cannot appeal to any feature of my experience to relieve me of my deception. Such features, as noted, are extremely important because they serve as marks that may distinguish or discriminate the truth from the deception. In this case, we have the state of dreaming and the state of waking experience; Descartes notes that "there exist no certain marks by which the state of waking can ever be distinguished from sleep" (23-24). I take it that this inability to distinguish is what really gives the dreamer argument its force.

There are two drawbacks to this kind of argument. The first is that there may actually be possible to develop some distinguishing marks. For instance, the dream might manifest irregularities that tip off the dreamer to fact that it is a dream. In a similar example, some characters in the movie the *Matrix* were able to tell a difference between reality and the computer program they were in by finding 'glitches' in the computer program known as the Matrix.[3] The second insufficiency with the dreamer argument is that it leaves unchallenged certain ideas that do not rely on experience—the obvious instances being from mathematics:

> We will not, therefore, perhaps reason illegitimately if we conclude from this that Physics, Astronomy, Medicine, and all the other sciences that have for their end the consideration of composite objects, are indeed of a doubtful character; but that Arithmetic, Geometry, and the other sciences of the same class...contain somewhat that is certain and indubitable: for whether I am awake or dreaming, it remains true that two and three make five, and that a square has but four sides; nor does it seem possible that truths so apparent can ever fall under a suspicion of falsity [or certitude] (25).

And so the dreamer argument only addresses ideas gained by perception; furthermore, it leaves the possibility that there might be some features of the perceptual experience that give us a clue about our deception.

I do not regard the first problem as really serious, for Descartes could just point out that *sometimes* there are no features of the dream or the computer program that allow us to distinguish between what is real and the deception, and we only must be concerned that we *sometimes* may be deceived. Nevertheless, this response is unnecessary, because Descartes' second thought experiment sufficiently addresses this concern and also the other one about mathematical ideas:

> The belief that there is a God who is all-powerful, and who created me, such as I am, has, for a long time, obtained a steady possession of my mind. How, then, do I know that he has not arranged that there should be neither earth, nor sky, not any extended thing, nor figure, nor magnitude, nor place, providing at the same time, however, for [the rise in me of the perceptions of all these objects,

and] the persuasion that these do not exist otherwise than as I perceive them? (25)

Now, instead of a dream, we are considering the possibility of being systematically deceived by a so-called 'evil genius.' First of all, this deception may be systematically perfect (at least an omniscient being could make it so), so that there are no distinguishing 'glitches.' But more importantly, an omniscient being of this sort would be able to poison my mind in such a way that I might accept 'four' as the answer for 'two plus three.' How could an epistemologist respond to such a logical possibility?

A Possible Aristotelian Response

Descartes' own solution, that an omnipotent being exists and could not be a deceiver, has enough important problems that it is not accepted as a plausible solution. But at least it *would* have been a solution; it is quite difficult to think of what form a possible solution could take. Because the real problem is about discrimination between other logically possible 'realities,' the putative knower must be able to distinguish his set of experiences from each alternate reality, each time he makes a judgment.

There are two responses that could be developed from Aristotle's work, only one of which I believe to be a response that Aristotle would actually endorse. It is possible to speak of a response in this case because Aristotle was not unaware of external-world skepticism.[4] One response could be based on a casual reading of the following passage, which might suggest that Aristotle's actual response is just to label any kind of external-world skepticism as 'absurd:'

> That nature exists, it would be absurd to try to prove; for it is obvious that there are many things of this kind, and to prove what is obvious by what is not is the mark of a man who is unable to distinguish what is self-evident from what is not. (This state of mind is clearly possible. A man blind from birth might reason about colors. Presumably therefore such persons must be talking about words without any thought to correspond) (*Ph.* II.1 193a4-9).

One plausible way to read this quote is that Aristotle is simply dismissing skepticism. He does appear to be addressing the strongest reconstruction of external-world skepticism, since he here recognizes that the central problem is really discrimination; but as he puts it, the skeptic is the one who cannot "distinguish what is self-evident from what is not" (lines 4-5). He proposes that this is analogous to a person born blind who reasons about colors.[5] He thus turns the point about discrimination around entirely on Descartes; instead of insisting that the evil demon hypothesis leaves us without a way to discriminate the demon-controlled world from a demon-free one, Aristotle says that such arguments show the ignorance of the skeptic.

On this interpretation, Aristotle simply starts with what is 'self-evident,' and dismisses any possibilities that are not self-evident if they would undermine the self-evident. This seems to be what G.E. Moore has in mind when he objects to skepticism on similar grounds: it is quite obvious that my hand is in front of my face, and so any skeptical argument that insists that I do not know if my hand is in front of my face has already condemned itself.[6] Likewise, it may appear that Aristotle is simply insisting that it is 'obvious' that nature exists.

However, I think he I making quite a different point in this passage—what he is referring to here is the distinction between kinds of dialectic. Aristotle is saying that it is absurd for the person who is trying to use dialectic to discover the definition of magnitude, for example, to attempt to prove that magnitude exists. As I argued elsewhere,[7] there is a difference between being a dialectician of the principles of *phusis* and being a dialectician of the principles of what must be assumed in order to engage in dialectic about *phusis*. Aristotle clearly endorses the method of dialectic is physics, as he himself engage in the process many times over in the *Physics*. However, there is a time and a place to suspend one's belief in what is obvious, and to give philosophical reasons in support of the obvious. This, of course, is entirely different than Moore's anti-skeptical method. Of course, Aristotle does not address anything like Cartesian skepticism, but he does indeed address the theory that insists that even though nature appears to have parts in motion, this appearance is deceiving:

> Now to investigate whether what exists is one and motionless is not a contribution to the science of nature...at the same time the holders of the theory of which we are speaking do incidentally raise physical questions, though nature is not their subject; so it will perhaps be as well to spend a few words on them, especially as their inquiry is not without scientific interest (*Ph.* I.2 184b26-185a20).

In this passage, Aristotle does say very clearly that an evaluation of monism is not useful for inquiry in physics; it should not, however, be entirely dismissed. I believe that the quote that seems to dismiss skepticism as 'absurd' at *Ph.* 193a4-9 is best read in this context. That is, he is not saying that arguments that attempt to undermine what is 'obvious' should never be addressed, only that they should not be addressed by the person engaging in an inquiry that presupposes what it obvious. So, for instance, if we were having a discussion about what magnitude might be, and Parmenides' ghost came into our midst to interrupt our inquiry with this challenge—'But how do you *know* that magnitude even exists?'—we would appropriately dismiss his question as absurd. We must rather presuppose the existence of magnitude in order to inquiry into its nature. But obviously, Aristotle does not suggest *never* addressing this kind of skepticism. He does so himself explicitly in the *Physics*, prefaced with the observation that "it will perhaps be as well to spend a few words on them, especially as their inquiry is not without scientific interest" (*Ph.* I.2 185a19-20).

Externalism and Internalism

External-world skepticism has generated many dozens of proposals from those who wish to remain optimistic about knowledge while recognizing the force of such arguments, and many of those responses have very little to do with each other except that they are responses to the same threat. But many of them do share a commonality, namely, that they are variations of externalism.[8] Dretske illustrates externalism (which he endorses) with an example. The knowledge claim, here, is the perfectly ordinary claim that there are cookies in the cookie jar in front of me. The skeptic, of course, will introduce any number of scenarios in which a condition exists that makes things other than what they seem; however:

> I do not have to know that no such condition exists for me to see that there are cookies in the cookie jar. If I had to know that no such condition existed in order to see whether there are cookies in the jar, there would be precious little, if anything, I could ever come to know by seeing. If there is, unknown to us, a Cartesian demon at work in the universe, deceiving us in random, unpredictable ways, we do not know much, if anything, about the world. Even when we are right (the evil demon doesn't fool us all the time), we don't know. Skepticism is true. Externalism tells us that whether or not skepticism is true, whether or not we know, depends not on our knowing there is no such demon, but on there not being one. That is something we may not know at all. It isn't even clear that we could know it...Indeed, if one is going to avoid skepticism, [externalism] seems to me inevitable.[9]

The move externalism makes is quite simple, but if it works, it makes all the difference. Cartesian skepticism hangs on the concept of discrimination; our failure to discriminate the reality that we believe ourselves to be in from other logical possible realities is thought to introduce skepticism.

This, however, only follows if we are responsible as knowers to discriminate this reality from others. 'Internalism' is the position that would insist that we have such a responsibility, and thus, we must *know* that we *know*, so to speak.[10] Thus, if internalism is true, we can only know that there are cookies in the cookie jar in front of us if we also know that we are not dreaming or being deceived by an evil genius, etc. The appeal of internalism is that it is more faithful to the traditional goals of epistemology; surely we do not know anything at all if we do not know whether we are being deceived by an evil genius. The appeal of externalism is that it sidesteps external-world skepticism without much effort. And, what is appealing about one theory is precisely what is unappealing about the other.

Goldman, a leading critic of internalism, believes that internalism is committed to the 'guidance-deontological' (GD) conception of justification. The 'guidance' idea is that justification is supposed to show us or guide us to confirm or reject certain beliefs. The 'deontological' element adds that we have a duty to believe what we are guided to believe. It is difficult (although not impossible) to separate these concepts because "the deontological conception, at least when paired with the guidance conception, considers it a person's epistemic duty to guide his doxastic attitudes by his evidence..."[11] As Goldman sees it, this is the commitment of internalism in general. This commitment implies that "the constraint that all justification determiners must be *accessible to*, or *knowable by*, the epistemic agent,"[12] which in turn implies what Goldman calls the knowability constraint on justifiers: "The only facts that qualify as justifiers of an agent's believing *p* at time *t* are facts that the agent can readily know, at *t*, to obtain or not to obtain."[13] There is a strong contrast with externalism on this point; externalism, as Dretske puts it, does not depend on knowing that there is no evil genius, but simply on there not being an evil genius. Clearly, this does not require any facts about an evil genius to be accessible to an epistemic agent—a strict requirement for an internalist.

The problem for internalism, as Goldman sees it, comes when the internalist must make sense of the kind of accessibility or knowability that must obtain of justifiers. The problem is a classic too much/too little dilemma. If internalism requires that the knowability be a strong kind, then there would be very little (or nothing at all) that we know, since many of our beliefs are in the form of memories. But if one goes the other way and allows this knowability to be weak in order to let in ordinary knowledge claims, this would avoid the more obvious skeptical problems, but only at the price of accepting many external forms of justification. Goldman believes that this dooms internalism.

This dilemma may be illustrated by an example that Goldman gives, of Sally, who has read about the health benefits of broccoli in the *New York Times* 'Science' section.[14] She then forms a belief about the health benefits of broccoli, which according to Goldman, is justified belief because she obtained her belief by reading a reliable source. Now, let's say that years later Sally has retained the belief in broccoli's health benefits, but has forgotten how she came by her belief about these health benefits. If the knowability required by internalism were strong, then Sally would no longer qualify as a knower about the health benefits of broccoli, because she has no direct access to her justification. If the internalist is willing to weaken the knowability standards a little (as Goldman thinks is appropriate), and allow the past acquisition to be a legitimate justifier, then the internalist has appealed to external standards. Hence, internalism fails, either because it leads inevitably to skepticism or to externalism.

Aristotle on Reliable Methods

Goldman allows another possibility, namely, to abandon the assumption that the accessibility in question be universal, and instead interpret the constraints as relativized to a particular agent. But Goldman rejects even this possibility:

If KJ constraints [the knowability constraints on justifiers] are agent relativized as a function of the differences in knowledge skills, this means that two people in precisely the same evidential state (in terms of perceptual situation, background beliefs, and so on) might have different epistemic entitlements...If one's epistemic duties or entitlements depend on one's knowledge skills...then compliance with one's duties requires knowledge of which skill one possesses. There are two problems with this approach. First, it is unlikely that many people—especially ordinary people on the street—have this sort of knowledge, and this again threatens large scale skepticism. Second, what is now required to be known by the agent is something about the truth-getting power of her cognitive skills—that is, the power of her skills in detecting justifiers. This seems to be precisely the sort of external property that internalist regard as anathema. How can they accept this solution while remaining faithful to the spirit of internalism?[15]

I believe that this quote does much to vindicate Aristotle's general views on knowledge. In chapter 1, I gave ten examples of statements about which we often say we know.[16] I then explained why nearly none of those count as instances of Aristotelian *epistēmē*. This is because Aristotle limits *epistēmē* to cases in which there is a demonstration that explains, carried out on the basis of first principles, and in the context of a science that is a theoretical science. I cautioned against the predictable reaction, which is to see these conditions as too restrictive. Perhaps, I suggested, these restrictions on *epistēmē* actually helpfully fortify knowledge from the attacks of skepticism.[17]

Goldman's remarks are instructive in this regard. Consider his reasons why agent-relativized knowability fails: 1) 'people on the street' will not have the requisite kind of self-reflective knowledge, and 2) the agent must know the reliability of her truth-getting skills, which looks much more like externalism than internalism. The second possibility may work quite well (and there is reason to believe Goldman himself endorses it), although it will not work for internalism, since it allows external constraints on justification. His first reason is that agent-relativized knowability violates Goldman's belief that knowledge is a pedestrian concept.

What has Aristotle said that is relevant for both of these problems? Consider Goldman's first reason. For Aristotle, *epistēmē* is not a mundane concept, even though *doxa* may be. This is because claims to *epistēmē* have very specific restraints, as noted, such that it is perfectly conceivable that a rational adult person may not have one bit of *epistēmē*. It is of course possible to have *doxa* about perceptual beliefs such as the cookies in the cookie jar, but that claim cannot be *epistēmē*. Goldman seems to think it is obvious that whatever knowledge is, regular people have it. Goldman does not specify what a person on the street may or may not know, but he would probably agree that a person on the street is not someone who is trained in the philosophical sciences (i.e., theoretical and practical sciences, although not productive). Thus, this person would not be well-versed in the methods necessary to obtain truths in that area. Aristotle, on the other hand, takes it as obvious that knowledge is only the result of a mind devoted to strict methods; to emphasize that this is supposed to be 'obvious,' he contextualizes many of his central epistemic claims by referring to *endoxa*, indicating that many of his views about knowledge are actually attempts to explain what is often said about knowledge.[18]

Goldman's second reason is that agent-relativized knowability commits one to externalism, because now we must consider justifiers legitimate even if they are not accessible to the agent. I do not feel particularly inclined to label Aristotle an 'internalist' or an 'externalist,' but I think it is worth noting that Aristotle's obsession with reliable methods far exceeds anything in contemporary epistemology. In fact, it is pretty obvious that someone seeking *epistēmē* must be thoroughly familiar with 'truth-getting' skills, to use Goldman's phrase. It would be quite inappropriate to start making claims of *epistēmē* unsystematically, or without a method. Instead, there is the method of *epagōgē*, which when followed correctly, results in *nous*. Then there is dialectic, which requires intense philosophical training, not to mention the method of demonstration, which depends on *nous* and is complicated enough to merit its own book—the *Posterior Analytics*.

Aristotle would certainly call these 'reliable methods.' Contrast these with the reliable methods introduced by Goldman, such as the method of getting knowledge by reading a claim in the 'Science' section of the *New York Times*. If this is a good example of what a reliable method is, then the traditional arguments against externalism—namely, that it solves the skeptic's challenge only by changing the very goals of epistemology—may be quite forceful. Consider the anti-externalist thought experiment introduced by Stewart Cohen.[19] Suppose there are two people, A and B, both inhabiting a world governed by an evil genius. A uses characteristically reliable ways to get beliefs, while B gets his beliefs by guesswork, superstition, and other such processes. What we should be able to say is that there is an important difference between the reliability of A's beliefs and B's beliefs. But since they both live under to systematic deception of the evil genius, they both have used unreliable methods. Hence reliabilism must be false.

By 'characteristically reliable,' Cohen just means the same thing as Goldman. It seems that when they refer to 'reliable,' they mean 'reasonable,' as in it would be reasonable to believe in the health benefits of broccoli by reading it in the *New York Times*, and not reasonable to reach the same conclusion after reading that same article in a tabloid. Based on this standard, Cohen's thought experiment has some intuitive force. It's worth wondering, however, if anything would be different if we consider Aristotle's standard of 'reliable,' which would demand the methods unique to and indispensable for the philosophical sciences. At least we can say that it we should not be surprised when the 'person on the street' is not in the possession of these reliable methods. Finally, it will be recalled that one problem with Gettier's argument was that his sense of justified meant simply 'reasonable,' and so his supposed examples of true, justified, belief were nothing like Aristotle's knowledge. Perhaps the weakness of Goldman's argument against agent relativized justifiers is that his kind of justifier must be 'reasonable' from the perspective of a person not educated in the sciences.

Notes

1. I am aware of the criticisms of the phrase 'external to one's mind.' I believe, however, that I can make all the points I need to make without entering the labyrinth of arguments that attempt to distinguish what is 'outside' one's mind from what it not.
2. Rene Descartes, *The Meditations and Selections From the Principles*, tr. John Veitch (Chicago: The Open Court Publishing Company, 1927).
3. *The Matrix*, Warner Bros., 1999.
4. Although the character of pre-Cartesian external-world skepticism is not the same as the skepticism I am considering here. See Gail Fine, "Sextus and External World Scepticism," *Oxford Studies in Ancient Philosophy* 23: 341-385.
5. Although the exact meaning of this analogy is not at all obvious.
6. G.E. Moore, "A defense of common sense," Contemporary British Philosophy, ed. J.H. Muirhead (London: Allen and Unwin, 1925), 193-223.
7. See pp. 59-66.
8. Fred Drestske, "Externalism and Modest Contextualism," *Erkenntnis* 61, no. 2/3 (November 2004): 173-186.
9. Dretske, 173-4.
10. Classic defenses of internalism include John Pollock, *Contemporary Theories of Knowledge* (Cambridge, NJ: Rowman & Littlefield, 1986), and Laurence BonJour, *The Structure of Empirical Knowledge* (Cambridge: Harvard University Press, 1987).
11. Alvin Goldman, "Internalism Exposed," *The Journal of Philosophy* 96, no. 6 (June 1999): 271-293, 273.
12. Goldman, 272.
13. Goldman, 274.
14. Goldman, 280.
15. Goldman, 286.
16. See page 11.
17. See page 11.
18. See pp. 30-31.
19. Stewart Cohen, "Justification and Truth," *Philosophical Studies: An International Journal for Philosophy in the Analytic Tradition* 46, no. 3 (November 1984): 279-295.

Chapter 10
The Problem of Intellectual Intuition

Introduction

The concept of intellectual intuition was central to Cartesian epistemology. For instance, he concludes his thought experiment concerning the melted piece of wax by making some observations about the kind of intuition that must be in play here:

> I must, therefore, admit that I cannot even comprehend by imagination what the piece of wax is, and that is the mind alone which perceives it. I speak of one in particular; for, as to wax in general, this is still more evident. But what is the piece of wax that can be perceived only by the [understanding or] mind? It is certainly the same which I see, touch imagine...But...the perception of it is neither an act of sight, of touch, not of imagination...but is simply an intuition (38).

This idea of intellectual intuition was important to the rationalist tradition, and takes center stage in Kant's critique of metaphysics. The basic idea of the critique is contained in the first lines of the *Critique of Pure Reason*. There he claims that "the capacity (receptivity) to acquire representations through the way in which we are affected by objects is called sensibility. Objects are therefore given to us by the sensibility, and it alone affords us intuitions" (A19/B33). Kant's critique begins here because he believes that whether metaphysics is possible or not depends on whether or not human cognizers have, in addition to our sensible intuition, an intellectual intuition that is able to access *noumena*.[1] He implies this connection in the *Prolegomena*:

> Objects of this kind are what are called *noumena* or pure beings of the understanding...if reason, which can never be fully satisfied with any use of the rules of the understanding in experience because such use is always conditioned, requires completion of the chain of conditions, then the understanding is driven out of its circle...and in that way, independent at last of the conditions of experience, nonetheless can make its hold complete. These then are the transcendental ideas (*Pro.* 4:332-333).

Kant's point here is that if we suppose that the understanding can intuit its own objects (i.e., things as they are, not simply things as they appear[2]), then the unconditioned ideas—whether they be God, the soul, or the world—are products are perfectly plausible arguments meant to explain the existence of the various *noumena*. When the conditioned is given in appearance, reason finds itself bound by a subjective law: "find for the conditioned knowledge given through

163

the understanding the unconditioned whereby its unity is brought to completion" (A308/B364). In Kant's language, they are simply given to us, not just given to us as a problem:

> If the conditioned as well as its condition are things in themselves, then when the first is given not only is the regress to the second given as a problem, but the latter is thereby really already given along with it; and, because this holds for all members of the series, then the complete set of conditions, and hence the unconditioned is thereby simultaneously given, or rather it is presupposed by the fact that the conditioned, which is possible only through that series, is given (A498/B526).

So his reasoning is that if we have a right to make metaphysical judgments or judgments about conditions that are themselves unconditioned, then we perceive *noumena* (things as they are in themselves); furthermore, if we can perceive *noumena,* then we must have an intellectual intuition in addition to our sensible intuition. As a matter of fact, Kant believes that human cognizers do not have intellectual intuition, and thus, that we do not have a right to make unconditioned judgments.

But why is Kant justified in believing that intellectual intuition is not an element of human cognition? Kant believes that the argument against intellectual intuition unfolds in the Transcendental Aesthetic and Transcendental Analytic. But in the first part of the *Critique*, we find much reasoning about the nature of human cognition based on the presupposition that humans do not have intellectual intuition, but no actual argument for this claim. If this is true, then one of Kant's most consequential positions on human cognition may be simply dogmatic. This is especially important for a thinker such as Aristotle, who argues that intellectual intuition plays a central role in human cognition.

Kant's Evolving Doctrine of Intellectual Intuition

In Kant's *Inaugural Dissertation*,[3] he says that

> *intelligence* is the *faculty* of a subject in virtue of which it has the power to represent things which cannot by their own quality come before the sense of that subject. The object of sensibility is the sensible; that which contains nothing but what is to be cognized through the intelligence is intelligible. In the schools of the ancients, the former was called a *phenomenon* and the latter a *noumenon*... It is thus clear that things which are sensible are representations of things as they appear, while things which are intellectual are representations of things as they are (*ID* 2:392-3).

That is, by intellectual intuition, "the concepts themselves, whether of things or relations, are given, and this is their real use" (*ID* 2:393).

Of course, Kant completely reversed himself in his mature work, as it became fundamental for the critical philosophy that the faculty of sensibility was, for humans, the only faculty that could intuit:

the capacity (receptivity) to acquire representations through the way in which we are affected by objects is called sensibility. Objects are therefore given to us by the sensibility, and *it alone affords us intuitions*; but they are thought through the understanding, and from it arise concepts. But all thought…must ultimately be related to intuitions, thus, in our case, sensibility, since there is no other way objects can be given to us (A19/B33, my italics).

Later in the first *Critique*, Kant explains his position on intuition through the distinction between *phenomena* and *noumena*:

appearances, to the extent that as objects they are thought in accordance with the unity of the categories, are called *phenomena*. If, however, I suppose there to be things that are merely objects of the understanding and that, nevertheless, can be given to an intuition, although not to sensible intuition (as *coram intuiti intellectuali* [by means of intellectual intuition]), then such things would be called *noumena*" (A248-9, my insertion).

For the critical Kant, the understanding has access to objects intuited by sensibility, but this means that its mode of access is always mediated. What Kant is considering in the following quote, as above, is *immediate* intuitive intellectual access:

with regard to appearances, to be sure, both understanding and reason can be used; but it must be asked whether they would still have any use if the object were not appearance (*noumenon*), and one takes it in this sense if one thinks of it as merely intelligible, i.e., as given to the understanding alone and not to the senses at all… The question is thus: whether beyond the empirical use of the understanding…a transcendental one is also possible, pertaining to the *noumenon* as an object—which question we have answered negatively (A257/B313).

The critical Kant argues that the understanding has an essential role to play in unifying the manifold of intuition (this is what he refers to here as its empirical use), but the question before us now is whether the understanding has any objects *proper to it* that it acquires through intuition (this is what he here calls its transcendental use, i.e., when an intellectual object is given to the understanding). This is the possibility that Kant ultimately rejects in the case of human cognition.

Kant sheds some insight on how his position evolved in a 1772 letter to Marcus Herz. There, he reminisced about his pre-critical days, when he believed that "[t]he sensuous representations present things as they appear, the intellectual representations present them as they are" (*PC* 72). The way he talked about the given-ness of intellectual representations was more or less typical of a rationalist, and already far away from general empiricism: "[i]n my dissertation I was content to explain the nature of intellectual representations in a merely negative way, namely, to state that they were not modifications of the soul brought about by the object...[i.e.] the way in which they affect us..." (*PC* 72). This is, in other words, simply to deny that any of the categories are "caused by the object..." (*PC* 72). Sometime after that, Kant second guessed his own project: "[h]owever, I silently passed over the further question of how a representation that refers to an object without being in any way affected by it can be possible" (*PC* 72). Specifically, the question he passed over was this: "...by what means are these things given to us, if not by the way in which they affect us?" (*PC* 72).

Kant's words there imply that even as a pre-critical philosopher, it was obvious to him that intellectual objects cannot affect us. But this raises an important issue, for if we assume that intellectual representations refer to (*noumenal*) objects, and thus are "given to us," yet do not affect us, "whence comes the agreement that they are supposed to have with objects...?" (*PC* 72). We can say positively that affection *is* an appropriate way to understand the relationship of sensibility to objects:

> If a representation is only a way in which the subject is affected by the object, namely, as an effect in accord with its cause, [then] it is easy to see how this modification of our mind can represent something, that is, have an object. Thus the passive or sensuous representations have an understandable relationship to objects... (*PC* 71).

Kant's epiphany that he discussed in this 1772 letter is clearly imported to the first *Critique*.[4] The memorable opening lines of the *Critique* proper state quite forcefully that the only way "we are affected by objects is...sensibility" (A19/B33). It may seem that this is blatant dogma; why does Kant just assert that the only capacity that can be affected by objects is sensibility? Kant comes close to addressing this issue in the chapter "Phenomena and Noumena." There he speaks of two ways to consider *noumena*:

> If by a *noumenon* we understand a thing insofar as it is not an object of our sensible intuition, because we abstract from the manner of our intuition of it, then this is a *noumenon* in the negative sense. But if we understand by that an object of a non-sensible intuition, then we assume a special kind of intuition, which, however, is not our own, and the possibility of which we cannot understand, and this would be *noumenon* in the positive sense (B307).

Kant is right to make this distinction, and he is right again to affirm that the critical philosophy only addresses *noumena* is the negative sense.[5] But this is precisely the problem. It is worth underscoring the point that the critical philosophy took flight when Kant first ruled out the possibility of *noumena* in the positive sense at the beginning of the *Critique*. Charles Parsons puts the matter this way:

> The capacity for receiving representations through being affected by objects is what Kant calls sensibility; that for us intuitions arise only through sensibility is thus something Kant was prepared to state at the outset. It appears to be a premise of the argument of the Aesthetic; if not Kant does not clearly indicate there any argument of which it is the conclusion.[6]

I think that Parsons is right to observe that Kant does not 'clearly indicate' the argument that led him to his doctrine that all intuition is sensible intuition. Although, as I have pointed out, Kant's 1772 letter at least gives us his train of reasoning: all intuition is by means of affection, only sensible objects affect us, and therefore all intuition is sensible intuition.

Kant certainly does not think that his denial of intellectual intuition to human cognition is dogmatic. For instance, he states that the transcendental deduction has proven that intellectual intuition is impossible:

> After what has been shown in the deduction of the categories, hopefully no one will be in doubt about how to decide the question, whether these pure concepts of the understanding are of merely empirical or also a transcendental use, i.e., whether, as conditions of possible experience, they relate *a priori* solely to appearances, or whether, as conditions of possibility of things in general, they can be extended to objects in themselves (without any restriction to our sensibility)... (A139/B178).

That is, Kant has proven to his own satisfaction that the pure concepts of the understanding do not have a transcendental use because *noumenal* objects are not "given to the understanding" by means of an intellectual intuition (A257/B313). For the sake of argument, let us grant the success of the transcendental deduction. Thus, we will say that Kant has indeed proven that the categories *do* have an *a priori* empirical use. But how has anything Kant has said so far proven that the categories *do not* have a transcendental use? What, exactly, is the problem with supposing that intellectual objects may affect the understanding?

The Connection Between Intellectual Intuition and Metaphysics

If one believes that human cognizers have intellectual intuition, then one presupposes that the understanding does not simply have the task of unifying the manifold given by sensible intuition. It has, in addition, what Kant called in the *Inaugural Dissertation* a 'real use,' namely, the cognition of objects that are given to it independently of sensibility. This amounts to a commitment to the human capacity to cognize (and not just think about) *noumenal* objects, which means that humans can cognize things as they are themselves: "...if we call certain objects, as appearances, beings of sense (*phenomena*)...we distinguish the way in which we intuit them from their constitution in itself..." (B306).[7]

Importantly, if human cognition has a right to make judgments about things as they are in themselves, then human cognition also has a right to make certain metaphysical judgments insofar as those metaphysical judgments are made for the sake of explaining those initial judgments. Certain judgments about God, the soul, and the true nature of the world, which Kant calls transcendental ideas, would qualify. In the *Prolegomena*, Kant says that

> Objects of this kind are what are called *noumena* or pure beings of the understanding...if reason, which can never be fully satisfied with any use of the rules of the understanding in experience because such use is always conditioned, requires completion of the chain of conditions, then the understanding is driven out of its circle...and in that way, independent at last of the conditions of experience, nonetheless can make its hold complete. These then are the transcendental ideas (4:332-333).

The key is the claim that 'the use of the rules of the understanding is always conditioned.' Kant notes that despite the complexities, the basic presupposition exposed by the Transcendental Dialectic is fairly straightforward: "if the conditioned is given, then the whole series of all conditions for it is also given" (A497/B525). The pre-critical ontologist believes that because conditioned objects are in fact given to us in sensibility, reason should be able to ascend to the unconditioned, because the unconditioned—that is, the final judgment grounding the series of conditions—must also be given. Kant names the position that leads reason on this misguided quest 'transcendental realism.'

The transcendental realist believes that the universe exists in space and time in itself, which requires her to make "modifications of our sensibility into things subsisting in themselves" (A491/B519). Thus, transcendental realism is simply rooted in the failure to appreciate that space and time are the conditions of sensibility, which according to Kant, implies that they are not features of the world in-itself. If this mistake is made, then it follows that when appearances are given, they are conditioned entirely by external, mind-independent reality; so to speak, space and time are presented to us by reality. Therefore the conditioned objects subsist in themselves, and are given to us on occasion of our having some experience of them. But transcendental idealism holds that "the objects of experience are never given in themselves, but only in experience, and they could never exist at all outside it" (A492/B521). The conditions of space and time come not from reality, but from the one doing the experiencing.

If one presupposes transcendental realism, then one has presupposed that any given object is conditioned by reality. Given such a presupposition, it is not only understandable but logically necessary to believe that the unconditioned is also given:

if the conditioned as well as its condition are things in themselves, then when the first is given not only is the regress to the second given as a problem, but the latter is thereby really already given along with it; and, because this holds for all members of the series, then the complete set of conditions, and hence the unconditioned is thereby simultaneously given, or rather it is presupposed by the fact that the conditioned, which is possible only through that series, is given (A498/B526).

In one sense, the judgment that the unconditioned is given to us is analytically true since "the concept of the conditioned already entails that something is related to a condition, and if this condition is once again conditioned, to a more remote condition, and so through all the members of the series" (A487/B526). So it is at least true by definition that the unconditioned is given to us *as a problem*, although the further inference that the unconditioned condition is a feature of reality is the assumption that Kant wishes to expose. The distinction between the unconditioned being given to us and being given to us as a problem is the same distinction that Kant highlights by characterizing the two ways to take this law, namely either as objective or subjective.[8] Kant's characterization of this principle as a law suggests that reason feels a special obligation to follow it. This is indeed what Kant means by calling the interpretation of it as an objective law a special type of error; he calls it the doctrine of transcendental illusion.

Accepting the idea of the unconditioned is a transcendental condition for giving unity to experience, and as such, we finite creatures always find ourselves under illusion. But if we become transcendental idealists, we understand that this principle cannot be used to acquire theoretical knowledge. Kant highlights this conviction in a series of rhetorical questions:

> take the principle, that the series of conditions...extends to the unconditioned. Does it or does it not have objective applicability?...Or is there no such objectively valid principle of reason, but only a logical precept, to advance toward completeness by an ascent to ever higher conditions and so to give our knowledge the greatest possible unity or reason? (A309/B366).

Aristotle on Intellectual Intuition

Kant's logic in his letter to Herz will be recalled: all intuition is by means of affection, only sensible objects affect us, and therefore all intuition is sensible intuition. Let's leave aside Kant's premise that 'all intuition is by means of affection' and focus on his assertion that 'only sensible objects affect us.' What has Aristotle said about affection that is relevant here? If empiricism is simply the theory that objects make our representations of them possible, then Aristotle is an empiricist, for he also considers the object the cause and our representation of it the effect. However, Aristotle's notion of intuition is more sophisticated than the empiricist account that Kant addresses in the Transcendental Analytic, for Aristotle believes that intuition is not only of sensible but also intellectual forms. He says that "mind must be related to the intellectual forms as sense is to the sensible forms" (*DA* III.4 429a15-18).[9] And since we have the sensible forms through intuition, the same general process is at work in the case of our grasp of the intellectual objects.

Charles Kahn argues that Aristotle makes this move because Aristotle believes, with Kant, that the intuition provided by sensation is indeterminate and cannot by itself account for experience. As Kahn explains, for Aristotle, "if we were restricted to the reception of sensible forms, all we could perceive would be colors and shapes"; that is, in order to turn the sensible forms into experience, the sensibility must be "enriched by the conceptual resources provided by its marriage with *nous*."[10] This is what Aristotle means when he says that "one perceives an individual, but perception is of the universal—e.g. of man, but not of Callias the man" (*Post Analytics* II.19 100a17). Perception, for Aristotle, is thus of the particular thing (which imparts the sensible forms) *but also* of the universals in which it partakes (which impart the intellectual forms).

What is quite clear from Aristotle's writings is that *nous*—and hence *epistēmē*—would not be attainable if there were not intuition of intellectual objects. Kahn's claim about Aristotle is more robust; he believes that experience would not even be possible without intellectual objects. If this is true, the objects that mind intuits, the intellectual forms, are necessarily intuited; if they were not, sense perception would not turn into meaningful experience. Kahn makes his claim in light of passages such as this:

> Perception of the special objects of sense is never in error or admits the least possible account of falsehood. Next comes perception that what is incidental to the objects of perception is incidental to them: in this case certainly we may be deceived; for while perception that there is white before us cannot be false, the perception that what is white is this or that may be false. Third comes the perception of the common attributes that accompany the incidental objects to which the special attributes attach...it is in respect of these that the greatest amount of sense-illusion is possible (*DA* III.3 428b17-26).

For Aristotle, there are three kinds of sense perception: there is first of all perception of sensible objects to which only one sense has access, such as color.[11] There is also perception of the common attributes, so called because they may be accessed by more than one sense, examples of which are number and magnitude.[12] Despite the differences, there is no reason to suppose that there is anything more than the sense faculties at work by themselves in these kinds of perception. Aristotle expresses this by saying these objects are "perceptible in themselves." (*DA* II.6 418a23-25). But there is a third kind (listed second in this passage), which is a kind of 'incidental perception.' One way that this kind is set apart from the first two because more than the sense faculties are needed: "We speak of an incidental object of sense where e.g. the white object that we see is the son of Diares; here because being the son of Diares is incidental to the white that is perceived" (*DA* II.6 418a20-23).

It stands to reason that if we cognize some being we know to be a son, and have a father, and be a human, and a male, etc., there must have already been perception by the noetic faculty, or as Aristotle would say, a perception of an essence that is robust enough to allow us to define that essence. For a true empiricist, however, the noetic faculty would not need to be involved in this perception—whatever kinds of perception are necessary for experience are all varieties of sense-perception. This doctrine, which I suspect would be endorsed by all or most who call themselves empiricists, is apparently rejected by Aristotle. He rejects this by classifying one kind of sense perception as 'incidental perception,' which is a kind or perception or intuition that cannot be entirely divorced from intellectual intuition. Without this distinction, the empiricist is left with nothing but perception and abstraction from that perception. Aristotle is a critic of this position.

This calls to mind Kant's criticism of empiricism because it focuses on the inability of the empiricist to explain the unity of sensation:

> Unity of synthesis in accordance with empirical concepts would be entirely contingent, and, were it not grounded on a transcendental ground of unity, it would be possible for a swarm of appearances to fill up our soul without experience ever being able to arise from it (A111).

Determinateness must obtain of sensation if sensation is going to turn into even minimal experience. The empiricist, by thinking that sensation might be unified by empirical concepts, asks the impossible of raw sensation. Kant has recourse to the categories because he believes that this determinateness can be explained only if the spontaneous *a priori* categories are involved in the synthesis, that is, if the synthesis has 'a transcendental ground of unity':

> If every individual representation were entirely foreign to the other, as it were isolated and separated from it, then there would never arise anything like cognition, which is a whole of compared and connected representations. If I therefore ascribe a synopsis to sense, because it contains a manifold in its intuition, a synthesis must always correspond to this, and receptivity can make cognitions possible only if combined with spontaneity (A97).

Kant appreciates the problem of the indeterminacy of sensation and posits the *a priori* categories as the ground of the unity of sensation. Kant no doubt believes that this criticism catches Aristotle's epistemology as well. However, Aristotle sees the very same problem, but instead posits a passive intuition of the intellectual form of the object.

It would be too weak, then, to say that Aristotle merely *avoids* Kant's criticism of the indeterminacy of sense data; it is more accurate to say that he *gives* this criticism. By recognizing that sensation must be complemented by the intelligible form of the object in intuition, Aristotle is acknowledging that sensation is not determinate in its own right; in addition, it must be complimented by intellectual intuition. Kant has said that

> [a]ppearances, to the extent that as objects they are thought in accordance with the unity of the categories, are called *phaenomena*. If, however, I suppose there to be things that are merely objects of the understanding and that, nevertheless, can be given to an intuition, although not to sensible intuition (as *coram intuiti intellectuali* [by means of intellectual intuition]), then such things would be called *noumena*" (A248-9, my insertion).

This analysis suggests that Kant's *noumena* (in the positive sense) and Aristotle's *ta noeta* are relevantly similar. They are 1) objects (or things),[13] 2) objects that are given in intuition, 3) objects that are inaccessible to the sensible intuition and therefore 4) objects that can only be intuited by the intellect; of course the difference is that for Kant, *noumena*, whatever their ontological status, cannot be accessed by human cognition.

Now it is certainly possible that Aristotle was wrong about intellectual intuition. But it seems clear, as Parsons wrote in his notes on the Aesthetic and I observed in the letter to Herz, that Kant simply does not take seriously the possibility of affection by intellectual objects, and thus never really argues against it. It seems, then, that Aristotle would have no real reason to take seriously Kant's conclusion about metaphysics derived from the first part of the *Critique of Pure Reason*, since that criticism depends on his dogmatic denial of intellectual intuition.

Conclusion

When Kant opened the *Critique of Pure Reason* by claiming that "objects are therefore given to us by the sensibility, and it alone affords us intuitions" (A19/B33), he was making a consequential claim. Indeed, this claim is the heart of his criticism of metaphysics in the tradition of transcendental realism. Thus it is quite important to notice that Kant does not actually explain why he believes this. I made some sense of this claim by referring to an earlier letter to Marcus Herz, in which Kant explains that he reversed his pre-critical acceptance of intellectual objects because intellectual objects could only be given to us by affection, and all affection is sensible. This, however, is exposed as a dogmatic claim when we consider Aristotle's substantial, unopposed arguments that there *is* affection by intellectual objects.

Notes

1. Many discussions of Kant recognize no difference between *noumena* and things as they are in themselves, i.e., apart from our consideration of them. This is justified in one sense, because for the mature Kant, *noumena* just *are* things-in-themselves, insofar as *noumena* are not objects of our sensible intuition (cf. B307). However, this conflation may obscure the truth that for much of the philosophical tradition, and for the pre-critical Kant, *noumenal* objects were in fact accessed by the understanding; that is, they were objects of a non-sensible intuition (Kant's distinction between positive and negative *noumena* is another issue). The question I am now considering is whether Kant is justified in concluding that we do not have access to *noumenal* objects, and thus, whether they can be justifiably called things in themselves.

2. Cf. *Inaugural Dissertation* 2:392-3.

3. Immanuel Kant, *The Cambridge Companion to the Works of Immanuel Kant: Theoretical Philosophy, 1755-1770*, Tr. and ed. David Walford in collaboration with Ralf Meerbore (Cambridge: Cambridge University Press, 1992).

4. I am not going to enter the notoriously difficult debate about Kant's mature position on the possibility of affection by things in themselves. Here, I am merely drawing a link between Kant's position on intellectual intuition discussed in his letter to Herz (namely, that intellectual objects are intuited, but that mode of intuition is not affection) and the assumptions that must be present in the Transcendental Aesthetic.

5. Cf. B309.

6. Charles Parsons, "The Transcendental Aesthetic," in *The Cambridge Companion to Kant,* ed. Paul Guyer (Cambridge: Cambridge University Press, 1992), 66.

7. Cf. A254/B310: "[t]he concept of a noumenon [is the concept] of a thing that is not to be thought of as an object of the senses but rather as a thing in itself..."

8. A306/B363.

9. This is my translation of: "...*hōsper to aisthētikon pros ta aisthēta, houtō ton noun pros ta noēta.*"

10. Kahn, 369.

11. *DA* 418a8-17.

12. *DA* 418a18-19.

13. In the *Inaugural Dissertation*, Kant also mentions that they could be relations of things or objects (2:393).

Chapter 11
Dialectic and Metaphysical Skepticism

Introduction

The form of this final chapter will be quite different from those that preceded it. My usual method has been to identify a problem that modern philosophy wrestled with, and then show that Aristotle's epistemology would have provided important insights, were it properly understood. But here, I want to describe a problem that Aristotle never appears to anticipate and does not have any obvious response to, and this is a problem with his method of dialectic. Kant and Aristotle have incompatible views on dialectic. For Aristotle, it is an irreplaceable philosophical method whereby one comes to know the truth of practical principles and certain kinds of natural principles; dialectic, since it produces truth, is an organon. In sharp contrast, Kant refers to dialectic as a 'logic of illusion,'[1] so called because it is a sophistical trick that uses formal or general logic as an organon, rather than its proper use as a canon[2] for detecting formal logical requirements.[3]

Part of this disagreement can be accounted for by observing that Kant and Aristotle have different definitions of 'dialectic.' As noted, Kant believes that dialectic is a style of general or formal logic, while for Aristotle, a dialectical argument is a deductive argument that uses *endoxa* as principles.[4] Their uses of the term, however, have at least one important similarity that allows their comparison. This is that Aristotelian dialectic is a way to test *endoxa*. One way to test an opinion is determine its logical consequences, and test those logical consequences directly. If the consequence is unacceptable, then we must reject the *endoxa* that we were testing. Kant also sees this as a central use of dialectic, and correctly identifies this style of argument as '*modus tollens*' (A791/B819); a *modus tollens* argument in the context of dialectic yields 'If p (in this case, my opponent's position), then q; not q (because q is self-contradictory or at least absurd); therefore not p (and so my opponent's position is false).' This is using dialectic as a canon, and both Kant and Aristotle would endorse its philosophical legitimacy at the general level.

Kant however, warns that logic must stop here, since it can decide the form of a claim if the claim happens to violate logic, but it cannot give us any more information about the content of the claim:

> the purely logical criterion of truth, namely, the agreement of knowledge with the general and formal laws of the understanding and reason, is a condition sine qua non, and is therefore the negative condition of truth. But further than this logic cannot go. It has no touchstone for the discovery of such error as concerns not the form but the content (A59-60/B84).

175

We would transgress Kant's proposed limits if we supposed that this *modus tollens* argument is part of a larger argument, and the real first premise is that 'either *p* or *r*,' where *r* is my position. Now, the effect of the first conclusion of the argument (therefore not *p*, i.e., therefore my opponent's position must be rejected) is to establish the truth of my position. In this, dialectic is used as an organon. For Aristotle, this is acceptable, and he himself relies heavily on this method.[5] For Kant, this argument style is acceptable in mathematics and to a certain extent in natural science, but it is not acceptable in metaphysics.

Kant's argument for his position may be found in the antinomies in the Transcendental Dialectic. In a letter to Christian Garve, he reuses one of his most well-known sayings in the context of the antinomies: they "woke me from my dogmatic slumbers" (*PC* 252).[6] Hume's skepticism about cause and effect—the original epistemological alarm-clock—motivated Kant to restore optimism about knowledge by showing why Hume was mistaken. But the antinomies should give rise to skepticism of dialectical reasoning in metaphysics:

> the dogmatic use of pure reason without critique…[leads] to baseless assertions that can always be opposed by others that seem equally plausible, and hence to skepticism…[A]ll attempts to answer these natural questions—e.g., whether the world has a beginning or has been there from eternity, etc.—have met with unavoidable contradictions" (B22-23).

The basic problem with using a *modus tollens* argument in metaphysics and then proclaiming victory is that the opposing argument can often just as well be subjected to refutation. For Kant, this indicates that there is something deeply wrong with presuppositions of the debate.

The Argument Style of the Antinomies

Kant divides the Transcendental Dialectic into three sections, namely the "Paralogisms of Pure Reason," "The Antinomies of Pure Reason," and "The Ideal of Pure Reason." Given the content of the first and third section, it is possible to believe that Kant is using the Transcendental Dialectic simply to show that typical arguments from the history of metaphysics are invalid, as opposed to showing why we do not have a right to make them. For example, the sentence that begins his critique of the metaphysical doctrine of the soul identifies the argument for the soul as a "transcendental paralogism," which "has a transcendental ground for inferring falsely due to its form" (A341/B399). In one case that Kant highlights here, if we expect to understand ourselves as substances, we may argue that "I, as a thinking being, am the absolute subject of all my possible judgments, and this representation of Myself cannot be used as the predicate of any other thing. Thus I, as thinking being (soul), am substance" (A348). The problem with that argument is that there is an equivocation on the concept 'subject,' and thus this syllogism only seems to extend our knowledge of ourselves if "it passes off the constant logical subject of thinking as the cognition of a real subject of inherence..." (A350). This syllogism, which has the initial look of validity, is invalid on closer inspection.

Similarly in the ideal of pure reason, Kant tries to show that the traditional arguments for the existence of God are invalid. He first turns his attention to the ontological argument, since he believes that all arguments for the existence of God ultimately depend on the ontological argument.[7] The ontological argument, in essence, argues that the concept 'God' is inseparable from the predicate 'being,' in the same way 'triangle' is inseparable from 'three-sidedness.' However,

> being is obviously not a real predicate, i.e., a concept of something that could add to the concept of a thing...In the logical use it is merely the copula of a judgment. The proposition God is omnipotent contains two concepts that have their objects: God and omnipotence; the little word "is" is not a predicate in it, but only that which posits the predicate in relation to the subject (A598/B626).

The particular arguments against the metaphysical claims about God or the soul are certainly important and interesting. However, they are not essentially related to Kant's general epistemological project of establishing transcendental idealism, for it is perfectly consistent to accept the force of these arguments and yet reject transcendental idealism. Conversely, it is possible to be convinced of transcendental idealism and yet believe that Kant has made some errors in these particular sections of the paralogisms and ideal.

The relevant point here is that if transcendental idealism is true, then it does not matter what kind of fallacies we made in our arguments about God and the soul. The only thing that matters is that God and the soul are unconditioned concepts; hence, we do not have to inspect the actual arguments about them to find out if they are good arguments. Guyer summarizes:

> The chief result of Kant's own critical philosophy [is] that concepts yield knowledge only when applied to intuitions, and as a result...all ideas of the unconditioned are fundamentally incompatible with the structure of our sensible intuition, which is always conditioned...In other words, it is the most fundamental characteristic of our intuitions that they are always conditioned by further intuitions, and so nothing unconditioned can ever be "given"...Therefore nothing unconditioned can ever be an object of knowledge for us.[8]

Thus it is true that the failure of the paralogisms and the ideal would not indicate that transcendental realism has failed, and the success of those sections does not count in favor of the success of transcendental idealism.

However, the argument(s) in the second section of the Dialectic, the antinomies, are of a different character entirely. Kant notes the asymmetry between the antinomies on the one hand and the paralogisms and ideal on the other in two ways. While the mistake of seeking an unconditioned judgment to ground conditioned judgments is common to all three sections of the Transcendental Dialectic, the antinomies are unique. They are first of all distinguished because they give this unconditioned judgment specifically in order to ground the "series of conditions of appearance" (A334/B391). Kant attempts to expose the root of any attempt to reach the unconditioned in cosmological debates. His project is to demonstrate that contradictory positions on the four main issues in cosmology can both be supported with sound arguments. Kant characterizes the four debates as follows (the first is in two parts):

> whether the world has been there from eternity or has a beginning; whether cosmic space is filled with beings ad infinitum or enclosed within certain bounds; whether anything in the world is simple, or whether everything can be divided ad infinitum; whether there is a generation or production from freedom, or whether everything is attached to the chain of the natural order; and finally, whether there is some entirely unconditioned and in itself necessary being, or whether everything is, as regards its existence, conditioned and hence dependent and in itself contingent (B509).

Unlike the paralogism and ideal, which argue that taking the unconditioned as a feature of mind-independent reality results in the beliefs in the soul and God respectively, here there are *two* ways of conceiving the unconditioned; furthermore, these two ways are contradictory. Karl Ameriks puts the matter this way in order to distinguish the nature of the conclusions of the antinomies from the claims made in both the paralogisms and ideal:

> cosmological claims, on the other hand, get us into contradictory theses that are resolvable only by transcendental idealism...Here the problem is not one of a lack of knowledge or detail; rather, for [cosmological] questions...there simply is no sensible answer about an ultimate nature.[9]

This means that the antinomies are able to offer a critique of transcendental realism that is unavailable to the other sections of the Transcendental Dialectic, and Kant himself appears to recognize this. This is why he says

> now the propositions of pure reason, especially when they venture beyond all boundaries of possible experience, admit of no test by experiment with their objects...: thus to experiment will be feasible only with concepts and principles...If we now find that there is agreement with the principle of pure reason when things are considered from this two-fold standpoint, but that an unavoidable conflict of reason with itself arises with a single standpoint, then the experiment decides for the correctness of that distinction (bxviii-bxix fn).

Here and elsewhere[10] Kant argues that if a debate can be shown to generate contradictory judgments, then the very presuppositions of that debate would have to be discarded. And if we grant that transcendental realism supplies the presuppositions that generate the antinomies and that transcendental idealism is the contradictory position, then the antinomies support transcendental idealism.

The result in each case is that we are forced to believe that the phenomenon in question cannot "exist in itself without relation to our senses and possible experience" (A493/B522). Kant summarizes the ideal pattern of discovery:

> if the world is a whole existing in itself, then it is either finite or infinite. Now the first as well as the second alternative is false...Thus it is false that the world...is a whole existing in itself. From which it follows that appearances in general are nothing outside of our representation, which is just what we mean by their transcendental ideality (A507-8/B535-6).

Thus, Kant believes that the antinomies are unique among the three divisions of the Transcendental Dialectic because the antinomies provide a defense of transcendental idealism, while the arguments in the paralogisms and ideal do not.

The Origin of the Antinomies

The antinomies come to exist because of the dialectical use of reason, which Kant will argue is always a misuse of reason. Kant's argument against the dialectical use of reason begins not when he turns in earnest to the topic in the Transcendental Dialectic but toward the beginning of the *Critique* in the section titled "On the division of general logic into analytic and synthetic." Kant begins by observing the importance and reliability of general logic. As such, the following premise summarizes Kant's view of logic:

> P1. General logic provides the rules for generating formally acceptable judgments and valid arguments.

Given this, the temptation to make the following inference is overwhelming:

> C2. Therefore general logic provides the rules for generating truth.

The conclusion seems innocent enough; after all, general logic certainly can be a guide for making claims in certain cases. For example, general logic would relieve me of the empirical chore of finding out whether it is true, as you claim, that you are both in the room and not in the room at the same time and in the same sense. The simple reason is that your judgment has violated one the two central principles of general logic—the law of non-contradiction, and thus, the *form* of the claim is wrong. Together with the law of the excluded middle, these laws provide the ultimate criteria for judging and inferring.

The problem, as Kant points out, is that such "criteria concern only the form of truth, i.e., of thinking in general, and are to that extent entirely correct but not sufficient" (A59/B84). So while we were justified in allowing the rules of general logic to tell us what must be *false* because it violates logical form (as in the case of your claim about being in the room and not in the room), no rules of logic can tell us the content of what is *true*: [t]he merely logical criterion of truth…is therefore certainly the…negative condition of all truth; further, however, logic cannot go, and the error that concerns not form but content cannot be discovered by a touchstone of logic" (A59/60-B84). Logic is therefore "the negative touchstone of truth"; it is negative because it can only tell us what claims about reality must be untrue, and it is a 'touchstone' because "one must before all else examine and evaluate by means of these rules the form of cognition before investigating its content in order to find out whether…it contains positive truth" (A60/B84-5). In the end, then, this is general logic in its analytic employment, since in this way "general logic analyzes the formal business of the understanding and reason…" (A60/B84).

However, general logic has a siren-like quality, and thus is liable to misappropriation:

> nevertheless there is something so seductive in the possession of an apparent art for giving all of our cognitions the form of understanding…that this general logic, which is merely a canon for judging, has been used as if it were an organon for the actual production of at least the semblance of objective assertions, and thus in fact it has thereby been misused. Now general logic, as a putative organon, is called dialectic (A61/B85).

Premise 1 above refers to the general use of logic as analytic and formal—a tool for eliminating judgments and inferences that violate the rules of thinking. But as Kant understands it, our realization that we possess the *a priori* rules for judging and inferring makes us power-hungry. General logic is properly a *canon* for judging and inferring the form of truth; we, however, use it to generate positive truth claims. General logic thus becomes an *organon* of truth. In other words, we pass silently from premise 1 to conclusion 2 without any attempt to justify our right to do so.

Kant adds, somewhat cryptically, that "even if a cognition accorded completely with its logical form, i.e., if it did not contradict itself, it could still contradict its object" (A59/B84). He has already explained the first part of this statement—we know an argument is bad when its form is invalid—but how could cognition 'contradict its object?' Although Kant will not clarify his last remark until later on in the *Critique,* it is certainly clear that he wants to establish "a critique of the understanding and reason in regard to their hyperphysical use" (A63/B88); that is, while the understanding and reason are necessary for experience (this is apparently their 'physical' use), they are also used beyond experience.

The Nature of an Antinomial Argument

What else makes an argument antinomial? We have seen Kant identify four theoretical[11] antinomies in the first *Critique,*[12] but without a rigorous definition of an antinomial argument, Kant has left us the task of finding the commonalities in these disputes. There are at least three different features of an argument that seem to motivate Kant to classify it as antinomial.

First, these positions must be contradictory and not contrary (or subcontrary), and this is everywhere emphasized by Kant. In fact, if the two traditional positions could be reclassified as contraries within the context of transcendental realism then these debates would be completely useless to Kant; it is specifically their transgression of the subjective rules of judging and inferring that we find our clue that some presupposition made by the arguers is wrong. That is, it is not interesting if we are arguing over the hygiene practices of Europeans, and you are able to prove your proposition that "Some French citizens smell good" and I can just as well prove my proposition that "Some French citizens do not smell good"; the obvious truth is that we are both right, and this is because our positions are sub-contrary, and not contradictory, as we may have believed at first. However, the fact that the opposed propositions 'The world had a beginning in time' and 'The world did not have a beginning in time' can both be supported by seemingly sound arguments is quite interesting; in Kant's considered opinion, it indicates that the presuppositions of our debate are wrong.

In this context, Kant argues that an antinomy *never* presents a genuine contradiction: "permit me to call such an opposition a dialectical opposition, but the contradictory one an analytical opposition" (A504/B532). The contradictions of the antinomies are not genuine contradictions, but rather mere 'dialectical oppositions' because the contradiction is removed by removing the presupposition of transcendental realism. In the case of the first antinomy, "...if I take away this presupposition,...and deny that [the world] is a thing in itself, then the contradictory conflict of the two assertions is transformed into a merely dialectical conflict...because the world...exists neither as an in itself infinite whole nor as an in itself finite whole" (A505/B533). Thus, without the presupposition of transcendental realism, these apparent contradictions are properly classified as contraries. Therefore, the positions in a debate may be both false (as in the first two antinomies) or both true (as in the last two antinomies); these oppositions are acceptable to logic.

The second common feature that Kant emphasizes is the rootedness of antinomial arguments in experience; that is, they begin with a phenomenon. As Kant says, "the entire antinomy of pure reason rests on this dialectical argument: If the conditioned is given, then the whole series of conditions for it is also given; now objects of the senses are given as conditioned; consequently, etc." (A497/B525). Whether it be our awareness of space and time, our observation of orderly causal processes, or our discovery of the (at least partial) divisibility of substances, antinomial arguments always begin with evidence that seems to demand a verdict; Aristotle would call these sorts of observations 'endoxa' because they are opinions based on reputable observations. Kant is sympathetic with this idea, for the evidence—that which is conditioned—is certainly "given to us as a problem" (A498/B526). But only those who presuppose transcendental realism go on to infer that because it is given to us as a problem, it is given to us

independently of the conditions of our sensibility and exists apart from our experience of it. In this way, our dialectical ascension begins with a phenomenon,
and because of the presupposition of transcendental realism, ends in the only
place where the realist can be satisfied: a theoretical judgment about the unconditioned condition.

Kant's identification of one particular antinomial offender has the effect of
emphasizing that the antinomies are rooted in experience: "...the famous Leibniz constructed an intellectual system of the world...by comparing all objects
only with the understanding and the formal concepts of its thinking"
(A270/B326). That means that if we follow Leibniz,

> ...we reflect merely logically, [and] we simply compare our concepts with each
> other in the understanding, seeing whether two of them contain the very same
> thing, whether they contradict each other or not, whether something is con-
> tained in the concept internally or is added to it, and which of them should
> count as given and which as a manner of thinking of that which is given"
> (A279-B335).

Kant takes these remarks to be illustrative of Leibniz' many metaphysical arguments, including this one about the nature of space and time:

> if I would represent outer relations of things through the mere understanding,
> this can be done only by means of a concept of their reciprocal effect, and I
> should connect one state of the one and the same thing with another state, then
> this can only be done in the order of grounds and consequences. Thus space [is]
> a certain order in the community of substances, and...time [is] the dynamical
> sequence of their states (A275/B331).

The general pattern is this: we begin with a given; in this case, the phenomenon
of space (or time). Then we begin seeking to account for the given. That is, we
attempt to identify what *must be true* in order to explain the phenomenon at
hand (the necessary conditions), and this is done through a process of logical
reflection. We finish by articulating an unconditioned ground for the appearance
in question; that is, we characterize "the inner constitution of things..."
(A270/B326). Leibniz certainly believed that his mundane familiarity with the
phenomenon of space together with his impressive familiarity with the rules of
logic allow him safely to infer that the nature of space was not some kind of
container as his rivals believed, but 'a certain order in the community of substances.'[13] Michelle Grier summarizes:

> Kant's criticisms of Leibniz in the Amphiboly chapter are designed to under-
> mine the attempt to draw substantive metaphysical conclusions about things in
> general (Dinge überhaupt) simply from the highly abstract concepts of reflec-
> tion and/or principles of general or formal logic (e.g., the principle of contra-
> diction).[14]

Kant's central point is that Leibniz happily ascends the ladder of inferences, carefully using the rules of logic to add one rung at a time as he goes, and arrives at what he believes must be the unconditioned condition of the given phenomenon. There are thus so far two relevant features of an antinomial argument: the apparent contradiction (i.e., dialectical opposition) of the positions, and the rootedness of the positions in the attempt to explain some feature of experience.

The Problem with Dialectic in Metaphysics

In addition to being contradictories and based in experience, the third feature that makes these arguments antinomial is that the proof of one position must consist of an attempt to undermine the other position. Kant sometimes calls this style of proof 'indirect' or 'apagogical,' as he does when naming the rules for pure reason at the end of the first *Critique*: "[reason's] proofs must never be apagogic but always ostensive...The apagogic proof...can produce certainty, to be sure, but never comprehensibility of the truth in regard to its connection with the ground of its possibility" (A789/B817). Kant, by further associating apagogical proofs with '*modus tollens*' arguments (A791/B819), identifies apagogical arguments as those that find a contradiction in the rival argument. The form of a *modus tollens* is 'If *p* (in this case, my opponent's position), then *q*; not *q* (because q is self-contradictory or at least absurd); therefore not *p* (and so my opponent's position is false).'

This sort of indirect argument was precisely what Kant was concerned with earlier in the *Critique* when he warned against the negative use of logic. There he said that "even if a cognition accorded completely with its logical form, i.e., if it did not contradict itself, it could still contradict its object" (A59/B84). Now, at the end if the *Critique*, Kant is in position to be clearer about how a cognition could contradict its object. He first asks us to consider a discipline where this sort of contradiction never happens: "in mathematics this subreption is impossible; hence apagogic proof has its proper place there" (A792/B820). The subreption to which he refers is the mistake of taking what is subjectively necessary for what is objectively valid. In mathematics, "it is impossible to substitute that which is subjective in our representations for that which is objective..." (A791/B819). Since mathematical objects are constructed by us, confusion between what is subjective and what is objective is impossible. Thus, mathematicians are justified in the use of apagogic proofs, but metaphysicians are not. The reason is that in metaphysics it *is* possible 'to substitute that which is subjective in our representation from that which is objective.' Unlike mathematical objects, we do not construct objects in the world as they are in themselves. This is just another way to describe the mistaken presupposition of transcendental realism because this position mistakes the subjective for objective by treating objects as we imagine them to be apart from our experience of them.

Besides mathematics, Kant mentions another discipline that might use apa-gogic proofs, namely, natural science. But there is one important difference be-tween the permissibility of apagogical logic in math and science, for while in mathematics its use is completely safe, it is not so in science; it only *tends* to be safe because there are other safeguards: "in natural science, since everything there is grounded on empirical intuitions, such false pretenses can frequently be guarded against through the comparison of many observations; but this kind of proof itself is for the most part unimportant in this area" (A792/B820). Kant's point is that the danger of an apagogical proof is mitigated in natural science because a future observation may make it obvious that the apagogical argument in question was wrong. But since metaphysical judgments are not liable to refu-tation by what is given in experience, there is no possible warning bell.

Does This Argument Present a Problem for Aristotelian Metaphysics?

Aristotle's argument for teleology in nature, to take one example, is para-digmatic of what Kant has been complaining about. The argument begins with a question Aristotle poses to himself: "...why should nature not work, not for the sake of something...but of necessity?" (*Ph.* II.8 198b15). Aristotle is consider-ing the two ways that a cause and its effect may be related: either the effect is the goal of the cause (and causal process), or it is not.[15] An initial observation is that in some cases, such as rain causing plant growth, it is clear that the effect (growth) is not the goal of the cause (rain): "what is drawn up must cool, and what has been cooled must become water and descend, the result of this being that corn grows" (*Ph.* II.8 198b19-20). If anyone would disagree that this is a mechanistic process, then he would also be obligated to believe that, for exam-ple, when that same rain storm spoiled crops on the threshing floor, the rain fell for the sake of ruining the crops (*Ph.* II.8 198b20-22).

Because a mechanistic analysis is quite sensible in this case, the physicist may be tempted to make it in the case of not just some but all natural events. She would then hold this proposition (here expressed but not endorsed by Kant): "all generation of material things is possible in accordance with merely mechanical laws" (*CJ* 5:387). Aristotle, of course, plans to argue the contradictory position that "some generation of such things is not possible in accordance with merely mechanical laws" (*CJ* 5:387). Aristotle reasons that if the effect is not the goal of the causal process, then the effect always arises through chance and spontane-ity. This, however, is not faithful to our observation of the way in which nature actually works: "natural things either invariably or for the most part come about in a given way; but of not one of the results of chance and spontaneity is this true" (*Ph.* II.8 198b35-199a1). The way we know that an effect is the coinci-dental result of a causal process is that the effect doesn't happen often. Natural things, however, are generated with regularity. Aristotle concludes, if then, it is agreed that things are either the result of coincidence or for the sake of something, and these things cannot be the result of coincidence or spontaneity, it follows that they must be for the sake of something...Therefore action for an end is present in things which come to be and are by nature (*Ph.* II.8 199a3-5).

Aristotle said it perfectly: his argument works *if* it is agreed that teleology and mechanism are the only possibilities for how nature in itself works; or, as Kant says, *if* they are "constitutive principles of the possibility of things themselves..." (*CJ* 5:387). That, of course, is the 'if' that Kant exploits. What Aristotle *has* done (arguably) is to show that mechanism, as a constitutive principle, is unable to account for the generation of all nature's effects. We should note that Kant agrees with this conclusion: "with respect to our cognitive faculty, it is just as indubitably certain that the mere mechanism of nature is also incapable of providing an explanatory ground for the generation of organized beings" (*CJ* 5:389). Kant's complaint is about what Aristotle has *not* done, which is to defend his own position directly by offering any kind of explanation of how teleology might work. In other words, the proof is apagogic and not ostensive. As Kant has pointed out, metaphysical arguments must work to avoid this danger because we are not doing math, but metaphysics; in mathematics, "it is impossible to substitute that which is subjective in our representations for that which is objective..." (A791/B819). In metaphysics, however, subreption is possible. Therefore, in order for Aristotle to deliver a decisive proof that he has not confused the subjective principles with objective ones, he must argue for teleology in nature directly and not by resorting to an apagogical argument.

Kant is now in position to ask whether the principle of teleology is constitutive of things themselves, or whether it is a nomothetic law, created by the reflective power of judgment for the sake of making judging possible. If it were not possible to construct an equally convincing argument for mechanism, we would not be able to answer Kant's question. But according to Kant, the mechanist can produce equally convincing reasons to discard teleology. We can consider Kant's words from the first *Critique* concerning the conditions for holding the distinction between appearances and things in themselves: since "we now find...[that] an unavoidable conflict of reason with itself arises with a single standpoint,...the experiment decides for the correctness of that distinction" (bxviii-bxix fn). Thus, these principles are best conceived as regulative, at once necessary and nomothetic, created by the reflective power of judgment for use by the determining power of judgment. In this way, the antinomial attack undermines this argument and Aristotle's other metaphysical arguments insofar as they are apagogical. If Aristotle has a reason to believe that metaphysical arguments can be fruitful, it is not obvious what it is.

Notes

1. A293/B349.
2. Epicurus appears to be responsible for the distinction between a 'canon' and an 'organon,' as he criticized the organon of Aristotle.
3. It is interesting that Kant believes that his use of the term 'dialectic' is in line with mainstream ancient philosophy, when it is in such clear contrast to how Aristotle used the word. See A61/B85-A62/B86.
4. See pp. 21-24.
5. See, for example, *Ph.* II.8. This passage will be under discussion explicitly in this chapter.
6. Immanuel Kant, *Kant: Philosophical Correspondence, 1759-99*, ed. and tr. Arnulf Zweig (Chicago: The University of Chicago Press, 1967).
7. A607/B635, A630/B658.
8. Paul Guyer, *Kant* (New York: Routledge, 2006), 133.
9. Karl Ameriks, "The critique of metaphysics: Kant and traditional ontology," in *The Cambridge Companion to Kant,* ed. Paul Guyer (Cambridge: Cambridge University Press, 1992), 254.
10. A490-7/B 518-25.
11. Kant also considers what he calls 'practical antinomies' in the second *Critique*. My discussion of antinomies will be limited to the theoretical ones.
12. B509.
13. Ariew, Roger ed., *Correspondence: G.W. Leibniz and Samuel Clarke* (Indianapolis: Hackett Publishing Company, 2000).
14. Michelle Grier, *Kant's Doctrine of Transcendental Illusion* (Cambridge: Cambridge University Press, 2001), 71.
15. Since these two ways to see the relationship between cause and effect represent teleology and mechanism, respectively, I take it that Aristotle's distinction is identical to the one Kant considers.

Bibliography

Allison, Henry. *Kant's Transcendental Idealism: An Interpretation and Defense.* New Haven: Yale University Press, 1983.

Ameriks, Karl. "The critique of metaphysics: Kant and traditional ontology." In *The Cambridge Companion to Kant,* edited by Paul Guyer. Cambridge: Cambridge University Press, 1992.

Ariew, Roger, ed., *Correspondence: G.W. Leibniz and Samuel Clarke.* Indianapolis: Hackett Publishing Company, 2000.

Aristotle. *Categories.* In *The Complete Works of Aristotle: The Revised Oxford Translation, Volume One,* edited by Jonathan Barnes. Princeton: Princeton University Press, 1984.

———. *De Interpretatione.* In *The Complete Works of Aristotle: The Revised Oxford Translation, Volume One,* edited by Jonathan Barnes. Princeton: Princeton University Press, 1984.

———. *Generation of Animals.* In *The Complete Works of Aristotle: The Revised Oxford Translation, Volume One,* edited by Jonathan Barnes. Princeton: Princeton University Press, 1984.

———. *History of Animals.* In *The Complete Works of Aristotle: The Revised Oxford Translation, Volume One,* edited by Jonathan Barnes. Princeton: Princeton University Press, 1984.

———. *Metaphysics.* In *The Complete Works of Aristotle: The Revised Oxford Translation, Volume Two,* edited by Jonathan Barnes. Princeton: Princeton University Press, 1984.

———. *Nicomachean Ethics.* In *The Complete Works of Aristotle: The Revised Oxford Translation, Volume Two,* edited by Jonathan Barnes. Princeton: Princeton University Press, 1984.

———. *On the Soul.* In *The Complete Works of Aristotle: The Revised Oxford Translation, Volume One,* edited by Jonathan Barnes. Princeton: Princeton University Press, 1984.

———. *Parts of Animals.* In *The Complete Works of Aristotle: The Revised Oxford Translation, Volume One,* edited by Jonathan Barnes. Princeton: Princeton University Press, 1984.

———. *Physics.* In *The Complete Works of Aristotle: The Revised Oxford Translation, Volume One,* edited by Jonathan Barnes. Princeton: Princeton University Press, 1984.

———. *Politics.* In *The Complete Works of Aristotle: The Revised Oxford Translation, Volume Two,* edited by Jonathan Barnes. Princeton: Princeton University Press, 1984.

———. *Posterior Analytics.* In *The Complete Works of Aristotle: The Revised Oxford Translation, Volume One,* edited by Jonathan Barnes. Princeton: Princeton University Press, 1984.

———. *Prior Analytics.* In *The Complete Works of Aristotle: The Revised Oxford Translation, Volume One,* edited by Jonathan Barnes. Princeton: Princeton University Press, 1984.

————. *Topics*. In *The Complete Works of Aristotle: The Revised Oxford Translation Volume One*, edited by Jonathan Barnes. Princeton: Princeton University Press, 1984.

Barnes, Jonathan. *Aristotle's Posterior Analytics*. Oxford: Oxford University Press, 1975.

————. ed. *The Complete Works of Aristotle: The Revised Oxford Translation*. Princeton: Princeton University Press, 1984.

————. ed. *The Cambridge Companion to Aristotle*. Cambridge: Cambridge University Press, 1995.

Berti, Enrico. "The Intellection of Indivisibles According to Aristotle, *De Anima* III 6." In *Aristotle on Mind and the Senses*, edited by G.E.R. Lloyd and G.E.L. Owen. Cambridge: Cambridge University Press, 1978.

Bolton, Robert. "Aristotle's Method in Natural Science: Physics I." In *Aristotle's Physics: A Collection of Essays*, edited by Lindsay Judson. Oxford: Oxford University Press, 1991.

BonJour, Laurence. *The Structure of Empirical Knowledge*. Cambridge: Harvard University Press, 1987.

Cohen, S. Marc. "Hylomorphism and Functionalism." In *Essays on Aristotle's De Anima*. Oxford: Claredon Press, 1992.

Cohen, Stewart. "Justification and Truth," *Philosophical Studies: An International Journal for Philosophy in the Analytic Tradition* 46, no. 3 (November 1984): 279-295.

Cooper, John. *Reason and Human Good in Aristotle*. Cambridge, MA: Harvard University Press, 1975.

Delbruke, Max. "How Aristotle discovered DNA." American Institute of Physics. Cambridge, MA, 1974.

Demoss, David and Daniel Devereux, "Essence, Existence, and Nominal Definition in Aristotle's *Posterior Analytics* II 8-10." *Phronesis* 33, no. 2 (1988): 23-38.

Descartes, Rene. *The Meditations and Selections From the Principles*, translated by John Veitch. Chicago: The Open Court Publishing Company, 1927.

Drestske, Fred. "Externalism and Modest Contextualism." *Erkenntnis* 61, no. 2/3 (November 2004): 173-186.

Fine, Gail. "Sextus and External World Scepticism." *Oxford Studies in Ancient Philosophy* 23: 341—385.

Freeland, Cynthia. "Accidental Causes and Real Explanation." In Aristotle's Physics: A Collection of Essays, edited by Lindsay Judson. Oxford: Claredon Press, 1991, 49-72.

Genova, A.C. "Kant's Epigenesis of Pure Reason." *Kant-Studien* 65 (1974): 259-273.

Gettier, Edmund. "Is Justified True Belief Knowledge?" *Analysis* 23, no. 6 (June 1963): 121-123.

Goldman, Alvin. "Discrimination and Perceptual Knowledge." *The Journal of Philosophy* 73, no. 20 (November 1976): 771-791.

———. "Internalism Exposed." *The Journal of Philosophy* 96, no. 6 (June 1999): 271-293.

Granger, Herbert. "Aristotle on Genus and Differentia," *Journal of the History of Philosophy* 22, no. 1 (1984): 1-23.

Grier, Michelle. *Kant's Doctrine of Transcendental Illusion.* Cambridge: Cambridge University Press, 2001.

Guyer, Paul. *Kant.* New York: Routledge, 2006.

Hankinson, R.J. "Philosophy of Science." In The Cambridge Companion to Aristotle, edited by Jonathan Barnes. Cambridge: Cambridge University Press, 1995, 109-139.

Harari, Orna. *Knowledge and Demonstration: Aristotle's* Posterior Analytics. Dordrecht, The Netherlands: Kluwer Academic Publishers, 2004.

Irwin, Terrance. "Ways to First Principles: Aristotle's Methods of Discovery." *Philosophical Topics* 15, no. 2 (Fall 1987): 109-134.

———. *Aristotle's First Principles.* Oxford: Claredon Press, 1988.

Judson, Lindsay. "Chance and 'Always or For the Most Part.' In *Aristotle's Physics: A Collection of Essays*, edited by Lindsay Judson. Oxford: Claredon Press, 1991, 73-100.

Kahn, Charles. "Aristotle on Thinking." In *Essays on Aristotle's* De Anima, edited by Martha Nussbaum and Amelie Rorty. Oxford: Claredon Press, 1992.

———. "The Role of *Nous* in the Cognition of First Principles." In *Aristotle on Science: The Posterior Analytics*, edited by Enrico Berti. Padua, 1981.

Kal, Victor. *Intuitive and Discursive Reasoning in Aristotle.* Leiden: E.J. Brill, 1988.

Kant, Immanuel. *The Cambridge Companion to the Works of Immanuel Kant: Critique of the Power of Judgment,* edited by Paul Guyer. Translated by Paul Guyer and Eric Matthews. Cambridge University Press, 1998.

———. *The Cambridge Companion to the Works of Immanuel Kant: Critique of Pure Reason*, edited and translated by Paul Guyer and Allen W. Wood. Cambridge: Cambridge University Press, 1998.

———. *The Cambridge Companion to the Works of Immanuel Kant: Theoretical Works After 1781,* edited by Henry Allison and Peter Heath. *Prolegomena* Translated and edited by Gary Hatfield. Cambridge: Cambridge University Press, 2002.

———. *Critique of Pure Reason.* Translated by Werner S. Pluhar. Indianapolis: Hackett Publishing Company Inc., 1996.

———. *Philosophical Correspondence: 1759-99*, edited and translated by Arnulf Zweig. Chicago: The University of Chicago Press, 1967.

Kosman, K.A. "What Does the Maker Mind Make?" In *Essays on Aristotle's* De Anima, edited by Martha Nussbaum and Amelie Rorty. Oxford: Claredon Press, 1992.

Kraut, Richard. "How to Justify Ethical Propositions: Aristotle's Method." In *The Blackwell Guide to Aristotle's* Nicomachean Ethics, edited by Richard Kraut. Oxford, UK: Blackwell Publishing Ltd, 2008.

Lear, Jonathan. *Aristotle: The Desire to Understand.* Cambridge: Cambridge University Press, 1988.

LeBlond, J.M. "Aristotle on Definition." In *Articles on Aristotle,* edited by J. Barnes, M. Schofield, and R. Sorabji. Gerald Duckworth & Company Limited, 1976.

Lenoir, Timothy. "Kant, Blumenbach, and Vital Materialism in German Biology." *Isis* 74, no. 1 (March 1980): 77-108.

Lescher, J. "The Meaning of *Nous* in the *Posterior Analytics.*" *Phronesis* 18 (1973): 44-68.

Longuenesse, Béatrice. *Hegel's Critique of Metaphysics.* Translated by Nicole J. Simek. Cambridge: Cambridge University Press, 2007.

McKirahan, Richard. "Aristotelian *Epagōgē* in *Prior Analytics* 2.21 and *Posterior Analytics* 1.1." *Journal of the History of Philosophy* 21, no. 1 (January 1993): 1-13.

———. Principles and Proofs: Aristotle's Theory of Demonstrative Science. Princeton: Princeton University Press, 1992.

Modrak, Deborah. "The Nous-Body Problem in Aristotle." *The Review of Metaphysics* 44, no. 4 (June 1991): 755-774.

———. Aristotle: The Power of Perception. Chicago: University of Chicago Press, 1987.

Moore, G.E. "A defense of common sense." In *Contemporary British Philosophy,* edited by J.H. Muirhead. London: Allen and Unwin, 1925, 193-223.

Norman, Richard. "Aristotle's Philosopher-God." *Phronesis* 14 (1969): 63-74.

Nussbaum, Martha. *Aristotle's De Motu Animalium.* Princeton: Princeton University Press, 1978.

Owen, G.E.L. "*Tithenai ta Phainomena.*" In *Articles on Aristotle: Vol. 1 Science,* ed. J. Barnes, M. Schofield, and R. Sorabji. Great Britain: Gerald Duckworth & Company Limited, 1975.

Parsons, Charles. "The Transcendental Aesthetic." In *The Cambridge Companion to Kant,* edited by Paul Guyer. Cambridge: Cambridge University Press, 1992.

Perelmuter, Zeev. "*Nous* and Two Kinds of *Epistēmē* in Aristotle's *Posterior Analytics.*" *Phronesis* 55 (2010): 228-254.

Plato. *Plato: Complete Works,* edited by John M. Cooper, associate editor D.S. Hutchinson. Indianapolis: Hackett Publishing Company, 1997.

Polansky, Ronald. *Aristotle's De Anima: A Critical Commentary.* Cambridge: Cambridge University Press, 2007.

Pollock, John. *Contemporary Theories of Knowledge.* Cambridge, NJ: Rowman & Littlefield, 1986.

Reeve, C.D.C. *Substantial Knowledge: Aristotle's Metaphysics.* Indianapolis: Hackett Publishing Company, Inc., 2000.

Reill, Peter. "Between Preformation and Epigenesis: Kant, Physiotherapy, and Natural History." In *New Essays on the Precritical Kant,* edited by Tom Rockmore. New York: Humanity Books, 2001.

Ross, W.D. *Aristotle's Prior and Posterior Analytics*. Oxford: Oxford University Press, 1949.

Sorabji, Richard. "Definitions: why necessary and in what way?" In *Aristotle on Science: the Posterior Analytics*, edited by Enrico Berti. Padua, 1981.

———. "Body and Soul in Aristotle." *Philosophy* 49 (1974): 63-89.

Walford, David, and Ralf Meerbore, editors and translators. *The Cambridge Companion to the Works of Immanuel Kant: Theoretical Philosophy, 1755-1770*. Cambridge: Cambridge University Press, 1992.

Wedin, Michael. *Aristotle's Theory of Substance*. New York: Oxford University Press, 2000.

———. Mind and Imagination in Aristotle. Yale: Yale University Press, 1988.

Westphal, Merold. "In Defense of the Thing in Itself." *Kant-Studien* 59, no. 1 (1968): 118-41.

Wubnig, J. "The Epigenesis of Pure Reason." *Kant-Studien* 60 (1969).

Index

accident, 15-17, 33-34, 44, 60-1, 83;
science of, 17-19
affection, 6, 74-5, 98, 106, 166-172
affirmation, 79, 82
aisthanesthai, 75-77
aitia. See cause
Allison, Henry, 131-2
Ameriks, Karl, 122, 178
ameson. See the immediates
antinomies, 176-181
archē. See principles
aporematic, 64
assertion, 80-90

Barnes, Jonathan, 28, 66, 137
belief. *See* opinion
Bolton, Robert, 64

canon, 174-5, 180,
cause, 14, 32-3, 58-9; formal and
material, 94-96; and representation,
116-8; and object 125-131, and *telos*,
184
chance, 16-20; and spontaneity, 184
Cohen, Stewart, 160
coincidence. *See* accident
compound, 36-7, 42-3
concept. *See noēma*
contact, 78-82, 85-9
contemplation, 78-9, 93-4, 96-102, 106-9
contingent, 17-9; and necessary, 40; and
intellectus ectypus, 134

deduction, 22-7, 46, 51, 141-9;
transcendental, 115-7
definiendum, 83
definition, 18, 23-8, 43, 52-5; as first
principles, 63-5; nominal, 59-61;
non-assertive, 81-6; as *thesis*, 65-7;
the 'what is it,' 79-81

demonstration, 1,2, 6, 22-7, 31, 44-7, 51-
3, 63-5, 75, 93-6, 109, 143-9
denial, 82
Delbrück, Max, xii
Descartes, Rene, xii, 6, 73, 123, 131,
153-5
dialectic, 7, 13, 22-6, 61-8, 156; Kantian,
175-6; in metaphysics, 183;
transcendental, 168, 176-9
dianoesthai, 76, 105-6
differentia, 60-2, 83-6
discursivity, 5, 107-8
doxa. See opinion
Dreske, Fred, 157

educt, 121, 130
eidos. See form.
empeira. See experience.
empiricism, 4-5, 63-8, 120; Kant's attack
on, 116-9, 136-7, 171; theory of
cognition, 126, 130
endoxa, 7, 23-32, 63-5, 89, 143, 159,
175, 181
epagōgē, 2-3, 13, 22-6, 51-3, 56-9, 62-3,
89, 93-4, 137
epigenesis
essence, 3-4, 17, 24, 33-7, 43-4, 56, 72,
75, 78-84, 87-90, 94-6, 170
eternity, 2-3, 7, 38, 40-4, 100, 104, 107
explanation, 2-3, 13, 15-9;
demonstrations without, 146-8;
pseudo, 26-7; primitive, 144-6; real,
148-9, though middle terms, 46-7;
unmiddled, 27, 69
experience, 52-6, 75; beyond, 178-180;
minimal, 171; person of, 64
externalism, 157-9

form, 35-7, 56, 65; without matter 75-6;
sensible and intellectual 77-8, as

cause 94, and external stimuli 97-8, 121

generatio aequivoca, 120, 129
genus, 33-4, 61, 65, 83-6
Gettier, Edmond, 141-150
gignōskō, 32
Goldman, Alvin, 142, 157-160
grasp, 6, 32, 60, 71, 86-90, 94, 146, 164
Guyer, Paul, 177

Herz, Marcus, 115-6, 126-7, 165, 170-2
hexis. See state
horismos. See definition
Hume, David, xii, 5, 116-9, 131, 176
hypolēpsis, 17, 29fn, 38, 88-9, 105
hypothesis, 63-8

images, 1, 74-5, 96, 106, 108-9
immediates, 27, 44-7, 144-7
incomposites, 79-81, 84
indivisibles, 80-84
induction. *See epagōgē.*
intellect, deliberative, 20-1; scientific, 20-1
intellectus archetypus, 125-9, 132-5
intellectus ectypus, 125-9, 134-5
internalism, 157-9
intuition, intellectual, 76-8, 87-9, 104-8, 127, 163,172; sensible, 76
Irwin, T.I., 24, 64

judgment, 17, 55-6, 76, 105; unconditioned, 177, 181; determinative power of, 133-5, 185; reflective power of, 132-5, 185

Kahn, Charles, xiii, 57, 73-4, 62, 108, 137-8, 169-170
katholou. See universal
Kosman, L.A., 107

labein. See grasp
LeBlond, J.M., 51-2
Leibniz, Gottfried, 122, 181-2
Locke, John, 117-8, 131
Longuenesse, Beatrice, 134-5

mechanism, 126, 133-5, 184
method, 22; of demonstration, 1, 22, 93-4; dialectical, 23-6, 175-7; of induction, 23, 51-2, 57-9, 63-7; reliable, 160; scientific, 94-96
modus tollens, 7, 175-6, 183
Moore, G.E., 156

necessity, 15-20, 39-44; *haplōs,* 40; hypothetical, 40-1; objective, 115; subjective, 116, 118-126, 136
noein, 3, 73-8, 97-102
noumena, 163-8, 172
noētos, 80
noēma, 80-90

oida, 32
opinion, 14-8, 23-4, 105, 175, 181
organon, 175-6, 180,
Owen, G.E.L., 24-5, 64

Parsons, Charles, 166-7, 172
paralogisms, 176-9
particulars, 20, 22, 36, 42, 51-3, 57, 75, 78, 84
phanatasmata. See image
phenomena, 32, 59, 165, 167
phronēsis, 2, 14, 17, 21, 24-5, 88-9, 109
Plato, 7, 36, 65, 118-9, 122, 141-2
Polansky, Ronald, 100-2
preformation theory, 120-3, 129, 138
primitives, 2, 22, 33, 44, 143-4
property, 61, 83

rationalism, 4, 116-119, 122-3, 125-6, 131, 136-8
receptivity, 5, 98, 121, 128-30, 134-5
reliabilism, 160
rēma, 4, 83-4
representations, 115-7, 122, 126-131 165-7
Ross, W.D., 33

science, 14-8, 25-6, 38-9, 63-6, 95; deliberative, 21; and metaphysics, 183; practical, 21, 24, 28, 39, 41-2; productive, 21, 24, 39, 41-2; theoretical, 13, 20-2, 24, 41-2, 45, 159
sensation, 3, 75-8; as indeterminate, 120, 169-171
sophia, 17, 93, 109
Sorabji, Richard, 40-4, 81-4
soul, 71-5

spontaneity, 5, 120, 128-131, 136-7, 184
spontaneous generation, 120, 136-8
state, 71, 75, 88-9, 99, 103
subreption, 7, 183-5
substance, 33-9, 42-3, 59-61, 71-4, 79, 88, 95-6, 99, 145-6
sullogismōs. See deduction
sumbebēkos. See accident.

technē, 2, 14, 17, 21, 24, 88-9, 109
teleology, 126, 133-5, 184-5
theōrein, 74, 98-100, 105-7
thigganein. See contact
touch, 3-4, 32, 80, 87-90
tuchē. See chance

universals, 20-2, 36, 51, 170; analyzed, 64; definitional, 2, 53-9; perceptible, 2, 52-9, 75-8